SAINT PAUL RETURNS TO THE MOVIES

Saint Paul Returns to the Movies

Triumph over Shame

Robert Jewett

William B. Eerdmans Publishing Company
Grand Rapids, Michigan / Cambridge, U.K.

NO LONGER PROPERTY OF
SEATTLE PACIFIC UNIVERSITY LIBRARY

© 1999 Wm. B. Eerdmans Publishing Co.
255 Jefferson Ave. S.E., Grand Rapids, Michigan 49503 /
P.O. Box 163, Cambridge CB3 9PU U.K.
All rights reserved

Printed in the United States of America

04 03 02 01 00 99   7 6 5 4 3 2 1

ISBN 0-8028-4585-1

Parts of Chapter 1 are adapted from "Honor and Shame in the Argument of Romans,"
in *Putting Body and Soul Together: Essays in Honor of Robin Scroggs*, ed. Virginia Wiles,
Alexandra Brown, and Graydon F. Snyder (Valley Forge, Pa.: Trinity Press International,
1997), pp. 258-73.

Chapter 3 is adapted from "*Babette's Feast* and Shaming the Poor in Corinth," *Dialog: A
Journal of Theology* 36.4 (October 1997): 270-76.

Chapter 6 is adapted from "Stuck in Time: Kairos, Chronos and the Flesh in *Groundhog
Day*," in *Explorations in Theology and Film: Movies and Meaning*, ed. Clive Marsh and Gaye
Ortiz (Oxford: Blackwell, 1997), pp. 155-65.

Chapter 10 is adapted from "The Gospel of Violent Zeal in Clint Eastwood's *Unforgiven*,"
Christianity and Literature 47.4 (Summer 1998).

For David and Sandy Rhoads,

  colleagues in the exploration of Bible and film

Contents

CONTENTS

**THE SHAMEFUL GOSPEL
AND THE PROBLEM OF REDEMPTION**

EPILOGUE

Preface

This book evolved slowly over a number of years, gaining its thematic center in 1994 when a preliminary form of Chapter 3 was presented in a worship service at Garrett-Evangelical Theological Seminary. Later presentations of other chapters were presented in sermonic form at the Nebraska Annual Conference of the United Methodist Church, at United Methodist churches in Whitehall and Claybanks, Michigan, and elsewhere. Lectures on these chapters have been delivered in summer school classes at Garrett-Evangelical, at the Charis Continuing Education event at Rainy Lake, Minnesota, at several ministers' retreats at Tipton, Indiana, at the School of Evangelism at Jacksonville, Illinois, in the form of the Cotner Lectures in Lincoln, Nebraska, and at a continuing education event of the Northern Illinois Conference of the United Methodist Church at Naperville, Illinois. Presentations have been shared with adult education series at Highland Park Presbyterian Church in Highland Park, Fourth Presbyterian Church in Chicago, Westminster Presbyterian Church in Munster, Indiana, St. Augustine Episcopal Church in Evanston, Trinity Lutheran Church in Evanston, United Church of Christ in Oak Park, and United Methodist churches in Orlando, Florida, Allison Park, Pennsylvania, and Rhinelander, Wisconsin.

Particularly helpful were the suggestions that came after presenting a form of Chapter 5 at a the opening session of the Upper

Midwest meeting of the American Academy of Religion and the Society of Biblical Literature. Suggestions and critical reactions from the ministers, teachers, and laypersons in these various sessions greatly influenced the development of this project. Ongoing conversations on the relationship of Pauline theology to the issues of honor and shame have also taken place on the Garrett-Evangelical faculty, in the Association of Chicago Theological Schools colleague group in New Testament, in the United Theological Seminary in Dayton, at Luther Seminary in St. Paul, and at the annual meeting of the Society of Biblical Literature. At a preliminary stage of the project, I was greatly aided by three students who did an independent study with me on the current literature of shame in the field of pastoral care: Carolyn Bowers, Laurel Phillips, and Anne Utterbach.

I am especially grateful for the careful reading of preliminary drafts of the manuscript by James B. Ashbrook, Robert Atkins, Russell Becker, Kay Bosworth, Keith Burton, Douglas Campbell, Neal Fisher, Gerald Forshey, David Fredrickson, Jeffrey Gibson, Paul Jewett, Linda Koops, Hubert G. Locke, Thomas Rand, David Rhoads, Glen and Lana Robyn, David deSilva, Sara Vaux, and Ed and Anne Wimberly. Appreciation is due to Robert Helmer for the careful job of creating the indexes. Given the risks of interdisciplinary work, I am certain that without the encouragement of friends, colleagues, and relatives, this project could not have been brought to completion. Errors in interpretation, of course, remain my responsibility, as are the translations of all biblical citations. Thanks also to Reinder Van Til and Dan Harlow for their editorial acumen and to Bill Eerdmans for supporting the publication of this sequel to *Saint Paul at the Movies*.

PROLOGUE

1. Uncovering Shame and Grace in Paul and the Cinema

Both to Greeks and to barbarians,
  both to the wise and to the uneducated I am under
    obligation,
hence my readiness also to preach the gospel to you who
are in Rome.
For I am not ashamed of the gospel:
  for it is the power of God for salvation to all who have
    faith,
  both to the Jew first and then to the Greek,
    for in it the righteousness of God is revealed
  from faith to faith, as it is written,
    "He who through faith is righteous shall live."

Romans 1:14-17

Introduction

It is widely acknowledged that films reveal the current state of mind in what is increasingly becoming a global village. Miriam Hansen, director of the Film Studies Center at the University of Chicago, articulates an assumption that matches my own experience: "Film has become the medium in which stories are told that tend to be central to the concerns, problems, preoccupations of a society. It is one way in which society reflects upon, communicates with, and negotiates the meaning of everyday experience, of changes, transformations of the world they live in."[1] Many of the films that have influenced my thinking reflect such a transformation. Some of them deal with the subjects of honor, shame, and righteousness, which until very recently were difficult to coordinate within the horizon of traditional biblical scholars like myself.

In this sequel to *Saint Paul at the Movies,*[2] I am continuing the experiment of bringing films and biblical texts into dialogue by means of an interpretive arch. This arch reaches between ancient and modern texts and stories. One end of the arch rests in the ancient world and the other in a contemporary cultural situation reflected in a particular film. In the films and texts I have selected for this volume, the themes of shame, honor, grace, and righteousness surface in surprising ways, shaking up traditional viewpoints and offering resources to understand the human project in our time. My method is to discern the conversation at each end of this arch, because both the biblical writers and the filmmakers interact with their cultural situations as they work with these themes, and these interactions throw new light on our current circumstances.

In the light of the historical-critical method, I understand Pauline texts as parts of larger conversations within the early church. By reconstructing these conversations on the basis of the stories that lie behind the text, I discover modern analogies not just to what Paul wrote but also to the situations he addressed. The method of these chapters is to interweave Pauline texts with modern stories and issues, allowing each side to throw light on the other. When I select a film whose themes correlate closely with a biblical text, I attempt to treat the film as a full partner in conversation with Paul. Although I am not a specialist in film criticism, I attempt to understand films within their cultural contexts. My method is that of biblical hermeneutics, aiming at the "fusion of horizons" between the ancient text and the contemporary situation. This is why Paul's discussion in Romans 1 about not being ashamed of the gospel, and its bearing on Greeks as well as barbarians, has so vital a connection with a certain strand of films.

Forgiveness and Shame in Film

Many films that are thought to have religious significance deal with individual sin and its ramifications: temptation, bad conscience, punishment, forgiveness and reconciliation. One thinks of *Amadeus, A Man Called Peter, Quo Vadis, David and Bathsheba, The Robe, Les Miserables, Pickpocket, Anna Karenina, The Scarlet Letter, Cry the Beloved Country, The Road to Heaven, Intermezzo, The Mission, The Forbidden Christ, East of Eden, The Informer, You Only Live Once, Diary of a Country Priest, A Man For All Seasons, Lilies of the Field, Cries and Whispers, Winter Light, Solaris, Nostalgia, Hamsun,* or *Dead Man Walking.* These and many other films operate out of the mainstream of the biblical interpretive tradition, assuming that the human dilemma is lack of will to achieve the good, resulting in inevitable failures to live up to the law or to high ethical ideals. This produces wicked behavior and a guilty conscience that must either be forgiven or punished. Shame in these films usually takes the form of embarrassment at being caught in sin. Grace in such films usually comes in the form of forgiveness for individual misdeeds. This matches the dominant theological paradigm of Western Christianity.

Films dealing with honor and deeper forms of shame have a very different texture: they feature social ostracism, low self-esteem, or emptiness on the one hand and arrogance, contempt, or overbearing behavior on the other. Some of the most prominent films of this type made in the United States deal with persons shamed by racial, cultural, or sexual prejudice, or by physical or mental impairments. Grace in such films takes the form of accepting the unacceptable, treating grotesque and repulsive persons as worthy human beings. This may represent a particularly pervasive stream of American filmmaking, but it is also found in films of other cultures. Americans seem willing to accept as leading characters persons of shameful intelligence in films like *Rain Man, Forrest Gump,* and *Sling Blade.* We appreciate stories of the shamefully wounded in *The Deer Hunter, The Best Years of Our Lives,* or *Born on the Fourth of July.* There is a well-established genre of films about the deaf that includes *The Heart is a Lonely Hunter, Bridge to Silence, Johnnie Belinda,* and *Children of a Lesser God. Philadelphia,* which deals with an AIDS victim who is fired because he has shamed the firm, was widely popular with American audiences. Films dealing with racial prejudice have long been a staple on the American scene, with classics like *Guess Who's Coming to Dinner, The Defiant Ones, A Raisin in the Sun,* or *In the Heat of the Night;* in *To Sir with Love,* the school children finally accept Sidney Poitier as a teacher despite initial prejudices, and in *Brother John* Poitier plays a kind of Christ figure. While these films have upbeat endings, other movies, such as *Birth of a Nation* and *Roots,* present more discriminatory scenes that reflect the history of American racism.

Class prejudice is the decisive burden in *The Young Philadelphians, Courtney Affair,* and *A Place in the Sun,* while distortions of the British class system surface in *Room at the Top* and *Look Back in Anger.* The issue of shame shifts to obesity in *What's Eating Gilbert Grape?* In *Elephant Man* and *Man Without a Face,* the heroes have grotesque physical impairments, and in *Delores Clairborn* the protagonist is an object of derision because she is ugly. In *Willow* the dwarf becomes the hero who redeems the king, while in *Gold Rush* the mistreated misfit continues to love his sweetheart until she finally is able to recognize his good qualities. In *The Fisher King* the homeless misfit is the redeemer, a role played by the alienated and tortured immigrant in *Fixer.* Paul Newman plays the role of a shamed prisoner who restores humanity to others in *Cool Hand Luke.* But there are many films in which shameful past events and discriminatory status continue to haunt the characters, such as *Spitfire Grill, Daughters of the Dust,* and *A Thousand Acres.* As in the Pauline letters, grace in these films takes the form not of forgiveness of individual sins but of overcoming dishonorable status. Despite their distance from, indeed sometimes their hostility toward, traditional religious faith, some of these films resonate with Paul's approach to triumph over shame, as recovered by recent research. They also deal critically with some of the social distortions of honor and shame that were characteristic of the ancient world with which Paul's letters interacted.

Honor and Competition in the Ancient World

The competitive center of the ancient systems of shame and honor was what Paul calls "boasting." This was a much more blatant, socially acceptable form of behavior than is conceivable for traditionally educated Americans, who are formed by an often disingenuous tradition of public modesty. Not so for the shapers of the Greco-Roman world. As E. A. Judge observed, "Self-magnification thus became a feature of Hellenic higher education."[3] By eliminating the culturally endorsed motivation of seeking honor through teaching and learning, Paul in effect radically alters the Greco-Roman theory of education.[4] Judge makes a similar case concerning the broad cultural tradition of public service. The assumption was that the quest for honor was the only suitable goal for life. "It was held that the winning of honor was the only adequate reward for merit in public life. . . . It therefore became a prime and admired objective of public figures to enshrine themselves, by actually defining their own glory, in the undying memory of posterity" by publishing memorials of their accomplishments.[5]

The explicit concern in ancient Roman society with the issue of honor is visible in its creation of what Judge has called "an aristocracy of esteem."[6] Ancient Romans used the term *gloria* to describe the aura that "arises from a person's successfully exhibiting himself to others,"[7] particularly in victorious political or military leadership. Such glory was viewed as intrinsic to the heroic person, raising him above the level of others. This was conveyed in expressions like "immortal glory" or "celestial glory" in that the superlative accomplishments would continue to resound after one's death. In contrast to Jewish thought, which reserved "glory" largely for descriptions of God, the Romans virtually restricted *gloria* to superior human accomplishments. Victorious military leaders were celebrated in religious processions, for example, that acknowledged the quality of immortal glory. Thus Ulrich Knoche contends that "the glorious man is raised up from the human to the eternal sphere: he does not become a [divine] hero but remains thoroughly human, indeed, remains a citizen."[8] Such glory depends, of course, on the recognition granted by other citizens to the "great man" for performing public service.

The glorious leader was thought to be capable of bringing the blessing of the gods upon the community; he was honored as the source of righteousness and prosperity. A sophisticated system of gradation in honor was established, in which the Roman senate voted appropriate rewards, offices, and celebrations for various levels of accomplishment in the fields of philanthropy or military strategy. The ambition of Roman leaders, who were usually drawn from leading families, was to gain ever higher levels of honor.[9]

The competition for honor was visible in every city of the Roman empire in which members of the elite competed for civic power through such activities as sponsoring games and celebrations, financing public buildings, and endowing mass food distributions. Public life in the Roman empire was centered in the quest for honor. There were inscriptions on every public building and artwork indicating to whose honor it should be attributed. Rome in particular was full of majestic public buildings such as temples, baths, fountains, and amphitheaters built to honor glorious leaders and triumphal occasions.[10] These ideas formed the center of the *Pax Romana* established by Augustus, whom Philo celebrated as the

> first and greatest benefactor to whom the whole habitable world voted no less than celestial honors. These are so well attested by temples, gateways, vestibules, porticoes. . . . he received his honours . . . with the magnitude of so mighty a sovereignty whose prestige was bound to be enhanced by such tributes. That he was never elevated or puffed up by the vast honours given to him is clearly shown by the fact that he never wished anyone to address him as a god.[11]

The propagandistic *Res Gestae* that Augustus published and inscribed in Roman temples throughout the empire celebrates his glorious accomplishments in bringing peace to the Mediterranean world and consolidating his rule under the fiction of democracy. Here one can see the elaborate gradations of honors he boasts of having received:

> In my sixth and seventh consulships, when I had extinguished the flames of civil war, after receiving by universal consent the

absolute control of affairs, I transferred the republic from my own control to the will of the senate and of the Roman people. For this service on my part I was given the title of Augustus by decree of the senate, and the doorposts of my house were covered with laurels by public act, and a civic crown was fixed above my door, and a golden shield was placed in the Curia Julia whose inscription testified that the senate and the Roman people gave me this in recognition of my valour, my clemency, my justice, and my piety. After that time I took precedence of all in rank, but of power I possessed no more than those who were my colleagues in any magistracy.[12]

The claims of having restored power to the senate and the Roman people, and of having only the collegial power of the magistracy were, of course, fictions. His position of supreme glory rendered it logical that total power would be placed in his hands, celebrated in the *Res Gestae* with language that is significant for the argument of Paul's most influential letter: *clementia* = "mercies" in Rom 12:1; *justicia* = "rightwising, righteousness, etc."; *pietas* = "piety" in Rom 1:18.

It is clear that Paul uses the Greek equivalents of these Roman terms to criticize and reverse the official system of honor on which the empire was based. He offers a new approach to mercies, righteousness, and piety, one that avoided the propagandistic exploitation of the Roman system. In the words of Dieter Georgi, "Here, in Romans, there is a critical counterpart to the central institution of the Roman Empire,"[13] that is, redemptive kingship (see Rom 1:1-3). Augustus is celebrated in the poetry of Virgil as the savior figure who ushers in "this glorious age." He receives the prophetic tribute: "He shall have the gift of divine life, shall see heroes mingled with gods, and shall himself be seen of them. . . . Enter on thy high honors . . . O thou dear offspring of the gods, mighty seed of a Jupiter to be!" (Virgil, *Eclogue* IV 11, 48) It is understandable that at Augustus' death in A.D. 14, he was voted *caelestes honores* ("eternal honors") by the Roman senate. In Everett Ferguson's words, "Deification at Rome . . . was a conferring of status; cult was a supreme form of honor."[14] In a similar vein, Claudius was voted apotheosis by the Roman senate when he was killed in A.D.

54. Nero, on his accession to the throne, was celebrated as the glorious leader who would usher in a golden age.[15] In every victory parade[16] and civic celebration in temple or coliseum, the Romans claimed superior honors for themselves and their rulers; they were firmly convinced that the gods had "exalted this great empire of Rome to the highest point yet reached on earth"[17] because of its superior virtue. In Cicero's memorable formulation, the Romans boasted of being *religione . . . multo superiores* ("far superior with respect to religious observance")[18] in comparison with the other nations they had incorporated into their empire. There are mild counterparts to such sentiments in American declarations or implications of superior virtue, but they hardly match the blatant quality of Greco-Roman boasting.

Paul's Critique of Boasting

In virtually all of his surviving letters, Paul counters the various forms of boasting that were characteristic of Greco-Roman culture, including its Jewish branches. The famous claim in Rom 3:9 that "Jews as well as Greeks are all under sin" is followed by a catena of scriptural citations that repeat no fewer than eight times that "no one" can claim honorable or righteous status or performance. James D. G. Dunn observes that the citations from the Psalms at the beginning of this catena "presuppose an antithesis between the righteous (the faithful member of the covenant) and the unrighteous. The implication is that when that presupposition of favored status before God is set aside, the scriptures serve as a condemnation of *all* humankind. . . ."[19] This undercuts the superiority claims of every system of gaining honor through performance or inherited status.

It follows that "no flesh will be set right before God by works of the law" (Rom 3:20). Dunn has moved the discussion of this verse beyond the denunciation of Jewish law popularized by the interpretative tradition undergirded by the Reformation. He describes "the function of the law as an identity factor, the social function of the law as marking out the people of the law in their distinctiveness. . . ." The problem is that "works of the law" served as an identity marker for those "whom God has chosen and will vindicate" and provided a method of "maintaining his status within that people."[20] There is a need to link these insights with the systems of gaining honor and avoiding shame in the Greco-Roman world, to allow a broader grasp of Paul's argument. It is not just the Jewish law that Paul exposes here, but law as an identity marker for any culture. Paul did not select the term "flesh" in this verse merely to critique "the equation of covenant membership with physical rite and national kinship,"[21] but to include the entire human race. In the face of the impartial righteousness of God, no human system of competing for glory and honor can stand.

The climactic formulation in Rom 3:23, that "all have sinned and fallen short of the glory of God," also has a bearing on the Jewish and Greco-Roman systems of shame and honor. It is widely acknowledged that Paul is assuming that Adam and Eve were originally intended to bear the glory of God, but lost it by eating the fatal apple. But the use of the verb "fall short" has not been sufficiently explained. An equivalent term is not employed in any of the Jewish parallels. This is a comparative term relating to the failure to reach a goal, to be inferior to someone, to fail, to come short of something.[22] The basic connotation is that of "deficit, which consists either in remaining below the normal level, or in being behind others,"[23] and hence of being in a position of deserving shame.

An important parallel to Rom 3:23 is 2 Cor 11:5 and 12:11, where "to be inferior to someone" is used in connection with the competition between Paul and his opponents known as the "superapostles."[24] To fall short is an honor issue: it resonates with the competition for honor within and between groups in the Greco-Roman world, and it echoes the wording of Rom 1:18-32 in terms of refusing to grant honor to God by choosing to worship the creature rather than the creator. Despite the claims of Jews and Greeks to surpass each other in honor, and despite their typical claims that the other groups are shameful because of their lack of wisdom or moral conformity, Paul claims that *all* fall short of the transcendent standard of honor. Dunn comes close to seeing this

11

issue, when he notes that Paul "reduces the difference between Jew and Gentile to the same level of their common creatureliness."[25] If all persons and groups fall short of the ultimate standard of honor that they were intended to bear, that is, "the glory of God," then none has a right to claim superiority or to place others in positions of inferiority.

The classic declaration of "justification by grace" in Rom 3:24, which I translate as being "set right through a gift by his grace through the redemption that is in Christ Jesus," is another issue that needs to be understood in terms of shame and honor. Righteousness, honor, and glory can be used as virtually synonymous terms, a point whose relevance can only be grasped if the traditional English translation for *dikaioumenoi* ("being justified") is replaced with its more adequate verbal equivalent, "being set right." To be "set right" in the context of the "righteousness of God" (3:21), and with reference to humans who have fallen short of the "glory of God," is to have such glory and honor *restored*. This is not an achievement but a gift of grace.

Paul is not suggesting that believers gain a comparative form of honor, so that they can continue to compete with others who remain shameful. Rather, in Christ they are given an honorable relationship that results in what 2 Cor 3:18 describes as an actual transformation derived from the mirror image of Christ in which believers change "from one degree of glory to another." In being honored by God through Christ who died for all, the formerly shamed are integrated into the community of the saints where this transformation process occurs under the lordship of Christ. This observation could be correlated with the recent work of Peter Stuhlmacher, James Dunn, and Richard Hays, which stresses that Paul understands the righteousness given to converted Jews and Gentiles "primarily in terms of the covenant relationship to God and membership within the covenant community."[26] Paul has in mind a new social reality: within the community of the shamed made right by the death and resurrection of Christ, there is no longer the possibility of any "distinction" (Rom 3:22) in honor.

Paul's crucial contention is that in Christ, rightful status is not achieved on the basis of any human effort. The threefold reference in Rom 3:24 to divine "grace," to the "gift," and to "redemption" through Christ makes it plain that no one gains this honorable, righteous status by outperforming others or by privilege of birth or wealth. In contrast to the hypercompetitive environment of the Greco-Roman world, including its Jewish component, this new status is granted by Christ only to those whose shame is manifest. While the Greeks boast in their wisdom, the Romans in their power, and the Jews in their conformity to the law, grace addresses the shameful void that motivates all boasting. By its very nature, therefore, honor granted through grace alone eliminates any basis of human boasting, which Paul explicitly states in 3:27: "Where is the boast? It is excluded!" In the words of Halvor Moxnes, the result is "to exclude false claims to honour."[27]

Paul's Surprising Use of the Language of Shame

The verses that introduce the formal argumentation of Paul's letter to the Romans, used in the caption for this chapter, contain some remarkable epithets. He employs Jewish and as well as typical Greco-Roman terms for shameful status. For example, in announcing his desire to visit Rome, Paul describes his hope to "reap some fruit also among you as among the rest of the Gentiles" (Rom 1:13). This is the second reference in Romans to non-Jewish peoples that employs the epithet used by Jews to distinguish shameful non-Jews, "Gentile."[28] The ethnically discriminatory potential of this formulation is enhanced by the next verse, which employs some of the most explicitly discriminatory language in the Pauline letters. The labels "Greeks and barbarians . . . wise and foolish" (Rom 1:14) articulate the social boundaries of Greco-Roman culture in a thoroughly abusive manner. As the definitive study of *barbaros* ("barbarian") by Yves Albert Dauge has shown,[29] this was a supremely discriminatory epithet in Greco-Roman culture. It was comparable to abusive racial terms like "nigger" or "gook" in American culture. When paired with its ideological opposite, "Greeks," which stood for the educated class in the Greco-Roman world, the term "barbarian" denotes the violent, perverse, corrupt, uncivilized element beyond and within the Roman empire that threatens peace and security. Similarly, the terms "wise" and "unwise/uneducated" depict the educational boundary between citizens of the empire and the shameful masses. But it is not just Paul's use of these epithets of honorable and shameful status that jars the reader; Paul undercuts the moral premise of the Greco-Roman world in proclaiming his indebtedness to the shameful as well as to the honorable representatives of the antitheses. Only Ernst Käsemann among modern commentators catches the revolutionary implications of Paul's formulation: "All earthly barriers are relativized. . . . as a messenger of the gospel he can uninhibitedly stride across the conventions and prejudices of the divided cosmos."[30]

The remarkable formulation in Rom 1:14 is followed by the antithetical formulation "to the Jew first and also to the Greek" in the thesis concerning the righteousness of God in Rom 1:16-17. This reverses the claim of ethnic priority that was probably being advanced by the Gentile Christian majority in Rome.[31] The reference to not being "ashamed of the gospel" (1:16) sets the tone for the entire letter.[32] As one can see from the parallel text in 1 Cor 1:20-31, the gospel was innately shameful as far as the various branches of Greco-Roman culture were concerned. The message about a messianic redeemer being crucified was a "stumbling block to Jews and foolishness to Gentiles" (1 Cor 1:23). A divine self-revelation on an obscene cross seemed to demean God and overlook the honor and propriety of established religious traditions, both Jewish and Greco-Roman. Rather than appealing to the honorable and righteous members of society, such a gospel seemed designed to appeal to the despised and the powerless. To use the words of 1 Corinthians once again, "God chose what is foolish in the world to shame the wise; God chose what is weak in the world to shame the strong. God chose what is low and despised in the world . . . so that no one might boast in the presence of God" (1 Cor 1:27-29).[33] There were persuasive social reasons why Paul should have been ashamed of this gospel; his claim not to be ashamed signals that a social and ideological revolution has been inaugurated, one that overturns the systems of honor and shame throughout the Greco-Roman world.

14

This revolution explains why Paul was able to use and to overturn the derogatory epithets that apparently were being used by partisans within the Roman churches to designate their rivals. Joel Marcus has shown that the references to groups as "circumcised" or "uncircumcised" (Rom 2:26-27; 3:30; 4:9; 15:8) should be translated literally as "circumcised glans" and "foreskin," both of which were "derogatory terms used by people in one group for people in another."[34] The language is comparable to "dickhead" as an abusive epithet in contemporary English. The politeness of modern translations disguises the element of shame that Paul is attempting to reverse. The apostle overturns the dishonorable status imputed to each group by claiming that "God will set right the 'circumcised glans' on the ground of faith and the 'foreskin' through that same faith" (Rom 3:30). These same groups are referred to in Romans 14–15 as the "weak" and the "strong," labels that reflect the superiority claims and the abusive disparagement that were poisoning relations in the church. That "weak" and "strong" in this context implied claims of both ethical and social superiority seems very likely, in light of the history and social status of the Roman house and tenement churches. But in place of the ordinary Greco-Roman assumption that the strong should dominate the weak while holding them in contempt, Paul argues that "we the powerful are obligated to bear the weaknesses of the powerless and not to please ourselves. Let each of us please the neighbor for the good, toward upbuilding. For also the Christ did not please himself, but as it is written, 'The reproaches of those who reproach you fell upon me'" (Rom 15:1-3). If Christ accepted the ultimate reproach of the cross, then bearing burdens for the shamed becomes a new form of honorable behavior.

Moving beyond Guilt and Forgiveness

Although I have been working intensively on Romans since 1980, it has only been in the last several years that the awareness of the theological significance of honor and shame has begun to dawn. Like other Pauline scholars, I was indebted to the traditional par-

15

adigm of guilt and forgiveness that has prevailed since the time of Saint Augustine. It stands as the central organizing principle in every commentary on Romans that I have studied. This highly individualistic paradigm places the individual believer at the center of Paul's thought, caught between the temptations of the flesh and the high ideals of the ethic of love, and therefore bound to fall into sin and guilt. The essence of grace, according to this traditional model, is forgiveness of sins.

For at least a decade, doubts have been growing in my mind about the adequacy of the traditional model of Paul's thought. The more I learned about the menial social status of most of the Roman congregations, the less likely it seemed that the conscience problems characteristic of later Western mentality could have been their major preoccupation. That both Jewish and pagan religions provided elaborate methods of gaining forgiveness and atonement for sins added to my disquiet about the paucity of explicit references to forgiveness in Paul's letters.

My interest was further stimulated by the increasingly wide-ranging discussion of honor and shame in the Mediterranean world.[35] On the basis of sociological, anthropological, and historical information, Bruce Malina has defined the ancient view of honor as "the value of a person in his or her own eyes . . . *plus* that person's value in the eyes of his or her social group. Honor is a claim to worth along with the social acknowledgement of worth."[36] In the competitive environment of the Mediterranean world, such honor was gained "by excelling over others in the social interaction that we shall call challenge and response."[37] This occurs only among persons of the same class, since superiority over those of lower status was assumed and did not have to be proven. The goal of a challenge, in arenas ranging from political power to religious reputation, was "to usurp the reputation of another, to deprive another of his reputation. When the person challenged cannot or does not respond to the challenge posed by his equal, he loses his reputation in the eyes of the public. . . . every social interaction that takes place outside one's family or outside one's circle of friends is perceived as a challenge to honor, a mutual attempt to acquire honor from one's social equal. . . ."[38]

16

The culture of honor and shame reflected in the New Testament, according to Malina, produced a personality type that was very different from modern, Western "individuals," whose self-identity is allegedly internal and self-directed. Mediterranean people had a "dyadic personality" (derived from the Greek word meaning "pair"); they understood themselves exclusively "in terms of what others perceive and feed back" to them.[39] This is visible in the New Testament, Malina contends, in that people are defined by their family and cultural group: Paul speaks to Jews and Gentiles, Greeks and barbarians, not to individuals. That certainly matches what I had discovered about the focus of Paul's argument in Romans and the other letters.

The recent publication of *Portraits of Paul* by Bruce Malina and Jerome Neyrey advances this analysis by incorporating evidence from the book of Acts and some of the Pauline letters.[40] Other scholars have made similar contributions. David deSilva has applied his thorough grasp of Greco-Roman literature to trace the role of honor and shame in the Epistle to the Hebrews and Paul's first letter to the Thessalonians.[41] Arthur Dewey has contributed an investigation of the theme of honor in 2 Corinthians,[42] while John Elliott has explored both shame and honor in 1 Peter.[43] The most decisive contribution to my understanding of Romans, however, came through reading "Honour and Righteousness in Romans," written by the Norwegian scholar Halvor Moxnes. He places the entire argument of Paul's most influential letter in the ancient cultural context of an "honour society" in which "recognition and approval from others" is central, which means that the "group is more important than the individual."[44] This contrasts with the dominant concern of Western theology and its interpretation of Romans, "in which guilt and guilt-feeling predominate as a response to wrongdoing."[45] He notes that the semantic equivalents of honor and shame play important roles in the argument of Romans; these include "honor," "dishonor," and the verb "to dishonor";[46] "shameless," "be ashamed," and "put to shame";[47] "glory" and "to glorify";[48] "praise" and "to praise";[49] "boast," "boasting," and "to boast."[50] This focus on honor and shame relates to the central purpose of the letter as Moxnes understands

it, "to bring together believing Jews and non-Jews in one community."[51]

To these references I would add the socially discriminatory
categories discussed above, such as "Greeks and barbarians, educated and uneducated" in 1:14, the twenty-eight appearances of the
potentially shameful epithet "Gentiles," and the categories "weak"
and strong" employed in 14:1–15:7. Even more prominent are the
twenty-five references to social gestures of honor in the form of
"welcome" and "greeting" of outsiders that dominate the last three
chapters. The word field of "righteousness/unrighteousness,"
which plays such a prominent role in the argument of Romans, is
also closely related to Jewish and Greco-Roman terminology for
honor and shame: "righteous" appears seven times; "righteousness," thirty-four times; "make righteous," fourteen times; "righteous decree," five times; "being made right," twice; "unrighteous-
ness," seven times; and "unrighteous," once.

The need to move beyond the traditional paradigm of individual guilt and forgiveness is particularly acute when we attempt
to understand the thesis of Romans. As visible in the caption at
the head of this chapter, Rom 1:16-17 declares the paradox of
power. Paul claims that in this shameful gospel the power of God
is revealed. I believe that Paul's claim that the gospel *is* the "power
of God" pertains to the reversal of the stereotypes of honor and
shame articulated in 1:14. The message of Christ crucified shatters
the unrighteous precedence given to the strong over the weak, the
free and well-educated over slaves and the ill-educated, the Greeks
and Romans over the barbarians. If the gospel that the world
considers shameful has divine power, it will prevail and achieve a
new form of honor for those who have not earned it, an honor
consistent with divine righteousness. All who place their faith in
this gospel will be set right, that is, be placed in the right relation
to the most significant arena in which honor is dispensed: divine
judgment. Thus the triumph of divine righteousness through the
gospel of Christ crucified and resurrected is achieved by transforming the system in which shame and honor are dispensed.

When the frequency of honor and shame terminology is compared with the single allusion to pardon in Rom 3:25, it now seems

clear that a mainstream has been confused for a minor current in the tradition of interpreting Pauline theology. It is time to move beyond the paradigm of individual guilt and forgiveness in understanding Paul. This book represents my first extended effort to articulate a new assessment of the triumph of grace over shameful status as the organizing center of Paul's thought.

Conclusion

Judging from the evidence in the Pauline letters and stimulated by the close study of certain films, I have come to the intuition that shame may be a deeper and more pervasive human dilemma than guilt, and also that grace is broader than individual forgiveness. Shame pertains not merely to what we have done but also to what we are, both as individuals and as members of groups. My impression is that some of the more prejudicial wounds of shame are rarely cauterized and almost never forgotten. But this intuition is almost impossible to confirm in the abstract: the memories of personal and collective failures and limitations, of abuse and discrimination, of feeling neglected, unloved, or unworthy, need to be brought into the light of day before their effect can be assessed. But the essence of shame is painful exposure of vulnerability, which we avoid at all costs. The root meaning for the terminology of shame in many languages is "cover" or "hide," and the basic shame phenomenon in every culture, including the Greco-Roman and Jewish cultures that produced the Bible, is the lowered, averted, reddened face, often hidden by one's hands. Beyond all other human emotions and reactions, shame is what we most instinctively hide.

Cinema has a unique capacity to uncover, to show the faces whose shameful features are usually disguised, both to ourselves and to others. In the darkness of a theater or the privacy of a video screening, we gaze at the uncovered faces on the screen, while our own faces remain unobserved. We deal with shame vicariously in this peculiar, modern ritual of watching the flickering images on the screen. We eagerly gaze time and time again at the embarrassing gaffes of our elected leaders or the stumbling of our Olympic skaters, while our own failures are carefully disguised from public view. While "uncovering shame" is extremely difficult for theology, and even for therapy, it remains the everyday stuff of cinema, which can provide a decisive aid in understanding and dealing with the wounds of shame in a manner congruent with Paul's legacy.

It follows that this book is an exploration of a seemingly preposterous proposition. Could it be that certain movies afford deeper access to the hidden heart of Paul's theology than mainstream theologians like myself have been able to penetrate? Are there insights in these films that would help us better to understand Paul's references to honor, shame, and grace, allowing us to come to terms with some of the deepest and most obscure dilemmas of the human heart, to confront them openly and redemptively? Conversely, could Pauline theology help us understand the deeper dimensions of *The Prince of Tides, Forrest Gump, Babe,* and *Shawshank Redemption?* Does it throw light on *The Firm* and *Groundhog Day?* Could it help us understand the interplay between honor, shame, and superheroic fantasies in *Mr. Holland's Opus* and *Unforgiven?* Can it help us grasp the theological depths of *Edge of the City* and *Babette's Feast,* revealing dimensions of grace that reach beyond the conventional parameters of individual forgiveness? And will this dialogue throw any light on the dilemma of religious faith in the current moment, so that the gospel message of the triumph of grace over shame can be caught afresh? This book is an effort to find out.

LOVE AND THE SECRETS
OF SHAME

2. The Exposure of Shameful Secrets in *The Prince of Tides*

Therefore if the whole church gathers together and all
speak in tongues,
    and outsiders or unbelievers come in,
        will they not think you are mad?
But if all prophesy,
    and an unbeliever or outsider comes in,
        he will be convicted by all,
        called to account by all,
        the secrets of his heart are disclosed,
and so falling on his face he will acknowledge God,
    declaring that God is really among you.

1 Corinthians 14:24-25

This passage provides a vivid glimpse into the life of the early congregations. When the Corinthian believers gathered together, it was probably in the context of a love feast in which the Lord's Supper was incorporated into a potluck meal.[1] Paul envisions a non-Christian neighbor drifting into the celebration and calculates how it would affect him. If everyone is wildly speaking in tongues, the visitor may well conclude he is viewing a typical mystery religion celebration of Bacchic frenzy in which divine madness is contagious. But if the community's prophets are holding forth, explaining the meaning of Christ's life, death, and resurrection and applying it to everyday life, it could result in the conversion of the outsider.

The most striking feature in this description of conversion is the matter of disclosing the secrets of the heart. The message of Christ crucified, which Paul had established as a model of early Christian proclamation according to 1 Cor 2:1-2, related to the peculiar structure of secrecy in that cultural environment. The shameful crucifixion of Christ evidently had the power to unlock secrets kept tightly locked within the human heart. But why should the revelation of secrets be understood as a crucial step in human transformation? This is a point left unexplained by most commentators, one that hardly ever surfaces in standard accounts of religious conversion. Yet it plays a central role in Pat Conroy's novel and screenplay that address us in this chapter.

The Prince of Tides[2] is the story of the Wingo family in Charleston, South Carolina, growing up on a tidal island with the burden of shameful family secrets that come close to destroying them all. The father is a brutal, bullying shrimp fisherman, the mother a manipulative, social-climbing beauty. She finally divorces her husband and ascends into the upper class by marrying a banker who had earlier bullied her son Tom. When Tom's twin sister Savannah attempts to commit suicide, Tom, played by Nick Nolte, is called to New York by Dr. Susan Lowenstein, the psychiatrist working with Savannah. She wants help in recovering the memory of family secrets that her suicidal patient has buried like "a splinter inside her, that she has neglected," to use the words of the doctor played by Barbra Streisand.

Shameful secrets festering inside Savannah almost kill her until she is helped to confront them. The most suppressed secret of all relates to "Callenwolde," the woods from which a rapist had stalked their mother and from which he later returned with two escaped convicts on a rainy night. They attacked the Wingo family while their father was off fishing, raping Tom, Savannah and their mother, Lila. The rapists are killed after being surprised by the return of the courageous elder brother, Luke Wingo. But Lila pledges her children to absolute secrecy as they bury the bodies on their remote island, lest the news about their shameful humiliation deepen the impression that they are a trashy family. It is only after Savannah unearths and painfully confronts this secret in the course of the story that healing becomes possible for her.

The Prince of Tides throws light on 1 Corinthians 14 by indicating why "the secrets of the heart" need to be exposed. It reveals that the secrets of shame are profoundly crippling and that they need to be brought to light before people can come to health. When we understand 1 Cor 14:24-25 in the light of its context in an ancient system of honor and shame, the social function of secrecy becomes transparent and the affinities between this text and the film become mutually revealing. In conversation with the film, I would like to explore why shameful experiences are buried with such vehement secrecy and why Paul assumes that the prophetic proclamation of Christ crucified and resurrected has the capacity to expose and heal the secrets of the heart.

Shame and the Secrets of the Heart

The standard commentaries on 1 Corinthians 14 attempt to explain this passage by concentrating on the conventional theme of individual sin and guilt. For example, Hans Conzelmann refers to Paul's "evangelization by uncovering the consciousness of guilt,"[3] while F. F. Bruce describes the gospel that is able to "pierce direct to his heart and conscience, expose his inmost secrets, and convict him of sin."[4] The sense of shame as exposure of guilty behavior in these commentaries reflects the preoccupation of Western theologians with individual conscience and the inner state of the self.[5] However, in the ancient world, keeping an evil deed secret prevents the shame of public exposure but does not guard against pangs of conscience. Rudolf Bultmann has a firmer grasp of the primacy of the public dimension of shame when he suggests that *aischynō* ("be ashamed") describes "not so much the state of soul of the 'shamed one', but the situation into which he is brought and in which he is exposed to shame and thus has to be ashamed."[6] In Greco-Roman culture, shame is primarily repugnant "in the external sense . . . as disgraceful in words and deeds or in appearances and afflictions" in the sociological sense.[7] It is not merely a matter of what one has done but who one is, how one appears in the public eye. Similarly, in New Testament usage, "the sense of *being put to shame* is . . . more pronounced than that of *being ashamed*."[8] The urgent necessity of maintaining secrets in such a cultural setting derives from precisely this fear of public exposure, of being put to shame. In the words of Albrecht Oepke, who has contributed the definitive article on the Greek word for "hide," "One conceals things of which one is ashamed,"[9] because if they are discovered, one's social standing is jeopardized.

The crucial place Paul gives to exposing human secrets is typical of biblical thought. In Rom 2:16 Paul refers to the last judgment as a time when "God will judge the secrets of humans," exposing the public camouflage that Gentiles as well as Jews erected to avoid shameful exposure. The prophet Jeremiah perceived that only God is able to penetrate these hidden reaches of the heart in which perversity is buried: "The heart is devious above all else; it is perverse — who can understand it? I the LORD test the mind and search the heart, to give to all according to their ways, according to the fruit of their doings" (Jer 17:9-10). The biblical premise is stated succinctly by in the Psalms: God "knows the secrets of the heart" (Ps 44:21). To counteract this propensity for shameful secrecy, the righteous are taught to pray for openness: "Search me, O God, and know my heart; test me and know my thoughts" (Ps 139:23).

The Prince of Tides deals not just with the secret of Callenwolde, but also the other shaming events that poisoned relationships in the Wingo family. For example, Tom remembers how his mother would tell him that he was the only Wingo who would amount to something. "You're my favorite. That's going to be our little secret," she says, "can you keep a secret?" Embarrassed by this favoritism and the stifling intimacy of his mother's bedroom where this conversation takes place, the boy wants to leave, but Lila won't let him go until he says he loves her. Tom turns away, reluctantly saying, "Love you, mamma." In reporting this incident to Lowenstein, Tom says, "It took me twenty years to tell Luke and Savannah about my secret. When I did, they just fell on the floor howling." Their mother had told the same thing to each. These dishonest, shaming secrets contributed to Tom's inability to love and trust others, making him the "defensive, closed SOB" he admits to having become.

The Wingo family secrets had to remain buried because their exposure would bring shame. When Dr. Lowenstein asks why Lila had burned Savannah's childhood journal, Tom replies, "Because Savannah was being disloyal, writing about our hideous family." Later in the film, when Tom tells his mother he is going to tell Lowenstein about Callenwolde, she replies: "I don't know what you're talking about." "Oh yeah you do, Mom, yeah you do," he says. She replies, "You made a promise never to speak about that. I expect you to keep that promise. . . . my life is private and I want to keep it private." Tom retorts, "Even at the expense of helping your own daughter?" He later is able to tell Lowenstein how they had buried the three rapists and cleaned up the house, while Lila kept everyone from ever knowing what happened.

> Momma said, "It's over, get these carcasses outside. This did not happen," she said. The minute we breathed a word about it was the minute she'd stop being our mother. Told us, "Morning will come and it will look nice in the sunlight."

After burying the rapists in the woods, Tom had gone back into the house to check on Savannah, who "was trying to do what Momma said, act like nothing had happened." But her dress was on inside out.

Henry Wingo, the father, came home for supper and was his usual bullying self, suspecting nothing. They sat around the dinner table, unable to converse, pretending nothing was wrong. "God help me," Tom recalls to Lowenstein, "the silence was worse than the rape." This seems incredible, given the scale of their humiliation and pain in being brutally raped. But to remain silent heightened the shame, and a secret on this scale was too much to bear.[10] Three days later, Savannah tried to kill herself. As Tom reports, "She could keep quiet, but she couldn't lie."

Tom's method of coping with the impossible burden of family secrets was to become pliant and polite. He tells Lowenstein that whereas Luke and Savannah were "incredible people . . . not for sale," he had become a "courteous Southern boy, did what he was told. I was responsible, normal, dull." He joked when threatened with the slightest exposure of vulnerability; he kept his distance from his own feelings and from close relationships with others; he had kept a stiff upper lip even after the death of his brother, Luke. But to use the words of a friend of mine who is involved in prison ministry, "secrets keep you sick."

Tom is depicted at the beginning of the film in a state of emptiness and despair. Talking with his wife on the beach, he tries to "calculate the exact moment" when everything in his life got so messed up, leading to his being fired as a coach and to the imminent breakup of his marriage. "My life's a mess, Sally," he says. In response to her statement that she no longer knows how he feels about her, Tom replies, "I don't know how I feel about anything anymore." Later he writes that he understands how Sally could feel about being married to "half a man. How could you not be disappointed?" As movie critic Jack Matthews describes him, "Tom buried his pain under so many layers of glib wit and phony philosophy that neither his wife nor his children can see the man beneath them."[11] At the center of this painful despair lay a myriad of shameful secrets, and it was only as they were exposed that he could gain wholeness.

In *Radical Honesty*, the psychotherapist Brad Blanton relates incidents reminiscent of Tom's dilemma. He tells of a bureaucrat in the Federal Bureau of Indian Affairs suffering from "terrible insomnia and chronic fatigue" who finally went to a therapist, who advised him to admit his other sexual liaisons to his live-in lover and "to reveal his disdain for various co-workers to their faces."[12] The exposure of these secrets had a remarkable effect, resulting in his marriage to his lover and a healthy reinvigoration of the bureau. "Now he continues to sleep well and feel lots of energy." Blanton says: "We are all terrible liars. People with notable stress disorders like ulcers, insomnia and spastic colitis are worse liars than normal people, although normal people are generally unhappy from lying, withholding, hiding, avoiding and evading." It's a cliche to ask what it takes to sleep at night," says Chicago psychiatrist Henry Evans:

> . . . but honesty is most often the answer. When we are not honest, we feel shame for not meeting personal standards and guilt for breaking the rules of our consciences. . . . When you rationalize, you are explaining things to the conscience. There is a lot of hiding from yourself and loss of awareness. You go around with the vague sense something is wrong, but you don't quite know why because you have convinced your conscience that everything is OK."[13]

We see this kind of chronic, crippling dishonesty in Tom's very first response to Dr. Lowenstein's question about earlier suicide attempts in his sister's life. She inquires about the attempt after their brother died, but Tom is evasive and angry. He knows very well that her first attempt at suicide occurred after the rape episode when they were thirteen. Lowenstein says that although she cannot be certain of a cure, "I'm not going to give up trying." When Tom admits he is resigned to Savannah's committing suicide, Lowenstein says this means he can no longer be of help. He is struck dumb for a moment and asks, "What do you want from me?" "Information" she replies, because "there are whole portions of her life that she has blotted out. I want you to be her memory, in a sense, to fill in the missing details." But Tom replies, "I spent my life trying to forget those missing details."

It is precisely this dishonest effort to forget that keeps both Tom and his sister sick. But the question is how to overcome the secretive habits of the heart, especially when they seem so essential to protect people from shame. Who would ever love and accept us if our shameful secrets were exposed?

"Prophecy" in Christological and Psychiatric Forms

The word "prophecy" is potentially misleading to modern readers, because in the biblical tradition it was not always a matter of predicting future events but of challenging and comforting the community. When Paul speaks of "prophecy" in 1 Corinthians 14, it seems close to what we today might identify as pastoral preaching or stating the truth in a group counseling session. He contends that prophecy of this type has the capacity to expose these secrets of the heart and cause religious conversion. The contrast, of course, is with "speaking in tongues," which is comparable to some forms of modern emotional peak experiences. Earlier in this chapter, Paul claims, "I thank God that I speak in tongues more than all of you" (1 Cor 14:18), but he prefers understandable speech in the congregational setting, "in order to instruct others" (14:19). But in the context of a public setting where uninitiated visitors appear, he fears something much more extreme, that the suspicion of religious mania will arise (14:24). He evidently assumes that Christian worship will be confused with pagan religious ecstasy.[14] This kind of experience can lead to amoral, irrational behavior while one loses conscious control, but it does not have the capacity to open up the secrets of the heart. Like contemporary drug experiences, it provides the illusion that one is temporarily released from the shameful present, caught up in a superhuman reality of some kind; but when one comes out of the spell, the depressing current circumstances reassert themselves, and one is less capable than ever of coping with that shame. Escapism vitiates the capacity to prevail over the legacies of shame.

The scholarly discussion of 1 Corinthians 14 has shown that Paul favors prophecy because it "is simply more effective in conveying salvation to the visitors."[15] The key to understanding its effectiveness is found in 14:3, where "the one who prophesies speaks to people to strengthen, encourage and comfort them."[16] Carolyn Osiek has explained this by elaborating the meaning of three nouns used in 14:3: of *oikodomē* as "being constructive" in relating to others; of *paraklēsis* as "encouragement," in the Garrison Keillor sense of making "shy people get up and do what needs to be done"; and of *paramythia* as "consolation," in the sense of "holding things together in a loving way in a difficult time or a time of pain."[17]

All this makes sense only if this kind of prophecy is explicitly

Christological. There is a distinctive shape to evangelical prophecy, which applies the message of Christ shamefully crucified on behalf of the shamed, but resurrected to the honor of all. This message produces a powerful expression of unconditional acceptance of the shamed, which in turn allows the secrets of each person's heart to come out into the open. If the love of Christ is unconditional, then there is no longer a need to disguise one's shame. This conveyance of the unconditional love of Christ was enhanced by the social context of such prophecy. In the atmosphere of mutual acceptance in the early Christian love feast, each participant was treated as an honorable equal, beloved by Christ. Walter Rebell in particular has pointed to the social context of the house church and the peculiar shaping of prophecy through "love" as the keys to this transformation.[18]

For Paul, Christian prophecy began with this message of Christ crucified for all. Paul then developed a critique of the various methods people develop to hide their shame. As Paul shows in Romans, such efforts always end up in hostility against God and in a symbolic willingness to crucify the Christ. His shameful death came as a result both of having identified with the shamed and of having exposed the proud. His death reveals that each human is engaged in a war with God in which we seek to honor the creature rather than the creator. Christ's resurrection proves that this revelation of the wicked idolatry of the human heart is true, and has been overcome by divine power. But Paul conducted this critique under the aegis of love, which demanded constructive, encouraging, and consoling discourse. It is closer to "individually shaped therapeutic conversation" than to the modern sermon.[19] Under the persuasion of such prophecy, the secrets of hearts are loosed from bondage. When they fly free, the process of human transformation begins to soar.

We encounter a modern form of this kind of prophecy in *The Prince of Tides*, with a therapist struggling for the truth in a context of love and commitment to the healing process. In the film's narrative voice-over, Tom describes his daily routine in New York City. In the mornings he would work with Lowenstein's son Bernard, to teach him how to play football. Then in the afternoons he would tell the Wingo family secrets. During one such conversation over dinner,

Lowenstein asks Tom if he has any idea about the "three stray dogs" that play such an ominous role in a children's book that Savannah wrote. The dogs are an obvious reference to the three rapists in the Callenwolde incident. But Tom evades and talks about his own dream, of walking through a blinding snowstorm and meeting Lowenstein. "What does it mean?" he asks. She reflects, "Blinding snow storm . . . maybe there's something you're afraid to see."

Under the guidance of Lowenstein's therapeutic insight, the truth finally comes out. Tom Wingo tells the awful story of the rape and its cover-up. When the doctor asks how he feels about bringing this family secret out into the open for the first time, he lies and jokes and says he feels all right, ghosts out of the closet and so on. She notes that he has really learned to "cover his pain." "You've done that all of your life," she wisely observes. He breaks down and cries for the first time while Lowenstein comforts him with motherly tenderness. She shares his tears while saying over and over again, "It's okay."[20]

Although the sources and inspiration of these two forms of prophecy are different, the process of exposing the secrets of the heart in an atmosphere of unconditional acceptance is strikingly similar. Both the Pauline text and the modern film throw light on each other, illuminating at the same time one of the deepest and most elusive aspects of human transformation: unraveling the web of lies and deceptions that attempt to guard the heart from shame.

Reproved and Called to Account

In 1 Corinthians 14:25 Paul details two dimensions of this prophetic activity that contribute to the disclosure of the secrets of the heart: "convicted by all, called to account by all." Both need to be interpreted in the light of the earlier reference to prophecy discussed above. The need for mutual accountability was grounded in the Christ event, which required a context of love and support that the church received day by day in the love feasts. Commentators are clear that this verse is one of the earliest accounts we have of Christian conversion.[21] But what kind of conversion? Robertson and Plummer's classic commentary sees here a three-stage process, a theory shaped more by the later tradition of revivalist preaching than by the actual language of this chapter. They posit the three stages of conversion as follows:

> (1) He is convinced of his sinful condition; (2) he is put upon his trial, and the details of his condition are investigated; (3) details are made plain to him.[22]

Rather than seeing the first step as an attack on human sin,[23] which is not mentioned in this passage, it is better to understand the first step in the light of 1 Cor 14:3, as interpreted by Osiek and Rebell. Encouragement and upbuilding on the basis of Christ crucified for the shameful are the first steps in opening the heart. Without this foundation, "being convicted by all, called to account by all" would only raise the defense systems of the human heart higher than ever. Grace is the key to this therapy, not judgment. What Paul has in mind, I think, is close to what Blanton calls the discipline of "telling the truth" and then finally "exposing the fiction" of one's imagined and public self. This process cannot even begin until unconditional acceptance has been conveyed in real and tangible forms.

There are several kinds of mutual accountability in *The Prince of Tides*, none of which is fully comparable to what Paul had in mind. One is Tom's coaching of young Bernard Woodruff. At first Bernard is so touchy that he cannot accept coaching at all, having been humiliated by the ballplayers at his private high school the preceding year, and feeling no affirmation from his parents in athletics. But Tom Wingo will only coach him on the condition that he show respect by saying "sir," that he follow orders without back talk, and that he put everything he has into the game. Within a few weeks, Bernard begins to shape up into a promising athlete. At the end of the summer, he heads off for the music festival at Tanglewood with new self-confidence.

A more significant embodiment of this principle of mutual accountability involves both Susan Lowenstein and Tom Wingo. The need for truth-telling becomes mutual, because after Bernard shuts his mother off again, Susan asks Tom what Tom thinks of her. He jokes with her in his usual, evasive manner: "You're rich, you've got it made, you're in the top one percent." She sees through this in an instant, retorting, "You're lying," which is in fact the case. Tom becomes quiet and reflective for a moment and then speaks the uncomfortable truth, "I think you're a very sad woman, Lowenstein." She replies, "I like it when you tell the truth. And I think you're the first friend I've made in a long time."

The most vivid episode of being "convicted" and "called to account" in *The Prince of Tides* concerns Susan Lowenstein's arrogant husband, the famous violinst Herbert Woodruff. He is verbally abusive to his wife while carrying on an affair with a young flutist whom he invites to parties at their home. Herbert holds Wingo in contempt because of Tom's Southern accent, his profession of coaching, and his success in developing a genuine relationship with Bernard. He invites Tom to a party of musicians, friends, and sycophants, and in order to shame him as a Southern boor, he plays a wickedly humorous rendition of "Dixie" on his Stradivarius violin. Then he rudely sends Tom off to fetch a drink. At dinner, Susan is emboldened to say that she can't believe that the musician who has been making love with her husband would come to the party. As the flutist stalks out, Herbert demands that Susan apologize. She replies, "I think you owe me an apology, you SOB." He replies, "Darling, where's your sense of humor?"

Meanwhile Tom Wingo slips out of the room and appears on the balcony, playing the role of the Southern crazy man as he holds Woodruff's Stradivarius over the edge of the high-rise balcony and tosses it up in the air with the confidence that only a gifted, experienced athlete could muster. Woodruff hastily apologizes to Susan in order to protect his most valuable possession. Then Tom demands and receives an apology for the insults he has experienced as a guest at their dinner party. He heads out of the apartment with the comment, "You all sure know how to give a party up here in New York City." His calm, effective presence has exposed the brutal contempt that makes Susan's life unbearable. But there is no hint that Tom's insistence on a minimal form of accountability has either the deep grounding or the kind of transforming effect that the apostle Paul had in mind.

This episode is followed by a brief love affair between Susan and Tom, one that Tom has to repudiate at the end, as he feels compelled to return to his responsibilities at home. This is a problematic aspect of the film, especially in light of the need to be "called to account" and "convicted" by all. It is a relationship between a family member of a patient and a psychiatrist that seems to be a perverse substitute for the prophetic truth-telling of gospel preaching based on genuine love that Paul had in mind.[24] In the end, Tom tells Susan that he has to go back. She says, "One of the things I love about you is that you're the kind of guy who will always go back to your family. I gotta find a nice Jewish boy; you guys are killing me." He goes home to pack up, and Savannah is shown writing a new book of poetry, dedicated to "Tom Wingo, my memory." Despite their mistakes, the Wingo twins and Susan Lowenstein have found their way through disclosing the secrets of the heart.

Conversion as the Discovery of God

A peculiar feature of 1 Cor 14:25 is that the disclosure of secrets is followed by the discovery that "God is really among you." I believe the logical connection between these ideas is visible in other Pauline passages. Prior to the exposure, abandonment, and cure of the secrets of the heart, each person and each group is suppressing the truth and playing god, seeking to enhance the honor of the "creature" rather than worshiping the "creator" (Rom 1:18, 25). It is God's love that freed the Corinthians from their corrupt secrets, so they could discover the truth about themselves and about God. The crucifixion and resurrection of Christ reveal the hostile idolatry at the center of these schemes to disguise shame. The gospel is able to cure the wounds that make such schemes seem so desperately necessary for human dignity. But until those wounds are brought out into the open and cauterized, healing is impossible. We remain caught in the throes of evil in all its dimensions as long as we worship false gods that promise "honor," or we ourselves play God's role.

In *The Prince of Tides* there is a discovery of transcendence, but not exactly the transcendence of God as Paul envisioned it. On their last night together in New York City, Tom and Susan are dancing slowly together, and he recalls, "I told her it was her doing that I could go back. Six weeks before I wanted to leave my wife, my kids. I wanted out of everything. But she changed that. She changed me. For the first time I felt I had something to give back to the women in my life. They deserve that." The scene shifts to the beach, where Tom and his wife embrace while his daughters run to join the hug. He returns to his coaching profession and reflects on what his trip to New York has meant:

> In New York I learned that I must love my father and mother in all their flawed, outrageous humanity, that in families there are no crimes past forgiveness. But it is the mystery of life that sustains me now. . . . At the end of every day, I drive through the city . . . and as I cross the bridge to take me home, I feel the words building inside me. I can't stop them . . . but as I reach the top of the bridge, these words come to me in a whisper. I say them as prayer, as regret, as praise. I say, "Lowenstein, Lowenstein."

The camera pans to that great tidal plain of Charleston linked by the bridge that bears the prince of tides back home. This is a saccharine scene in some ways, overlaid with sentimental music and lacking in full plausibility. Yet it is striking that this film, which otherwise makes no explicit reference to religion in any form, was felt to require a mystical framework to correlate with the remarkable transformation in the Wingo family. Lowenstein's miraculous ministrations somehow blend with the primal power of the tide, producing a cinematic climax that is effective emotionally if not intellectually.

The early Christians crossed a similarly mysterious bridge in every love feast that celebrated the one who died for the sake of the shamed, a death that led them to accept each other as family, despite "all their flawed, outrageous humanity." They were led to believe that the transcendent reality that holds the universe together, moving the tides in their rhythms, was the love of God that exposed and cured the secrets of their hearts. No matter what rivers they had to cross and what burdens they were given to carry, they sang Christ's praises as their most valued, most beloved companion. So I find myself in the end humming a hymn of our century as I cross my bridge toward home, celebrating that same Lord: "In the cross of Christ I glory, towering over the wrecks of time. . . ."

3. *Babette's Feast* and
Shaming the Poor in Corinth

But in [these] instructions, I do not commend you, because when you come together, it is not for the better but for the worse. For, in the first place, when you come together in church, I hear that there are divisions among you. . . . When you meet together, it is not the Lord's supper that you eat. For in eating, each one goes ahead with his own meal, and one is hungry and another drunk.

What! Do you not have houses to eat and drink in?
Or do you despise the church of God and shame
those who have nothing?
What shall I say to you?
Shall I commend you in this?
No, in this I will not praise you!

For I received from the Lord what I also delivered to you, that the Lord Jesus on the night when he was betrayed took bread, and when he had given thanks, he broke it, and said,

"This is my body which is for you.
Do this in remembrance of me."

In the same way after supper [he took] the cup, and said,

"This cup is the new covenant in my blood.
Do this, as often as you drink it,
in remembrance of me."

For as often as you eat this bread and drink the cup, you proclaim the Lord's death until he comes. . . . So then, my brothers and sisters, when you come together to eat, wait for one another. If any one is hungry, let him eat at home, lest you come together to be condemned.

1 Corinthians 11:17-18, 20-26, 33-34

Introduction

In 1 Corinthians 11, Paul criticizes the Corinthians for violating the Lord's Supper by starting to eat before others arrive and by not partaking of the same food and drink. Does this kind of behavior not "show contempt for the church of God and shame those who have nothing?" he asks (1 Cor 11:22). Their behavior violates the love feast in so fundamental a manner that they are not really eating the "Lord's Supper" at all (11:20).

Why was Paul so upset? What was the underlying relationship between the references to shame and the celebration of the common meal that led to his sense of outrageous violation?

I approach this text with the premise that shame may be more basic than guilt in understanding the human dilemma. As we have seen in Chapters 1 and 2, guilt is the status we enter into after violating a rule or doing wrong to someone. Shame includes the embarrassment we feel in getting caught. But at a deeper level, shame is felt when others demean us on prejudicial grounds, not because of what we have done but because of our identity, whether it be our race, our culture, our gender, our ability, or our religion. The most damaging form of shame is to accept and to internalize such evaluations, leading us to believe that we are worthless, that our lives are without significance.

It is clear that most of our traditional theologies and liturgies

39

concentrate on individual sin, by offering forgiveness for our failing to live up to the law. But I would like to concentrate here on the broader strand of New Testament thinking that offered an antidote to shame by conveying that, in God's eyes, those held in contempt by society were really "somebody." I would like to sketch the inclusion of the shamed in early Christian meals, the grounding of this inclusion through the shameful death of Christ on the cross, and the problem of shaming fellow believers in Corinth. Along the way I would like to link these themes with *Babette's Feast*,[1] a film that reveals the transforming potential of overcoming shame and emptiness by sharing a meal together.[2]

The Inclusion of the Shamed in Corinth and Denmark

There is considerable evidence that the love-feast system in Corinth welcomed persons whom Corinthian society held to be shameful in the sense of lacking honor or social prestige. In chapter 1, Paul asks the Corinthians:

> Consider your own call . . . . : not many of you were considered wise, not many were powerful, not many were of noble birth. . . . God chose the weak things of this world, things that are not, to reduce to nothing the things that are, so that no one might boast in the presence of God. (1 Cor 1:26-29)

Boasting was the name of the game in Greco-Roman society. Honor came to those with high intelligence, wit, and culture; it was the privilege of those with political, economic, or social power; and it was granted to anyone of noble birth. But an honor and shame society has only so much honor to go around: those receiving none, like most of the members of the Corinthian church, were held in contempt. They and their children were taught to be ashamed; as far as the public was concerned, their lives were worthless. Yet, Paul reminds the Corinthians that it was precisely such people who were invited into the Corinthian church by the message of Christ crucified. They were converted when they discovered that Christ had died on their behalf, and that they were deemed worthy by his act alone to enter into the love feasts celebrated in various homes and shops around Corinth.

One of the most powerful expressions of this theme of the transforming feast is the Danish film *Babette's Feast*. The film tells the story of a banquet organized and given by a Parisian cook, Babette, for a small, pietistic congregation. The group had been founded by a minister whose two daughters had renounced their talent, their beauty, and all chances at marriage in order to continue their father's work after his death. Martina and Philippa now care for the sick and gather the small group together for simple services in the spirit of the departed founder.

Babette had arrived in 1871 as a refugee from the massacres in Paris, which destroyed her family. Babette, played with magnificent reserve by Stéphane Audran, becomes the family cook; her only contact with France is the annual renewal of a lottery ticket. Unbeknownst to the sisters, Babette had been the most famous chef in Paris, but she "watches with a stiff-upper-lipped stoicism as the sisters show her how to make the codfish and ale-bread soup that constitutes their main diet."[3] While they are intent to make their food as unappetizing as possible, she not only humanizes their life by small improvements in their diet, but also saves them money by her wise stewardship of the household. When the sisters plan an anniversary celebration in honor of their father, she asks to be allowed to prepare the dinner.

Martina and Philippa had envisioned a simple meal, fitting their ascetic lifestyle. But Babette has recently won 10,000 francs in the lottery, so she proceeds to spend the entire sum on one sumptuous meal. It is to be served on proper silver platters with proper linen tablecloths, with table decorations that would suit the finest French restaurant, with wines perfectly selected to match the extraordinary fare.

The eight members of the congregation, who have been bickering sourly with each other for years, show up at the dinner, having resolved not to enjoy the taste of any of this extravagant food lest it bring them too close to the sensual pleasures of the flesh. They are joined by a former suitor of Martina, Lorens Loewenhielm, and his aunt, making a table of twelve. Loewenhielm is now an honored general who has become despondent about the empty triumphs of his life experienced after leaving the congregation years earlier.

The story relates the gradual transformation that comes over everyone enjoying the feast, as the members of the community begin to savor the wonderful food and wine. The crotchety members begin to overcome secret but long-felt grudges, and the general discovers the gift of life once again. In the words of James Wall, writing in *The Christian Century,* "The feast becomes an experience of grace . . . in which conflicts are resolved once they are seen from a transcendent perspective."[4] It is the banquet itself that provides this transformation. The shame that their piety had sought to alleviate is simply overwhelmed by the power of abundant love.

Our Corinthian text deals with a Lord's Supper that is expected to convey a similar kind of transformation, where the source of the love is explicitly stated. It comes through the gospel message about the death of Christ. This leads to the second theme in our text that I would like to explain.

How the Crucifixion of Christ Overcomes Shame

There is a striking concentration on the death of Christ both in the description of the sacramental meal in 1 Corinthians 11 and in the references to Paul's gospel in chapter 2. "For as often as you eat this bread and drink the cup," says Paul, you Corinthians "proclaim the Lord's death until he comes" (1 Cor 11:26). In a similar vein, Paul reminds the Corinthians that he had not preached "lofty words or wisdom," enticing them with visions of honor, but had instead "decided to know nothing among you except Jesus Christ, and him crucified" (1 Cor 2:1-2).

This may be a little hard for us to grasp, for the cross has become an emblem of honor today. We wear polished crosses as jewelry; we "lift high the cross" and bear it into our services with pride. But in the first century the cross was the supreme emblem of shame.[5] To be crucified was to be stripped naked and nailed up high, where one's vulnerability and agony were exposed to public contempt. As we can learn from the Gospel accounts of Jesus' death, crucifixion was as much a ceremony of shame as of torture. In a Jewish culture that avoided any exposure of private body parts, crucifixion was shockingly obscene. Furthermore, only the most shameful elements of society were subject to crucifixion. If you were a Roman citizen, you would not be executed in this way; crucifixion was for slaves, prisoners of war, revolutionaries, and bandits.

For most of the members of the Corinthian house and tenement churches, the cross of Christ meant not only that he had suffered the death they were in danger of experiencing, but also that he suffered it on their behalf. It was Jesus' ministry to the shamed, to the marginalized "people of the land," to the prostitutes and the mentally and physically impaired that led directly to his death. He struggled against the religion and politics of contempt that he knew would shortly propel his country into a cataclysm of violent warfare and ethnic cleansing. His love for the shamed led to his execution by means of the most shameful, obscene method of death on a cross. So when the assembly of the formerly shamed Corinthians share their sacramental love feasts together, they remember Jesus' body and blood given for them, and "proclaim the Lord's death until he comes." They do so with joy, because his shameful death has overcome their shame, transforming them into God's beloved family, entitling them to dance and sing.

One problem in understanding these basic connections is that traditional celebrations of the sacramental meal bypass the element of shame. Our communion liturgies deal much more directly with individual guilt and forgiveness. Paul reports the original words of Jesus as follows: "This cup is the new covenant in my blood. Do this, as often as you drink it, in remembrance of me" (1 Cor 11:25). The same wording is found in the earliest Gospel, in Mark 14:24. But traditional liturgies always employ the altered wording of Matt 26:27-28: "This is my blood of the covenant, which is poured out for many *for the forgiveness of sins*." This moves away from the original issue of shame[6] to the more conventional religious topic of sin. In taking this direction, our standard communion liturgies encourage an introspective, guilt-ridden spirituality. This explains why traditional communion services often tend to be avoided by persons whose problems are deeper than sin, who feel that their lives are without promise or hope, that nobody respects them.

Babette's Feast points toward this deeper, more original significance of the Lord's Supper. It is the shameful death of the crucified one that overcomes our shame by letting us experience the boundless love of God.[7] Babette's most distinctive recipe, *cailles en sarcophage* ("quail entombed"), symbolizes this supreme gift of death for the sake of life.[8] Christ takes up the ultimate weight of shame to lift our heaviest and most secret burden, the feeling that no one loves and respects us. Like Babette, he prepares banquets for the most awkward of guests. But unlike Babette, he comes out of the kitchen to join our celebration as genial host and storyteller. He leads us to laugh at our folly and at the "wisdom of the world," which overlooks the deepest truth of all, that God loves each and every one of us whether we deserve it or not.

The Distortion of the Love Feast in Corinth

Paul's anger about the Corinthian love feast focused on the reappearance of the cultural habits of shame and contempt. He is furious that the prestigious members of the Corinthian church "show contempt for the church of God and shame those who have nothing" (1 Cor 11:22). As reconstructed by Gerd Theissen,[9] the wealthy patrons of Corinthian house churches were arriving at their usual banquet time, in the late afternoon, before the slaves and artisans had completed their twelve-hour workdays. The rich brought their own expensive meats, pastries, and wine; they sprawled over the couches in the dining hall. By the time the poorer members of the congregation arrived, the rich were tipsy and everything but the slave food had been eaten up. The rest of God's family were left to eat their skimpy diet of bread, vegetables, and water outside the dining hall. More recent studies by Peter Marshall[10] and Raymond Pickett confirm that the "antitheses of honour and shame"[11] lay at the root of this social conflict. The rich were exhibiting "individualistic self-indulgence which is predicated on distinctions of status and wealth."[12]

After reiterating the tradition of the Lord's Supper, in which a new covenant of equals was established by Christ's blood, Paul insists that the Corinthians "wait for one another" so that they can all partake of the same food in the love feast (1 Cor 11:33). If they do not, they will "eat and drink judgment against themselves" (1 Cor 11:29), because they will have fallen back into the cultural habits of honor and shame that discriminate against the marginalized and pit the elite in vicious competition with each other. By reverting back into the habits of the "world" that crucified Christ, the Corinthians will "be condemned along with the world" (1 Cor 11:32). Nothing less than the salvation of both the elite and the marginalized is at stake in this matter: unconditional grace strikes at the privilege of the rich just as it overcomes the deficit of the poor. The love feast celebrates the equality and unity of everyone redeemed by the cross: male and female, Greek and Jew, slave and free, rich and poor, liberal and conservative.[13]

Babette's Feast helps us understand the profound impact of the early Christian love feasts. Since the communion services in contemporary churches are almost exclusively focused on individual forgiveness of sins, usually in a somber, formal setting, the spontaneous joy that marked the early church is alien to us. In its extravagance and its indirect strategy of human transformation, this film throws light on 1 Corinthians 11. The feast depicted in the film conveys to each participant, whether rich or poor, wise or foolish, that God's grace is infinite. It transcends the positions of social honor while overcoming the shame of the dishonored. Here are the memorable words of the general at the end of the meal, the one who alone recognized the supreme artistry of Babette's cooking:

> My friends, we have been told that grace is to be found in the universe. But in our human foolishness and short-sightedness we imagine divine grace to be finite. . . . But the moment comes when our eyes are opened, and we see and realize that grace is infinite. . . . Grace, brothers, makes no conditions and singles out none of us in particular; grace takes us all to its bosom and proclaims general amnesty.[14]

If grace is really so boundless, then the lives of all people sharing the meal are infinitely honored. In the wondrous atmosphere of Babette's banquet, everyone is able to experience the extravagance of divine love. Grace comes to the foolish and shortsighted, to persons who have seemingly lost their chance for fulfillment in life, and even to the general, who has "sought to cut a brilliant figure in the world of prestige"[15] only to find the emptiness of achievement. What remains puzzling, however, is how such grace addresses the peculiar problem of shame within the small congregation itself.

Shame and Renunciation in Sectarian Piety

The piety of the small Christian community in Denmark depicted in *Babette's Feast* reveals a distortion in honor and shame quite different from the situation in Corinth. While rejecting the folly and wisdom of the world, the sectarian form of Christianity portrayed in *Babette's Feast* represents an extreme version of the introspective, guilt-ridden spirituality that marks traditional Protestant celebrations of the Lord's Supper or Roman Catholic celebrations of the mass. The founder of the congregation is portrayed as a strict Lutheran pastor who has radicalized the tradition of Hans Nielsen Hauge, the leader of the pietistic awakening in nineteenth-century Scandinavia. The founder rejects worldly standards and sensual pleasures in all of their forms, believing that shameful pollution can only be countered by renunciation. The pastor's followers call him the "Master" of this "world-denying" creed;[16] his daughters Martina and Philippa are named after Martin Luther and his successor Philipp Melanchthon, and have been raised to conform to the pietistic ideals.

When Martina and the handsome young soldier Lorens Loewenhielm fall in love, she feels compelled to renounce sexual fulfillment even in the form of marriage. When Philippa's magnificent voice is trained by M. Achille Papin, the acclaimed tenor visiting from Paris, she feels compelled to abandon any hope of personal fulfillment through artistic endeavors. When her father conveys the message that she will not be taking further voice lessons, "he looks positively happy"[17] for the first time in the film, while Papin's hopes are shattered. The "Master" is proud of having controlled the impulses toward pleasure and personal fulfillment even when they surfaced in the most benign way in his daughters. The two sisters are henceforth "doomed to remain in their virginal state according to both God and their father's will. They will live out their dry, spinster-like existences for the rest of their narrow lives, a living projection of their father's missionary zeal," in the words of reviewer Eva Kissin.[18]

These perverse episodes of renunciation are consistent with the rejection of all earthly pleasures, including the taste of good food and the smell and sight of flowers. There is not a single flower box in the window of these austere Danish houses. The daughters and the other members of the sect have been taught that worldly pleasures of any sort are inherently evil, and this has resulted in a radical dualism between body and spirit. Shame for the entire physical world stands at the center of this narrow piety. A fierce pride infuses those who, like the "Master," have successfully achieved honor by this renunciation. Yet each sectarian is wary lest any lapse in renunciation catapult one back into shame.

The sect and its founder are correct in the perception that worldly standards of honor lie at the heart of the human dilemma. There is truth in the founder's warnings about opera singing and soldiering, that the quest for honor through achievement is certain to be empty and perverse. But the problem lies not in the physicality of the world: it is not vocational achievement, sensual delight, or sexual fulfillment in themselves that cause our dilemma, but their involvement in wicked systems of honor and shame. Thus, focusing the piety of a group on renunciatory moralism is simply to erect an even more distorting system of honor and shame. Since honor can now be achieved only through obedience to the moralistic code, any departures from it have to be disguised. The mask of world-renouncing piety has to be worn by all. Every lapse has to be brought to light. This causes chronic alienation in the small community. Every member of the sectarian community is depicted as guarded, suspicious, and quarrelsome. But the deepest theological problem is reflected in the language of the film itself: to restrict divine approval to those who renounce pleasures is fatally to curtail any idea of "infinite grace." Grace is effectively limited to the matter of forgiveness for sad failures in renouncing sensual pleasures, while the natural human yearnings to enjoy the physical world become ever more hatefully shameful.

When the supplies for Babette's banquet arrive, the ascetic piety of the congregation leads to bewilderment and shock. They look on with horror as the sea turtle and the quails are brought ashore, along with wine and truffles and caviar and other dangerous pleasures. That these sumptuous supplies arrive from Roman Catholic France further marks them as an invasion of "papist gluttony."[19] Martina "had a nightmare in which she saw the memorial dinner turn into a witch's sabbath."[20] This is the clearest expression of the dualistic premise of the sect's piety, that sensuality is demonic. The sisters call a congregational meeting and reluctantly agree to carry through with the memorial meal, but only on the condition that no one should taste or speak of the food or drink, lest the demonic threat of pleasure be given a chance to prevail. In the words of Isak Dinesen's short story, on which the screenplay of the film is based:

> "Even so," said a white-bearded Brother, "the tongue is a little member and boasteth great things. The tongue can no man tame; it is an unruly evil, full of deadly poison. On the day of our master we will cleanse our tongues of all taste and purify them of all delight or disgust of the senses, keeping and preserving them for the higher things of praise and thanksgiving."[21]

1 Corinthians 11 throws light on the inner dynamics of *Babette's Feast*. The problems of alienation, dullness of spirit, and lack of appreciation for the essential goodness of creation that mark the members of the small circle of believers in Denmark cannot be alleviated by stricter adherence to the rules of the community or by more pious concentration on religious practice. The suppression of human desires and physical pleasure reflects a deeply rooted shame for the body and the physical world that can only be addressed by an overpowering experience of material and spiritual grace. The impact of the meal on the guests, captured by the skillful camera work in Gabriel Axel's film, is explicitly detailed in Dinesen's short story:

They only knew that the rooms had been filled with a heavenly light, as if a number of small halos had blended into one glorious radiance. Taciturn old people received the gift of tongues; ears that for years had been almost deaf were opened to it. Time itself had merged into eternity. Long after midnight the windows of the house shone like gold, and golden song flowed out onto the winter air. . . . They realized that the infinite grace of which General Loewenhielm had spoken had been allotted to them, and they did not even wonder at the fact, for it had been but the fulfillment of an ever-present hope. The vain illusions of this earth had dissolved before their eyes like smoke, and they had seen the universe as it really is. They had been given one hour of the millennium.[22]

As David Denby observes, the film does not overdo the impact of the meal on the reluctant sectarians, by depicting them as drunk or gluttonous. "For though they are all seduced — no, ravished — by the meal, they have no idea what they've experienced. Sensuality overwhelms them, and they aren't even aware of it. They feel themselves spiritually renewed, and they stop quarreling; they become more Christian in their behavior toward each other."[23] The wondrous meal melts their deadened hearts, overcoming the encapsulation of shame, thereby allowing genuine reconciliation to occur. Diane Edwards describes the results:

The two quarrelsome old women are able to smile and befriend each other once more; the two old farmers acknowledge that they have cheated one another in a time long past; and the guilt of the two lovers is forgotten and covered over by a single long kiss. When the banquet is over the guests depart, the snow lies thick upon the ground, covering and sealing all that is underneath. Light in hearts and spirits, the men and women join hands and begin to circle around the well as they sing a final hymn.[24]

As film critic Richard Schickel observes, "In all of film there is no happier ending than this one: an artist achieving transcendence, her audience learning for the first . . . time the transforming power of art."[25] But more than art is involved here, despite Babette's claim that the meal is nothing more than an expression of her artistry:

"I am a great artist, Mesdames, and a great artist is never poor."[26] In and yet beyond the food itself, the guests discover what the Corinthians had been sharing before they got off track and allowed the ancient system of honor and shame to corrupt their meals.

Conclusion

I believe that the meal at Corinth and the meal in Denmark throw light on each other, and on our situation today. The cultural background of the eucharistic meal, despite its various distortions, is required to explain the transformation in *Babette's Feast*, for despite her artistry, there is no hint that her famed work in the Parisian restaurant had ever produced such an effect. Although the general had earlier experienced her masterful preparation of *cailles en sarcophage* in Paris, it had no power to jar him away from the quest for honor. But on the other side, the film shows that there is a need to infuse contemporary celebrations of the Lord's Supper with the spirit of Babette's banquet. There are times when the Lord's Supper should be celebrated as a love feast, an actual meal in which sensual pleasure and fellowship are combined. We who are accomplished and honored need to share in a meal that accepts everyone as equals. We who feel demeaned need opportunities to celebrate the honor that Christ died to restore. We who have lost touch with the joy of life through laborious religious and moral exercise need the superabundance of material grace to break through our defenses.

It is almost impossible to convey this transforming experience in abstract, theoretical terms. Yet even when a chef like Babette is not available to "transform a dinner into a love affair," the combination of Lord's Supper and meal may suffice. The combination could recapture what Hans Josef Klauck and Peter Lampe have shown, that the original "words of institution" about the bread and the wine were used as the frame that opened and closed actual meals in the early church.[27] Perhaps there is a basis here for reinventing church potluck suppers in which the one crucified in shame plays host to the shamed.[28]

Gaining a sense of worth at its most basic level comes most naturally when we eat together, moving beyond the normal boundaries of friends and families. When this occurs, communities and individuals find wholeness and a restoration of health. They are enabled to escape for a time from the distortion of a competitive world, in which honor and shame are dispensed ruthlessly to the damnation of all. They are released from the shame they feel about their unworthy and imperfect physical bodies; they are enabled to transcend the false achievement of honor through ceremonies of renunciation. A new world is created when the one shamed by the cross is allowed to host the banquet, saying, "This is my body that is for you. . . . This cup is the new covenant in my blood," the covenant of equals. When we allow ourselves to discover this God-given medicine for shame, we find what it really means "to proclaim the Lord's death until he comes" (1 Cor 11:26).

4. Shame, Love, and the Saga of *Forrest Gump*

If I speak with the tongues of humans and of angels,
   but have not love — I am a noisy gong or a clanging
      cymbal.
And if I have prophecy and understand all mysteries and
      all knowledge,
   and if I have all faith so as to remove mountains,
      but have not love — I am nothing.
And if I use all my property for feeding others,
   and if I hand over my body that I might boast,
      but have not love — I gain nothing.
The love is patient; kind is the love;
   not envious, not boastful, not arrogant, not behaving
      shamefully,
      not self-seeking, not irritable, not keeping record of
         wrongs,
   not rejoicing at wrongdoing but rejoicing in the truth,
      always forgiving, always believing, always hoping, always
         enduring.
The love is never defeated.
   But where there are prophecies — they will come to an
      end;
   where there are tongues — they will be silenced;

where there is knowledge — it will come to an end.
For we know in part and we prophesy in part,
    but when that which is perfect comes, what is in part
will come to an end.
      When I was a child, I spoke as a child,
      I thought like a child, I reasoned like a child,
        but when I became a man, I put an end to childish ways.
For now we see in a mirror darkly,
    but then face to face.
Now I know in part;
    then shall I fully know,
        even as I am fully known.
And now faith, hope, and love remain, these three;
    but the greatest of these is the love.[1]

1 Corinthians 13:1-13

Introduction

The Academy Award–winning film *Forrest Gump*[2] throws an extraordinary light on the puzzling state of the American mind. Its surprising power and appeal derive in part from its affirmation of simple virtues in the context of a battered public arena. In a hilarious manner, achieved partly through trick photography, Gump (played by Tom Hanks) participates in all of the crucial events that have sullied public life in the last thirty years. The film allows us to laugh at the foibles and tragedies of the past without losing faith in a simplistic, characteristically American system of ethics, derived in no small measure from a long-standing preoccupation with the celebration of love in 1 Corinthians 13. Only Gump remains true to these simple virtues of belief in God, doing one's best with one's abilities, loving one's family and friends, and expecting the best of others. This film displays the triumph of love. But is this story of love that prevails credible only because its protagonist is a simpleton?

Gerald Forshey captures the crucial problem in this depiction of a redeemer figure who is "a man with a low intelligence quotient

. . . the innocent who has never sinned, has accepted his victimization with equanimity and patience, and has prevailed despite his limitations. Some benign destiny seems to watch over him."[3] Can we really believe in a destiny in which such simple love prevails? Does the fickle feather of fate really favor fools who love? Or should the country and the church continue to follow the currently more popular modes of seeking honor and holding fools in contempt as the foundations of social interaction?

Agape Transcends the Honor System

The question of whether love transcends the honor system is central to 1 Corinthians 13. Gordon Fee in particular has pointed to the recapitulation in this chapter of issues in the Corinthian controversy.[4] The Corinthians were competing against each other in claiming superior status for themselves, their own house church, and their particular charismatic gifts. The issues of social divisiveness in Corinth were related to the invasion of the cultural values of competition into sacramental and group relationships. Margaret Mitchell's recent analysis of the argument against discord in the letter shows how Paul uses common warnings about the destructive aspects of the competition for honor that lies at the center of such discord, which is reflected in this passage.[5]

1 Corinthians 13 begins with references to the prestigious charismatic gifts of prophecy, speaking in tongues, and miracle working, and then moves on in verse 3 to spectacular expressions of philanthropy. Paul shows that, with the dawn of the new age, love transcends all of these prestigious gifts with which humans can compete and gain their superior honor. Although not highlighted by commentators because of traditional inattention to the ancient system of honor and shame, the matter of boasting is prominent in this passage, with explicit references in verses 3 and 4.[6] Note, however, that it is not love in general, but "the agape" that is finally in view here, that is, love grounded in the Christ event and experienced daily in the early Christian love feast. In order to counter the tradition of generalizing and romanticizing

love, I have translated the definite article when Paul employs it, "the love," indicating explicitly Christian love.

The theme of support for the love feast is particularly prominent in 1 Cor 13:3, which literally refers to dividing up one's property into morsels of food to eat[7] and selling oneself into slavery to provide funds to feed others.[8] Although unworthy misfits were given equal honor in such love feasts, there is no presumption of a Forrest-Gump-type of innocence in 1 Corinthians 13 or anywhere else in Paul's writings. This is agape-love with blood dripping from the cross, because Christ's death for the sake of others was its foundation and supreme embodiment.[9] Agape transcends and abrogates the competition for honor; therefore, the argument in this passage is that none of the prestigious charismatic gifts, not even the most lavish form of Christian philanthropy, is valid without love. Adolf von Harnack pointed to the crucial link with honor: "Without love all reason for glorying, even the greatest, is profitless."[10]

The opposition between love and social glory runs through *Forrest Gump*. From his opening conversation with strangers on a bus stop bench, the audience recognizes that the hero is unintelligent, with a kind of shameless openness to conversing with total strangers. As he begins to tell his life story, we see the young Forrest Gump being fitted with special shoes and braces. In a line that echoes ironically through the rest of the film, which plays this person of low status off against presidents and superstars, the doctor says, "His legs are strong but his back is as crooked as a politician."

The braces quickly become an object of derision, deepening Gump's failure to measure up to the standards of society. While walking home from the doctor's office, his brace-shoe is caught in a grate, and his mother asks people why they are staring at his braces. Mrs. Gump, played by Sally Field, tells him not to accept this contempt: "Don't let anybody ever tell you they're better than you, boy. If God intended us all to be the same, he'd have made us all with braces on our legs." She insists that he is not different from anyone else, despite his low IQ of 75. She induces the principal to place Forrest in a regular classroom. When he gets on the school bus the first time, the students won't give him a seat until a girl in the back of the bus invites him. Although she comes from an abusive family, Jenny teaches him to climb trees and to read, and she becomes his only friend.

The tension between love and honor is particularly sharp later in the film in the interaction between Gump and his platoon leader, Lieutenant Dan Taylor (played by Gary Sinise), who comes from a family that has suffered a casualty in every American war. After leading his platoon into an ambush in Vietnam, "Lieutenant Dan," as Gump calls him, doesn't want to be rescued by Gump, because his survival would dishonor his family tradition of noble sacrifice. While recuperating from the loss of both legs, he falls into the kind of despair that Gump's cheerful comments prove unable to dispel. On the premise that life without public recognition of honor is not worth living, the lieutenant drags Gump out of bed one night in the hospital and berates him: "You listen to me: we all have a destiny; nothing just happens. It's all part of a plan. I should have died out there with my men [in Vietnam.] But now, I'm nothing but a goddamned cripple, a legless freak. Do you know what it's like not to be able to use your legs?" Gump replies, "Yes sir, I do." Lieutenant Dan doesn't believe him, and he continues the attack: "You cheated me. I had a destiny. I was supposed to die in the field. With honor. That was my destiny. And you cheated me out of it. . . . This wasn't supposed to happen to me. . . . What am I gonna do now?"

Without the culturally scripted quest for honor, Lieutenant Dan assumes that life has no purpose and no meaning. On the same premise, he later accosts Gump because this fool has received a Congressional Medal of Honor for rescuing several men of his platoon, including Lieutenant Dan. The irony here is that the very one not seeking honor receives it, in the form of fame, recognition, wealth, and the highest military award. While simply trying to do his best and to follow the dictates of agape as conveyed by his mother, he receives honors that are all the more ludicrous because he takes them so much in stride. Heeding the admonition, as it were, not to "hand over his body that he might boast," he quietly gives away the money earned from his shrimping business and the investment that his partner Lieutenant Dan made for them in a "fruit company," which turns out to be a founding investment in Apple Computer stock. The millions he earns from the fickle feather of destiny are used to fix up his mother's house, to provide for the family of his best friend, Bubba, who was killed in Vietnam, to endow a hospital, and to build a new church for a black congregation.

The idea of agape overcoming the boundaries of honor and encouraging generous relations between persons is itself the product of a cultural tradition shaped in part by the ideals of early Christianity as expressed in writings such as 1 Corinthians 13. Early Americans attempted to extend the ideals of a democratic, loving church into the society as a whole. This is why historian Sidney E. Mead called the United States "the nation with the soul of a church."[11] The ideals of a community shaped by charity are reflected in the philosophy of Josiah Royce, who was very conscious of its source.[12] So the theme of this film has run full circle, as it were. Having originated as a biblical paradigm, and been incorporated in early American ideals of character development that departed from the domineering drive for honor in royalist Europe, disinterested love has long since been secularized and in part tacitly repudiated by the elitist trends of modern American life. Now it suddenly reemerges in a figure so simplistic that it is given a ludicrous kind of credibility. Must one be subnormal in intelligence to follow the way of agape? Gump would certainly not be able to explain either the sources or the contours of the love he so mythically embodies. He does not even appear to be aware of the supreme irony of his name, Forrest, which was taken from the infamous Ku Klux Klan founder, Gen. Nathan Bedford Forrest, who violently opposed the extension of civil rights to blacks in the period after the Civil War. So how is this kind of love defined, in the film and in our text?

The Character of Love as Embodied in Gump

The leitmotif of the film is Forrest's poignantly stated declaration to Jenny, played by Robin Wright, "I know what love is." Earlier in the film, when Jenny is being harassed by a crowd in a striptease joint, Gump gallantly comes to her rescue. She is embarrassed and says, "You can't keep doing this all the time." Gump replies, "I can't help it, I love you." She replies, "You don't know what love is." This language surfaces again later in the film when he asks Jenny, "Will you marry me. . . . I'd make a good husband." When it is clear that she is not willing, he goes on: "Why don't you love me, Jenny? I'm not a smart man, but I know what love is." This is the truthful center of the film, because this person of low IQ, who hasn't a romantic or seductive bone in his body, knows that the essence of love is taking care of people, defending them against assault. This is the deeper moral dimension that Jonathan Romney misses when he complains that "Gump is imbued with absolute infantile goodness, a global caritas. . . ."[13] Yet this central theme is highly problematic, because Gump's love seems so blind, so uncritical, and so lacking in social awareness. It functions mainly in the most private arenas, having no bearing, for example, on the purpose for which Gump soldiered in Vietnam. In this sense, *Forrest Gump* appeals to the current American audience because it privatizes love, overlooking all the complex issues of public policy. Could the message of this film be clarified by bringing it into critical interaction with 1 Corinthians 13, from which the idea of love's centrality derives?

"The love is patient and kind," writes Paul. Kindness and patience are the "passive and active responses toward others"[14] that the agape type of love elicits. It respects the integrity of other people, refusing to treat them simply as targets of one's ego gratification or rage. But the provision of the definite article, "the love," makes it plain that it is not some romantic and privatized love that is in view here, but Christian love, with its historic source in the public ministry of Jesus, and with its primary social embodiment in small groups of converts who are celebrating the "love feast" in places like Corinth.

The film reflects Paul's wording but reduces its range to the romantic relationship between Gump and Jenny. Despite being abandoned by Jenny repeatedly, his letters unanswered and his clumsy attempts at affection repudiated, Gump responds with patience and kindness: "I would never hurt you, Jenny," he says after protecting her from being slapped at an antiwar rally. But there is no hint that such kindness might also extend to the Vietnamese people for whose preservation the rally was being held.

Love is *"not envious,"* Paul writes, which means that it does not participate in the rivalry for status. In the Corinthian situation, rivalry was reflected in divisions within the community over the alleged superiority of their teachers.[15] In the film, those around Gump are depicted as envious of the success of others, as for example in the case of Lieutenant Dan's feelings about the Medal of Honor. At one point Jenny reveals that she wants to be a "famous singer, like Joan Baez." Jenny describes her desire to stand alone on a stage with a rapt audience admiring her. She asks Forrest what he wants to do, because he seems to have no such drive for honor and distinction. Envy is simply not part of his makeup, nor is jealousy, even when Jenny repeatedly goes off with other men. Compared with erotic love, whose orientation to self-fulfillment evokes envy and jealousy, agape eliminates the possibility of envy because it is oriented to the fulfillment of the other person.

Love is *"not boastful, not arrogant,"* says Paul. The rare word *perpereuetai,* translated here as "boastful," often has the connotation of "windbag" or "braggart."[16] The term used to depict arrogance, *physioō,* literally "puffed up," is applied earlier in the Corinthian letter to the charismatic leaders who vaunted their possession of the divine spirit and superior knowledge (1 Cor 4:6, 18-19; 5:2; 8:1). Since agape derives from the experience of unearned love from God, there is no longer a necessity to prove oneself by "self-seeking." Paul had used this expression, "seeking its own advantage," in 1 Cor 10:24 and 33 with reference to the "strong" members of the congregation imposing their standards on the "weak." Agape thus counters the boastful character traits that marked both individual and group behavior in the Greco-Roman world, traits that were ruining the Corinthian church by competition and conflict.

None of the remarkable achievements of Forrest Gump comes as a result of a conscious desire for his own advantage. When Gump's mother reports the offer of a $25,000 fee to endorse a ping pong paddle, after he had been a champion in China and elsewhere, he says, "I like using my own paddle." But she persuades him to hold the paddle with the picture of Mao on it, and he earns the money, which becomes the basis of his fortune. In another scene Gump relates the first time he met an American president, at a White House reception for college football stars. The only thing that impressed him was the huge selection of free refreshments. After drinking fifteen Dr. Peppers, he stands in the receiving line, where President Kennedy asks him how it feels to be a football hero. Gump replies, "I need to pee." If our hero is "puffed up," it can quickly be relieved, and there is no hint of boasting or bragging here.

The problem with this story of the first becoming last and the last first, which echoes the New Testament understanding of agape, is that it limits the critique of social competition to the private arena. The film suggests no bearing on the perversion of American public life through which Gump blithely drifts, deadly episodes brought on by national arrogance, military bragging, political posturing, and selfish economic advantage. Even if agape-love remains impossible fully to embody in public life, as Reinhold Niebuhr taught us to understand, its usefulness as a critical resource should not be disregarded.

In a sense, Gump's innocently asocial behavior might seem to counter the next hallmark feature of love that Paul mentions, *"not behaving shamefully."* It is clear from Paul's concern about "shaming the church" discussed in the last chapter, and from his discussion of gender behavior in 1 Cor 11:2-16, that he was intent on having the Christians at Corinth live up to the best standards of decent behavior. But he was also in the business of redefining those standards on a more egalitarian basis, as we shall see in Chapters 5–11. In fact, despite his social awkwardness, Gump steers clear of shameful personal behavior. While Jenny gets thrown out of college because she posed for *Playboy*, and enters into various forms of debasing experimentation with sex and drugs, Gump resists an offered union with a prostitute and remains virtuous in every way. While the antiwar protesters whom Gump joins in Washington, D.C. are always using what he calls "the F-word," he avoids foul language. But the avoidance of shame in the public arena is touched upon only indirectly through the cynical eye of the camera as it records leaders and soldiers and national crises in the most unflattering light.

The four characteristics of agape in 1 Cor 13:5-6 that relate to interpersonal relations are greatly at variance with typical behavior in Paul's time: *"not irritable, not keeping record of wrongs, not rejoicing in wrongdoing but rejoicing in the truth."* In the honor-shame society in which Christianity was emerging, personal irritations and affronts were matters always to be revenged; to forget them was to cease the quest for honor, to accept shame. In typical Greco-Roman homes and apartments there was an evil eye painted to face the entrance, with the message *kai su,* "and the same to you too." It meant, in effect, "If you bring evil here, this evil eye will make it bounce back on you, and in that we will rejoice." Early Christianity was in the process of opting out of this cycle of honor and vengeance, threat and counterthreat, in which every advancement by one's neighbor was thought to bring dishonor on competitors. Any "wrongdoing" against a competitor was considered legitimate, and slander was the rule of the culture.

In the privatized world of this film, the wrongs that Forrest Gump suffers, especially from Jenny, are mostly restricted to the realm of personal slights. Although they were best friends as children, Jenny repeatedly jilts Gump, refuses to read his letters, and treats him like dirt. Even after seducing him, she runs off to bear his child without any word to him of her whereabouts. Then after seeing him on TV in his coast-to-coast running spree, Jenny invites him to visit her in Savannah. She is now a waitress and has a nice apartment. After apologizing for whatever she ever did to him, she explains that she had been mixed up for a long time. Her babysitter brings their little boy, Forrest, named after his daddy. Gump hesitates and seems to feel he has done something terribly wrong in siring this child, who might carry his defective intelligence. She says, "You didn't do anything wrong." He is worried that his son will be as slow as his father, but she replies that little Forrest is one of the smartest children in the class. He goes to talk with his son, sitting down on the floor with him to watch *Sesame Street*. His ability to "rejoice in the truth" is continued through the end of the film, as he becomes a responsible parent to this child. But there is only the slightest hint that celebrating the truth might be relevant in the public arena through which Gump moves in scene after scene, in which wrongdoing has so frequently been celebrated in the past thirty years.

In the end, the film sustains the idea that Forrest Gump's kind of love prevails, because Jenny returns to Alabama with her child, seeking the father who would care for him after her inevitable death from AIDS. She has painfully discovered what love really is, having lived through the false allures of the hippie movement and the drug scene, returning to decent, simple values as a parent before returning to Alabama to marry Gump. Is it possible to sketch the religious foundations of these values that the film seems to embody?

Religion and Love's Endurance

The interaction between 1 Corinthians 13 and *Forrest Gump* is particularly challenging because of the usual translation of the rhetorical series in verse 7: "Love bears all things, believes all things, hopes all things, endures all things." By taking the ambiguously plural neuter *panta* ("all") as the object of the verbs, translators make Paul into an uncritical imbecile who allows himself "to be fooled by every rogue, or to pretend that he believes that white is black."[17] Such an undiscriminating stance is inconsistent with the argument in the chapter as a whole, which places agape in a critical role, superior to all other theological principles.

I believe Jean Héring was on the right track in translating *panta* as an adverbial accusative of limitation meaning "at all times."[18] Thus I suggest the translation "always forgiving, always believing, always hoping, always enduring." The point is not "that love always believes the best about everything and everyone, but that love never ceases to have faith; it never loses hope. This is why it can endure."[19] This outlook helps us to understand why Paul was able to prevail despite the discrimination, abuse, dangers, and controversies in his career, including the anguished conflict with the Corinthians. He was convinced that it was not theological, rhetorical, or charismatic sophistication that finally counted, but agape based on the love of God revealed in Christ. This provides the deepest level of sophistication and discrimination, available to all, and accessible even to persons of low IQ.

The religious faith underlying *Forrest Gump* gains some contours in the episode of Gump rushing home from the shrimp boat to be with his mother, who tells him, "I'm dying . . . it's my time. I was destined to be your momma, and I done the best I could." Forrest replies, "You did good." His mother says, "I happen to believe you make your own destiny. You have to do the best with what God gave you." Gump asks, "What's my destiny, Momma?" She says, "You got to figure that out for yourself." This belief in a divinely ordained destiny, never fully visible, yet calling people to responsible love, is linked with Mrs. Gump's belief that "miracles happen every day." Earlier in the film, when boys throw rocks at the young Forrest, he has to run away with his braces and learns to outrun his persecutors on their bicycles, running out of his braces. From that first day on, he runs everywhere he goes. When boys later throw stones at him and yell "Stupid," he outruns a pickup truck, ending up on the football field, and thereafter becoming a football star in high school and college. None of this, including the fortune that ensues, moves him from his basic stance: "I know what love is." But that the nation as well as the individual might persevere in this conviction seems far from the message of this film.

The link of love with Jesus is suggested in the cynical question Lieutenant Dan poses, "Have you found Jesus yet?" Gump replies, "I didn't know I was supposed to be looking for him, Sir." Taylor complains that all the "cripples" at the Veterans Administration center can talk of nothing else, and that a priest told him with regard to the loss of his legs, "God is listening, but I have to help myself. If I accept Jesus into my heart, I'll get to walk beside him in the kingdom of heaven." Gump simply replies in a quiet voice, "I'm going to heaven, Lieutenant Dan." When he reveals his plan to fill Bubba's vision of becoming a shrimp boat captain, Dan says with utter cynicism that when Gump gets to be that captain, "I'll come down to be your first mate."

Sure enough, after Gump buys the shrimp boat, Dan shows up in his wheelchair. They fail to catch many shrimp, and he advises Gump cynically, "Maybe you'd just better pray for shrimp." So Forrest faithfully continues to attend a black church, where a charismatic choir is celebrating and praising God. Then a hurricane strikes while they are out on the sea, which destroys the other shrimp boats. "After that, shrimping was easy," Gump reports. The two misfits, one with religious faith and the other utterly cynical about faith, end up with twelve boats, and start the "Bubba-Gump Shrimp Corporation," which becomes fabulously lucrative. It confirms the faith held by the Gump family, that "love is never defeated."

The gradual transformation of Dan's religious outlook surfaces later in the film when he says, "Forrest, I never thanked you for saving my life." Gump reflects to himself, "He never actually said so, but I think he made his peace with God." At the end of the film, Dan is seen attending Gump's wedding in Alabama, immaculately dressed and with a smile on his face. He has accepted a new set of artificial legs and comes in with his fiancée, Susan, on his arm. From her Vietnamese appearance, it seems that Dan has made his peace with the disastrous war as well.

The film leaves us with a clear alternative: a simple love grounded in a divine destiny that leads one to always forgive, believe, hope and endure on the one hand, and a cynical sophistication that proves destructive to all on the other. Before his transformation, the highly intelligent Dan cannot forgive Forrest for the insult to his honor; he does not believe in miracles or prayer; he has no hope for his own future, drifting into an oblivion of sexual depravity and alcohol; he is unable to endure, resisting the restoration of his limbs and hating the restrictions of life in a wheelchair.

The various cultural cycles of cynical disbelief in the past thirty years are all shown in this film to be similarly hollow and ineffective: the crooked politicians and coaches, the venal pop entertainers, the mindlessly obedient army, and the self-absorbed stars of the counterculture. The message of Forrest Gump and 1 Corinthians 13 is that genuine love endures, while the cynicism gripping the leading shapers of our culture appears both empty and ludicrous.

Conclusion

Does destiny really favor mindless love? Does religion require that intelligent believers suppress their capacity to make distinctions? Or to use the rhetoric of Paul's poetry (1 Cor 13:11), should we continue to speak as a child, think as a child, and reason as a child? The irony of this film and our text is that true maturity has little to do with intelligence or social achievement, but has everything to do with growing up in agape. When Paul spoke of giving up childish ways, he meant giving up the ways of the world, the competitive drive for honor that has divided the church and that will corrode every relationship. Maturity requires abandoning the cultural scripts of honor and contempt and learning a new way to think and reason and speak.[20]

In addition to Lieutenant Dan, the person who best embodies this kind of change in *Forrest Gump* is Jenny, who began to give up her childish ways in returning to Alabama. She finally brings herself to admit, "Forrest, I do love you." When they make love for the first time, at her initiative, Forrest doesn't seem to understand the implications. She then distances herself again, having returned his Medal of Honor and the other gifts he had entrusted with her. But at the end of the film, Jenny restores contact with her lifetime friend, revealing that she is sick and soon will be unable to take care of her son. It is mature, parental love that ultimately leads her to return home in response to Gump's invitation: "I'll take care of you." She then asks the question of responsible love, "Will you marry me, Forrest?" So there is a great wedding celebration on the house lawn in Alabama. The spirit of agape has made the fulfillment of romantic love possible.

The crowd of black and white friends gather for the wedding, and then after a scene of walking through the countryside together, Forrest is bringing a meal to Jenny of her sickbed. She asks whether he was scared in Vietnam." He says, "Yes, except when the rain stopped enough for the stars to come out; then it was nice." He then recalls having seen the reflections of a mountain on a lake while running in the American West: "I couldn't tell where heaven stops and the earth begins, it was so beautiful." When Jenny says she wishes she had been there, Gump replies that in his mind she was with him all the time.

There is a distant echo here of the early Christian agape, the love feast in which Christ was thought to be present in remembrance, and in which the kingdom of heaven seemed present on earth. We see evidence of this celebratory phenomenon in the wording of the Lord's Prayer, used in those early celebrations by small groups of believers. The literal translation is "give us this day the bread of the morrow,"[21] meaning "may the bread of the kingdom of God, the messianic banquet that will unite all peoples and tribes,[22] be given to believers 'today' as they share their humble food together." The erasure of the boundary between heaven and earth and of the barriers between people of various ethnic and economic groups produced an ecstatic, celebratory, and at times boisterous atmosphere in the early Christian celebrations of the agape meal. The overcoming of ethnic, economic, and gender barriers (see Gal 3:28) that marked these early celebrations of the agape meal is reduced to the scale of a small nuclear family in this riveting film. Jenny is buried under a tree near the Gump home, while her husband is left to care for their son. In the soliloquy in front of his wife's grave, Gump reflects that he doesn't know whether Lieutenant Dan or his momma was right about destiny, or whether they are just "floating around accidental like on the breeze, but I think maybe it's both. Maybe both happen at the same time." Stephen Brown is right in concluding that "Forrest's encounters suggest that there is no such thing as accidents. Life is held together by one who watches over us."[23]

In the final sequence, Gump is sitting with his son at the roadside waiting for the yellow school bus, when a feather drops out of the book that young Forrest is taking to school for show-and-tell. At the beginning of the film, Gump had placed this feather in the Curious George book that his mother had read to him and that he continues to carry around as a kind of loving anchor to his destiny. Now he remains rooted at the bus stop, anchored to the destiny of agape as he waits for his son to return. The feather floats away on the breeze, gracefully spinning and turning across the sky of an America that is having difficulty discerning where its true destiny leads. At the end of one of the most sophisticated pieces of trick photography in the annals of cinema, the feather finally sticks to the lens and abruptly blots out the film. It fixes the question of destiny on the eye of the audience. It forces us to consider whether we have become so enamored with the fickle fates of honor and contempt, of arrogance and self-seeking, that we have lost sight of where our true destiny might lie. Can it really be that "the greatest of these is the agape"?

TRANSFORMING
THE PROUD AND
THE SHAMED

5. *Mr. Holland's Opus* and Letters Written on the Heart

Are we beginning to recommend ourselves again?
    Or do we need, as some do, letters of recommendation
to you or from you?
You yourselves are our letter,
    written on our hearts,
        to be known and read by all,
and you show that you are a letter of Christ,
    delivered by us,
        written not with ink but with the Spirit of the living
        God,
        not on stone tablets but on tablets of human hearts.

2 Corinthians 3:1-3

Introduction

In the climactic scene of *Mr. Holland's Opus*,[1] a music teacher is being celebrated for thirty years of inspirational teaching. Mr. Holland (played by Richard Dreyfuss) is being forced out of Kennedy High School because of budget cuts in the arts, and he feels that his life has been a failure because he never fulfilled the dream of completing and performing his own symphony, his magnum opus. One of his former students, acting as the master of ceremonies, concludes by saying that "each one of us is a better person because of you. We are your symphony, Mr. Holland. We are the melodies and the notes of your opus. And we are the music of your life." The auditorium filled with his former students and colleagues erupts with applause.

This is a moving scene, especially for those of us who have been influenced by a great and devoted teacher or pastor.[2] But as I heard these lines, I found myself thinking of Paul's comment in 2 Corinthians: "You yourselves are our letter, written on our hearts, to be known and read by all. . . ." Paul was the first writer in Western culture, so far as I can tell, to develop the metaphor about persons held dear to the heart constituting the most effective letters. Is this merely a fortuitous allusion? Or is there a deeper resonance between this text and *Mr. Holland's Opus*? Is there a message in that resonance that could throw light on the role of honor in our vocational motivations? I would like to explore these questions by taking up first the idea that such letters are publicly accessible, readable by all.

You Yourselves Are Our Letter

The background of Paul's reference to the Corinthians as his letter of recommendation is the competition with the superapostles, sometimes translated "superlative apostles." I rely on the work of Dieter Georgi, Gail Corrington, and particularly Jeffrey Crafton's study, *The Agency of the Apostle,* to conclude that most of 2 Corinthians deals with the challenge posed by these invading superapostles.[3] Following Georgi, I believe they brought a "divine-man" orientation from which they criticized Paul's lack of speaking ability and personal charisma, his troubled relationship with various authorities, and his reluctance to tout his visionary experiences.[4] They arrived in the midst of the ongoing conflicts within the congregation, and they encouraged alienation from its founder. Paul responds to the invading missionaries' use of letters of recommendation showing their "sufficiency" in miracle-working, visions, oratorical ability, and allegorical interpretation.[5] David E. Garland aptly summarizes the superapostles' answer to the question "Who is sufficient for these things?" (2 Cor 2:16): "We are, and you are not."[6] These letters proved them worthy of the honor of being successful evangelists; honor was measured as success.

Paul doesn't have any letters of recommendation, and his leadership record is admittedly spotty. His career has been marked by many reverses (2 Cor 11:23-29); his congregations tend to fall into factions (1 Cor 1:10-17); he has frequent difficulties with authority figures (Gal 2:1-14), repeatedly landing in jail; he keeps moving around from church to church; and he puts people to sleep with his sermons (2 Cor 10:10; Acts 20:9). By charging that he has no letters to prove his sufficiency as an evangelist, the accusers have placed Paul in a position of shame.

Rather than commending himself, Paul appeals to the personal relationships he has established with the Corinthians. He claims in 3:1 that he needs no such letters as the superapostles display; he has turned away from a life of fame and self-commendation. This is anchored in his grasp of the theology of the cross, which dominates 2 Corinthians. The shameful crucifixion of Christ exposed the hostile futility of worldly standards of honor and fame. Like Paul, Jesus had devoted himself to persons rather than to reputation. Jesus was executed as a friend of "publicans and sinners" who stood outside of the law, as one who placed a priority on redemptive relationships with prostitutes, tax collectors, and menial fishermen. So when Paul became convinced that this crucified Jesus was resurrected, it caused him to toss the contents of his résumé in the trash. He recalls this proud record in Philippians:

> If anyone else has reason to be confident in the flesh, I have more . . . as to the law, a Pharisee; as to zeal, a persecutor of the church; as to righteousness under the law, blameless. Yet whatever gains I had, these I have come to regard as loss because of Christ. (Phil 3:4-7)

Persons beloved by Christ now became the center of his vocation, setting him free from the destructive, empty quest for human honors. He is free from the yearning for prestige that drives the superapostles. His "sufficiency" is entirely dependent on the grace of God rather than on his own abilities or achievements.[7] This is why he can claim that the Corinthians are a letter "written on *our* hearts." This pronoun deserve close attention: letters of recommendation aim to convince *you* that I am worthy. But if *you* are the letter written on *our* hearts, the whole process is reversed. It is no longer *you* who are required to honor *us*, but *you* are in the position of honor in *our* heart.[8] Personal relationships replace the quest for honor at the center of the human motivational system.

The story of *Mr. Holland's Opus* is also one of turning away from fame and reputation and turning toward persons. As the movie opens, Glen Holland and his wife Iris harbor the hope that he will become a rich and famous composer. After his first day as a music teacher in John F. Kennedy High School, Iris is rubbing his back and calculating how much money they will save with his new job and hers. "In four years we should have enough for you to quit and do nothing but compose music. You'll become famous and make us rich."

The film depicts the painful process of this family's gradual shift from the quest for fame toward service to others. For a long time Glen hates teaching and his students, but he is forced by circumstances to keep at it: an unexpected baby arrives, and the family needs to buy a home with the savings earmarked for the future of fame through musical compositions. But after a disastrous start Holland comes to love teaching and becomes absorbed by his students. In Janet Maslin's words, "Mr. Holland's real opus is a generous life."[9] The end of the film has an auditorium full of former students who recognize this generosity, confirming that they were his letter, written on the heart. One of his former students, a clarinetist by the name of Gertrude Lang, now the governor of the state, makes the speech that links this film with 2 Corinthians 3:

> Mr. Holland had a profound influence on my life, yet I get the feeling that he considers the greater part of his own life misspent. Rumor had it that he was always working on that symphony of his, and this was going to make him famous, rich, probably both.

But Mr. Holland isn't rich, and he isn't famous, at least not outside of our own little town. So it might be easy for him to think himself a failure. And he would be wrong. Because I think he has achieved a success far beyond riches and fame. Look around you. There is not a life in this room that you have not touched. And each one of us is a better person because of you. We are your symphony, Mr. Holland. We are the melodies and the notes of your opus. And we are the music of your life.

This film — and Paul's words — reminds us where the deeper meaning and satisfaction of life reside. What should be our most glorious opus? Our work? If we happen to be teachers, our writing and scholarly projects? If ministers or administrators, our success in moving up the ladder toward larger and larger responsibilities? If we work in large organizations, our status and rank compared with others? If we are in business, our share of the market and our profits? If we are employees and laborers, our wages and the approval of our supervisors? Or the lives of persons we serve?

A Letter Known and Read by All

The second theme to be explained is that this letter, written on a person rather than a page, becomes "known and read by all." Especially in the light of Georgi's work, the contrast is between superhuman interpretation, accessible only to a few, and publicly accessible information, available to all and readable by all. Paul's grasp of the theology of the cross leads him to reject esoteric elitism. The cross grounds his concern for the maturation of all, for if no one is saved by works and superior status, then all are equally saved by grace. The superheroic apostles who invaded the Corinthian church, in contrast, claimed exclusive access to truth because of their superior abilities. Only they could read and interpret the divine letters in the heavenly message book, so to speak. In Georgi's words, this ability "could also serve as an incentive to trust in the leadership of these capable persons, who knew the way to a special spring which poured forth the most

primal power of all, a power whose influence could be felt everywhere and always."[10]

I think these super interpreters would have felt right at home
in our contemporary educational environment, taking their place
among our esoteric superstars. The highest mark of sophistication
these days is to be able to baffle everyone but the elite insiders in
a particular hermeneutical or scientific speciality. But Paul's gospel
shatters such boundaries of honorable status and access, placing
everyone in a position of equality before God. He is committed to
the most democratic form of education: that which is "known and
read by all."

Mr. Holland's Opus offers a particularly apt embodiment of this
issue, which lies at the heart of pedagogy. Should music be made
accessible to average students, or should they be forced to subordinate their taste and interest to "the classics"? At the beginning,
Holland comes to his music appreciation class dressed very formally
and pushes students to take their seats more quickly. He functions
as the master of a sophisticated tradition that not a single student
at first can even understand. The students are completely unre-
sponsive to his first question about defining music. As he has them
open the text while he reads the definition aloud, students drop
off to sleep. Then the scene shifts to his first orchestra rehearsal,
in which students are playing the opening of Beethoven's Fifth
Symphony dreadfully out of sync and out of tune. He responds in
a condescending way to this appalling exhibition of musical incom-
petence; after the cacophony dies out, he says unconvincingly, "It's
good."

Months later Holland begins to find common ground with the
musical taste and experience of his students, demonstrating how a
contemporary rock tune is simply an alteration of a Bach sonata.
His students suddenly perk up, and hands fly up all over the
classroom. He comes home to tell Iris in amazement that it was
great fun. He begins to refine a pedagogy that is able to convey his
love and mastery of music to students.

Later in the film Glen Holland is called in to explain why he
is teaching the students "rock and roll." "Is this a problem?" he
asks, and the vice-principal says, "Yes, it is a problem." He goes

on to assert that pop music lacks discipline, that Holland should be pushing the classics. Holland replies with a pedadogical commitment to music that can be "known and read by all," one that resonates with the depths of 2 Corinthians: he will use anything from Bach to Billy Holliday if it "will help me to teach a student to love music." As the legalistic vice-principal scowls, the principal (played by Olympia Dukakis) replies, "A reasonable answer, Mr. Holland."

The matter of making music accessible to all confronts a particularly acute barrier with Holland's son, Cole, who is deaf. While Iris takes vigorous steps to learn sign language, Glen remains blocked by bitter disappointment at being unable to communicate with a child who lacks access to the music that is his lifelong passion. This impasse reaches a climax at the time of John Lennon's death, when Glen refuses to explain how he feels on the assumption that Cole could not possibly know about music, much less about Lennon. In the angry confrontation that follows, Cole indicates that he does know about John Lennon and about music, and that his father could teach him more. "But you care more about your students than you do about me."

Later Glen sees his son tuning up the family car while feeling vibrations by placing a rod between the engine and his head. Glen decides to visit the school for the deaf to discover ways to convey music to people with hearing deficits. He stages an imaginative musical celebration in which the deaf students sit up in front of the orchestra watching the flashing strobe lights that match the rhythm and intensity of the music. They are thrilled with the new accessibility this affords. Holland sings a song to his son, signing as he goes along. "Beautiful, beautiful, beautiful, beautiful boy." The next scene has Cole sitting on the loudspeakers enjoying the blues, and later in the film, Cole writes that he has been appointed professor of music at the school for the deaf. Through imagination and dedication, music has become a letter known and read by all, including those who cannot hear.

So what kind of discourse do we follow in our teaching, preaching, mentoring, and childrearing? The kind that throws honor back upon us, showing our brilliance, our mastery of knowledge unavailable to the uninitiated? Such discourse reveals that we care more about being admired by others than we do about the people themselves, to paraphrase Cole's criticism of his father. To commit ourselves to a form of service, to a kind of language and music "known and read by all," means that we place a high priority on meeting people's needs where they are. It places us on the same level, revealing that we have grasped the reality that, since Christ died for all, all are equal. This brings us to the central dialectic between tablets of stone and the human heart.

Tablets of Stone versus Human Hearts

It is amazing that Paul could leap from the simple metaphor of persons as letters into the profound theological discourse that follows. It involves a dialectic between messages inscribed on human hearts or on tablets of stone. As Carol Stockhausen has reminded us, this dialectic was already present in the Old Testament: Jeremiah and Ezekiel refer to the covenant written on the heart in contrast with the covenant on tablets of stone in Exodus 34 and 36.[11] The word "heart" refers to "the center of human personhood,"[12] understood, from a Judaic point of view, not as a physical organ but as "the inner person, the seat of understanding, knowledge, and will . . . the 'place' of the person in which the encounter with God is realized."[13]

My study of Paul's anthropological terms shows the central place of the heart in his thinking. This term "belongs to the earliest ascertainable level of Pauline anthropology. It depicts man as a whole, viewed from his intentionality; the heart as the center of man is thought of as the source of will, emotion, thoughts and affections."[14] In using this term, Paul refers to the center of emotional and intellectual attachment, evoking the deep, personal relationships his ministry established. The early Christians became family; they referred to each other as brother, sister, child, mother, or father, reflecting the new familial relationships being established in house and tenement churches of the Pauline mission.

In contrast, the superapostles worked with the ordinary means of honor and shame, seeking to sweep their audiences off their feet by rhetoric, authority, and charisma. What they wanted was recognition of their super performances. Instead of a family in which leaders and followers were bound together by love and mutual support, they desired a congregation of admirers. They would have been more successful in some of our modern, televised megaministries than Paul could ever have been.

Let me try to explain this contrast between "heart" and "tablets of stone." The letter was "written on our hearts," that is, on the hearts of Paul and his colleagues. Paul allows the personal concerns and development of each to preoccupy him. We see this in every letter, but most succinctly in the catalogue of hardships in 2 Corinthians:

> In toil and hardship, through many a sleepless night, hungry and thirsty, often without food, cold and naked. And besides other things, I am under daily pressure because of my anxiety for all the churches. Who is weak, and I am not weak? Who is made to stumble, and I am not indignant? (2 Cor 11:27-29)

At first Glen Holland's attitude is much closer to that of the superapostles. Within four or five months of his joining the faculty, his principal asks him to serve on a textbook committee that will meet at night, but Holland is above that sort of thing. He has the priorities of fame when school hours are over. Principal Jacobs comments: "I've never seen a teacher run for the parking lot at the end of the day with more speed and enthusiasm; you ought to be the track coach." Holland replies that he has never been late and does his duty to the best of his abilities. Jacobs explains: "A teacher has two jobs. Fill their minds with knowledge, yes. But more important, give those minds a compass so that knowledge doesn't go to waste." She suggests that his own internal compass is stuck, because he has been overlooking the deeper meaning of his vocation. He has not yet found the direction to the human heart.

In the course of time Holland becomes absorbed with the needs and orientation of his students, sometimes to the detriment of his family. In one angry confrontation with his wife, he admits he is pulled both ways, but music teaching is now his life. He spends his evening hours grading papers and writing arrangements for student performances. His compass is set for life, aimed not at fame but at meeting the needs of his students.

Paul's letter develops the antithesis with "tablets of stone," based on the law and authority. Paul goes on to deal with the religion of commandments as a "ministry of death" (3:7) in which "minds were hardened" and "veiled" (3:14-15). The letter of the law kills, Paul claims, "but the Spirit gives life" (3:6). Behind this language lies Paul's conviction that a religion of law quickly produces gradations of honor, and for those who fall short in the competition, abject shame. At its deepest level, hardness of heart is a sickness caused by the law that lures us into competitive achievement.[15] Paul's approach rests on his understanding of the cross and resurrection of Christ. The Spirit of Christ frees individuals and groups from the law by sharing their shame, bearing its burden, and exposing its death-dealing effect. By conveying unconditional acceptance that overcomes shame, the hardened heart softens, opens up, and comes alive again.

In Mr. Holland's Opus, Vice-Principal Walters, the crewcut legalist, wants Holland to stick with the classics, the "tablets of stone" so to speak, even if students hate it and become as impervious and asleep as stone itself. Early in the film, Holland wants the same thing: he repeatedly tries to instruct the clarinetist Gertrude note by note, and tries to drum music theory into other students. The results are deadening. He sarcastically reads back the answers to questions on the music appreciation class test. "Question: name an American composer. Answer: Johann Sebastian Bach." Holland reads the ridiculous answers back to the students to shame them into better performance. He threatens to go over the questions one by one, "until you get them right." It is a dismal exercise in boring failure as he passes out Fs with hard-hearted vengeance. This is a classic form of pedagogy by the law, enforced by the threat of sending kids to the principal's office.

Gradually and painfully, Mr. Holland learns how to relate to students' current musical taste, to connect it to classical music, and to teach a love and understanding of all music. The students who at first were unengaged in his class become alert, excited, and alive.

It is the town that ultimately reverts to tablets of stone as it eliminates the arts for budgetary reasons. In the confrontation with the school board over this issue, Holland predicts that the students will soon have nothing to write about. Life without the arts is a ministry of death, veiling children in a life of law without imagination and fantasy.

Yet neither the film nor Paul advocates an abandonment of the discipline of the law. Once the heart gets attached to the music, Glen is able to teach his musicians to play in tune and on the beat, making truly beautiful music. For example, Holland attempts to teach an athlete, Lou Russ, to play in the band so he can make a passing grade and stay on the wrestling team. The only possibility for someone with no aptitude for melody is to play the bass drum, but Russ was also born with absolutely no sense of rhythm; he simply can't hit the drum on the beat. Holland tries one technique after the other, dancing, moving Russ's foot to the beat by hand, even beating on his football helmet while Lou attempts to match the beat on the drum. Gradually, the teacher's persistence begins to pay off, because the band is playing "The Stars and Stripes Forever" and Holland stops to say, "Congratulations [Mr. Russ], you found the beat." The athlete beams and the band applauds. Then the marching band is shown, playing a new rock march, and the crowd goes crazy dancing. The beat becomes contagious when it is not simply a matter of law, when it becomes an expression of the heart in tune with the times.

Paul's analysis of the relationship between gospel and law allows genuine personhood to emerge from behind the facades erected by honor and shame. Such ministry allows "glory" to reappear (3:9-11) and removes the veil from individual faces (3:14), establishing "freedom" (3:17) under the lordship of Christ. This is the opposite of the lordship of law and custom. Similarly, Holland gradually learns to allow the hearts and voices of his students to arise, to shake free from convention, to come into their glory. The key episode is with the terribly tense and obsessive clarinet player, Gertrude. After months of frustrating private lessons, she decides to quit. She has practiced for three years and still cannot play a single line without screeching. "Is it any fun?" Holland asks. "I wanted it to be," she sadly replies.

Suddenly Mr. Holland has an intuition: "You know what we have been doing wrong, Miss Lang? We've been playing notes on the page." "Well, what else is there to play?" she replies. "There's a lot more to music than notes on a page," he responds. "Playing music is supposed to be fun. It's about heart. It's about feelings, and moving people, and something beautiful, in being alive, and it's not about notes on a page. I could teach you notes on the page. I can't teach you that other stuff." Then he has her pick up her clarinet and play without the music. She already knows the notes, but doesn't trust herself to play. She tries, but again overblows her instrument to make an awful screech. He then asks if he can pose a personal question, which he hopes will expose her personal identity: "When you look in a mirror, what do you like best about yourself?" She smiles, "My hair," which is long, auburn, and well kept. "My father always says it reminds him of the sunset." Then Mr. Holland adopts a new strategy: "Play the sunset. . . . Close your eyes." Amazingly, Gertrude begins to make the first real music of her life.

At the core of this dilemma is Gertrude's failure to live up to the high standards of performance held by her family. Her parents and siblings are all talented, but she is a nobody, unable to do anything right. Before the breakthrough, Gertrude bursts into tears because she is "terrible. . . . I just want to be good at something. . . . I'm the only one in my family who can't. . . ." She breaks off, unable to finish the sentence. Her shameful worthlessness is literally unspeakable.

When Gertrude is enabled to join her heart with the notes, she begins to make music, to come out of her shell, and to become a real person. It's not that she will ever become a musician, but that she has begun to locate her own voice, to overcome the burden of shame. A later scene has the whole orchestra playing swing music, and Gertrude is playing the clarinet solo, beautifully. To paraphrase Paul's language later in the 2 Corinthians passage, the veil over her mind has been removed and she moves into freedom. It is a freedom that later results in her becoming a responsible political leader of her state, able to speak her mind eloquently in the final celebration when she describes how much Holland's teaching has meant to her.

A similar case involves the beautiful singer Rowena Morgan, who auditions for a musical review and becomes a star. In the rehearsal she sings "Someone to Watch Over Me," and Holland takes a break to ask her, "What do you think the girl is really feeling here?" "I don't know," Rowena replies. He explains, "You have to know, or you can't sing it. This song is wistful, Miss Morgan; it's about a woman who's alone in a very, very cold world. And all she wants, more than anything, is to have someone hold her close, to tell her that everything's going to be all right. It's about the need for love . . . in your gut." Rowena tries it again, and the magic begins.

In time Rowena develops an affair of the heart with Holland because he has helped her discover her talent and vocation, because of her feeling of indebtedness to her inspired teacher. He encourages her to find freedom in a move to New York, supporting her without seducing her, a rather unusual feature in current cinema, but one that Paul would heartily endorse.

So how do we want to draw the letters of our life? On tablets of stone? Or on human hearts? The former offers far more prestige, if the society's standards of honor and shame are taken into account. Messages inscribed on stone are permanent. The symphony written on paper or recorded in the studio has a solidity that generations yet to come can admire and emulate. The book or building or scientific experiment that we create give the appearance of standing the test of time. In every field there is far more prestige attached to stone tablets than to the fleeting, elusive messages inscribed on human hearts. Reflections on this film and this text confront each of us with the question: Which kind of glory should we seek, the glory of our own fame and success, or the glory that emerges as others become free? This leads to the final issue: Who is it that finally writes the message on the heart?

A Letter of Christ Written by the Spirit

"You are a letter of Christ," Paul writes. He is trying to explain that the evidence of Christ as the one who sets people free from the law and from the burden of shameful status is visible in their own conversion. All Paul did for the Corinthians, he insists, was to "deliver" the letter,[16] whose message was written into their own lives by Christ and his gospel. But the superapostles were claiming that the crucial letters pointed to themselves. "What these letters prove," they argued, "is that the church needs leaders like us to take charge. Inspired leaders make an inspired church."

The difference between Paul and the superapostles is clarified by Jeffrey Crafton in *The Agency of the Apostle*. He observes that, in 2 Corinthians 2,

> Paul never places himself in the role of agent; rather it is God who acts through him. In contrast to the intruders, who operate as agents and therefore point to signs of legitimacy and carry letters attesting to their qualifications . . . , Paul is to be judged only by the results of his presence. In a show of rhetorical brilliance Paul engages the Corinthians in his argument by naming *them* as the sign of his agency. *They* are the proof of his apostolic effectiveness, of his authenticity.[17]

The social system of honor and shame leads us all to desire the status of agent. We want to act in such a way as to gain honor compared with others. But if we are set free to be the agency of God's power, then whatever we accomplish accrues to God's honor rather than our own. Paul's whole point is that Christ has freed him from the vicious necessity of being always on center stage, acting always so as to gain honor for himself. The death and resurrection of Christ had freed him from the compulsion to be number one. Thus Paul can be truthful about who is finally responsible for human transformation: it is the "Spirit of the living God" who alone is capable of inscribing the transforming gospel message on the human heart. Only the power of the Spirit is capable of opening up the hardened heart, to set us free from the compulsion to gain status, to live up to the expectations of others. Grace frees us to use our gifts freely, creatively, in the service of others. It releases us from the obsession to compete for honor.

Paul's point has some similarity to Holland's reluctance to take credit at several points in the film: the music is more powerful than he is; it only has to be freed up for people to begin to communicate with it and revel in its joys. He just helps students remove the barriers to their own effective communication, teaches them to play and march together, and lets the spirit of the music take the fore, to the inspiration of all.

This is why the final celebration of the film is jarring and unexpected. Holland is heading out of the high school building for the last time, accompanied by his wife and son, when he hears strange noises from the auditorium, which should be empty now that the school year is over. He is surprised by the former members of his orchestras and bands gathering to celebrate his life and to perform his American symphony for the first time. It is a tear-jerking climax in the film, but it leaves us with a problematic expectation that we too should receive such eloquent accolades if we do well in our professions. Reviewers caught the somewhat false, soupy note in this ending.[18] It allows fame to win in the end: Holland is celebrated as a superstar, the center of the attention of a large group of applauding people, including the governor and all of his former teaching colleagues, even the principal who has just fired him.

If we were to place this ending in the context of 2 Corinthians, it would be as if the superapostles gained their victory in the end, as if Paul himself became a superstar, applauded by all. Adoration of the "agent" prevails over a sober recognition of "agency." And when that occurs, the entire break that Christ made with the system of human commendation is fatally undermined. Granted, Holland is honored not for the symphony, which he thought would bring him fame, but for his devotion to students over the years. Nevertheless, Paul's viewpoint seems healthier than the anticipation evoked by the conclusion of *Mr. Holland's Opus*.

Paul carries through with the critique of self-commendation by insisting: "Not that we are competent of ourselves to claim anything as coming from us; our competence is from God, who has made us competent to be ministers of a new covenant . . . (2 Cor 3:5-6). The superapostles are really advocates of the old covenant of competition for honor. But it is Christ, rather than any human agency, who must receive the final credit, for Christ was the one who refused to seek superior status for himself. As Philippians 2 says, "He emptied himself, taking the form of a servant." Christ reversed the system of seeking honor that has corrupted the human race since Adam's fall, thereby setting free all who accept his message, free from the quest for admiration. This was accomplished by granting humans an acceptance so unconditional that we need not spend our lives seeking adulation.

There is a story my father used to tell that embodies this issue, moving it beyond the realm of cinematic fantasy and biblical reconstruction. It concerns a minister in New England who lacked leadership ability but loved the people in his parishes. A tiny, unassuming man with a sqeaky voice, Brother Draper had to be moved to a different church every year or two because of complaints. At the end of his disappointing career in the 1920s, he was moved back to the small town in northern New Hampshire where he had endured hostile rejection some years before. The state tuberculosis sanitarium was located several miles outside of town, on a remote mountaintop; prior to the development of antibiotics, rest and mountain air were thought to be the only cure for this otherwise hopeless disease. Draper regularly called on patients there.

On Easter morning, Brother Draper rose very early and picked tiny bunches of wild flowers for everyone in the sanitarium that he had been visiting. Being too poor to own a car, he walked out to the sanitarium and placed the flowers in each room before returning for his own church service. The parishioner relating this story to my father was so deeply moved that she rose from her bed and kissed the place on the floor where his shadow had fallen. Brother Draper may have been a failure; no auditorium ever celebrated his opus. But he showed that these hopeless patients were a letter written on his heart, "written not with ink but with the Spirit of the living God."

Conclusion

In light of this dialogue between Paul and *Mr. Holland's Opus,* can we allow Christ's letter written on the heart to preserve us from the yearning to be famous, to be remembered as great and heroic? If a celebration of our vocation does come, can we accept it without taking it too seriously, without being ruined by it? If it does not come, can we live without the fame of our symphony's publication and performance? Can the silent caress of a passing shadow on the floor be enough for us even though the world views us as failures?

Here is the gospel's bottom line: a replacement for the status gained through outstanding performance is ours already, in Christ's "new covenant" of grace. We do not need the endorsement of those we serve resounding through the auditorium, because in Christ we already have divine endorsement that is not dependent on our achievements. With this we are set free from the law, free from the tablets of stone, free from hardness of heart, free from the tyranny of the record book, free from bondage to the bottom line, and thus free to serve in whatever field we are called to make our opus. Such work has already been hallowed, before we even put our hand to the task, because Christ has inscribed it, "not with ink but with the spirit of the living God."

Since the final meaning of life is what God has done for us and not what we ourselves accomplish, the most appropriate response would be to praise the One who is the source of all our music. The best choice would be a word drawn from one of our most ancient songs, originating at least three thousand years before the dawn of what Western culture calls "classical music." It is a word whose melody is now unrecoverable, although its verbal articulation is shared by Jews, Muslims, Christians, and other thankful people around the globe to express the core of our common humanity, a word directed toward the source of the most essential messages inscribed on the human heart: "Hallelujah!"

6. The Deadly Deception of the Flesh in *Groundhog Day*

Do not be deceived; God is not mocked.
  For whatever a person sows, that he will also reap.
For the one who sows to his own flesh will from the
flesh reap corruption,
  but the one who sows to the Spirit will from the Spirit
reap eternal life.
And let us not grow weary in doing good,
  for in its own time we shall reap a harvest if we do not
    give up.
So then, as we have time, let us do good to all people,
  and especially to those of the household of faith.

Galatians 6:7-10

Introduction

There is an intriguing expression in Gal 6:10 that addresses the central premise of *Groundhog Day*,[1] the story of a television weatherman by the name of Phil Connors who "gets stuck in time."[2] He feels caught in an endless cycle of repetition reminiscent of the despair felt by many people in Paul's time. Paul moves against the

88

cultural stream in promising that "in its own time we shall reap a harvest if we do not give up." The expression *kairos idios* ("in its own time") in the final verse of this passage from Galatians implies that there are moments that are appropriate, distinctive, and non-repetitive, designed by God for the harvest. Translations like the Revised Standard Version render this "in due season." In the world as God intended it, we do not go on planting a crop day after day, or cultivating and weeding day after day. Rather, planting is followed by cultivating and nurturing and then by harvesting. Time is going somewhere because God intends it so.

But Phil Connors is out in Punxsutawney, Pennsylvania, for the fourth year in a row, watching the same groundhog come out of the same hole, and seeing the same people in the same celebration. He is arrogant, bitter, and cynical, as contemptuous of his colleagues on the camera crew as he is of the citizens of Punxsutawney. His orientation leads him to view the yearly celebration of the groundhog's emergence as a sign that there is really no "tomorrow." There is no "proper time," no "due season" for moving on. This throws his whole life into a tailspin. He discusses this burden with some fellows at the bar early in the film: "What would you do if you were stuck in one place, and every day was exactly the same, and nothing that you did mattered?" The guys at the bar look off into the distance for a moment, and then one of them says, "That sums it up for me." Their lives also have no "proper time" for moving past planting and cultivating into some kind of fulfillment, into the harvest. They feel they are stuck on a treadmill for the rest of their lives. To use Paul's language, they have devoted their energies to "sowing to the flesh," and now they are "reaping the corruption" of emptiness.

Does *Groundhog Day* throw light on the links between time, flesh, and the quest for gratification and honor, or between sowing and reaping through "doing good"? As the starting point for our reflections, let me begin by sketching the distinctive view of time reflected in this text from Galatians.

The Biblical Approach to Time

In the last fifty years scholars have made much of two Greek words for time found in the New Testament: *chronos,* meaning linear time, from which our word "chronology" comes; and *kairos,* meaning the "appointed time" or the "time for decision."[3] The standard Greek term for cyclical time was *chronos,*[4] with the same hour appearing each day, moving as relentlessly as Phil Connor's schedule — waking with that same six o'clock alarm every morning and going through the same routine each day. Through the miracle of film, the same day is repeated over and over again like a recurrent nightmare. The Pittsburgh weathercaster goes to the same small town in Pennsylvania to a Groundhog Day celebration that happens day after day. He steps into the same pothole of icy water, has the same conversations with the same people, and celebrates the same stupid groundhog coming out of the same hole. As Jonathan Romney writes, this film "may be the purest nightmare movie Hollywood has ever produced — potentially endless repetition, just for its own sake."[5] This is *chronos* in its most painful form.

The other word used in our Galatians text is *kairos,* that is, "significant time" or "fulfilled time."[6] In Jörg Baumgarten's formulation, "*chronos* designates a 'period of time' in the linear sense, while *kairos* frequently refers to 'eschatologically filled time, time for decision.'"[7] Although we do not have different words in English, we all know the difference between everyday time, when we follow our routines, and special times such as birthdays or anniversaries. Some of us remember the day we decided to marry our spouse, or when we got the new job offer, or when we moved into a new house. The audience of Galatians would have been even more sensitive to this set of terms than we are, because their educational system was dominated by the study of rhetoric, the art of appropriate speech. They were taught that there was a proper moment to say a specific thing. The ancient education system was very concerned to train people in timeliness.

The idea of "proper time," the "time of fulfillment," plays a key role in the New Testament. Christ is the one who ushers in a new time; salvation moves believers off the treadmill. Thus Paul urges the Corinthians in 2 Cor 6:2, "Behold, now is the acceptable time; behold, now is the day of salvation." Since "at the right time Christ died for the ungodly" (Rom 5:6), the present moment of decision is fraught with significance. The early Christians had the sense that the present time is moving quickly toward the end of the world, that the "time is shortened" (1 Cor 7:29) in which there is an opportunity for conversion. Thus the present is "the decisive moment" in which sides must be taken.[8]

The Bible teaches the significance of being responsive to time. The formulation of Ecclesiastes 3:1-8 places this idea in classic form:

> For everything there is a season, and time for every matter under heaven:
> a time to be born, and a time to die;
> a time to plant, and a time to pluck up what is planted;
> a time to kill, and a time to heal . . .
> a time to embrace, and time to refrain from embracing. . . .
> a time to love, and a time to hate;
> a time for war, and a time for peace.

Learning to live, according to this view, depends on discovering how to tell time. As Bill Murray reveals in playing the role of Phil Connors in *Groundhog Day*, if you try to embrace when it is not the time for embracing, you are sure to get a slap in the face. Whether the issue is planting or making war, life requires that people act in accordance with the demands of constantly changing circumstances.

Paul intensifies this usage by using *kairos* ("proper time" or "fulfilled time") to refer to the final period of history inaugurated by Christ, pointing to the coming time of judgment (1 Cor 4:5; 1 Thess 5:1) as well as to the current moment of decision (1 Cor 10:11). "The Pauline understanding of time culminates in the interpretation of the future determined by the present . . . [and] the present determined by the future."[9] In Paul's view, the way people respond to life in the present shapes the kind of future they will have. By placing their faith in Christ, they grasp the significance of the present routine because it leads to a future called "eternal life." So from the Pauline point of view, this is what a film like *Groundhog Day* is really all about, even though the filmmakers and actors may not have fully understood these implications themselves. To live according to the flesh is to be stuck in *chronos,* to repeat the same mistakes day after day, to face the same defeat time after time. To live according to the spirit, in response to the love of Christ, is to enter the realm of *kairos,* to find fulfillment in the midst of daily routines.

The barrier to fulfillment is what Paul calls the "flesh" — which we can think of as willful self-centeredness, intent on the achievement of honor in competition with others. "Flesh" deceives us, deludes us, keeps us thinking that our attitudes and actions have no consequences. So we lock ourselves in cycles of deadly repetition that lead to despair. This is why Paul issues the strong warnings that open our text, describing what we might call the deadly deception of the flesh.

The Deadly Deception of the Flesh

"Be not deceived," Paul writes; "God is not mocked. Whatever you sow, that you will also reap. The one who sows to his own flesh will from the flesh reap corruption, but the one who sows to the Spirit will from the Spirit reap eternal life" (Gal 6:7-8). Paul writes these words to Galatian Christians who are still inclined to believe that the self-centered lifestyle popularized by society will have no effect on their future. Paul evidently fears that they will interpret their baptism as a sign that their future is assured and that therefore it no longer matters how they behave or think.[10] Paul warns that such illusions will have deadly consequences.[11] He is arguing for what we might call the principle of accountability.

Paul's idea of the flesh struggling against the Spirit derives from his conviction that the old age of sin stands in conflict with the new age of Christ, and that this conflict rages inside each person at times. The flesh is the realm of self-centered pleasure, related primarily to the pleasures of public approval and honor. It leads people to think that they can gain fulfillment by manipulating others or proving their superiority by surpassing others. In the ancient world, as in the contemporary one, the culture of the flesh was competitive, cut-throat, exploitative, and self-centered. The market for honor in the Greco-Roman world was extremely small,[12] so everyone had to struggle to achieve status. Behavior in the realms of religion and ethics was oriented not to intrinsic ends, for the most part, but to the goal of gaining honor. By contrast, the realm of the Spirit being ushered in by Christ was cooperative, caring, and noncompetitive. These two realms have been in conflict ever since the time of Christ, the one leading to death and the other to life. Paul wanted the Galatians to know that if they reverted to the behavior of the flesh taught by their culture, the consequences would be disastrous.

The question of whether current attitudes and behavior have future consequences is a central theme in the film and is a central problem for current Americans. We tend to understand freedom as a kind of release from constraint. We receive signals on every side that we should just "do it," because consequences can always be fixed. Life is a comedy with happy endings if we just work the system. Phil Connors is depicted as a successful person deceived about time and its consequences, about his own arrogance and its deadly future. While complaining of being stuck in a situation where every day is a repetition of the last, he is actually caught in the web of the flesh and fails to grasp his situation. The basic illusion is discussed before the repetition of *Groundhog Day* begins. "What if there were no tomorrow?" Phil asks the guys at the bar. They reply, "That would mean there would be no consequences, no hangovers, and we could do whatever we want." So the film depicts Phil living out this deception. Once he discovers that he will wake up the every single morning to the same Groundhog Day, he begins to live recklessly. As Matthew Giunti observes, "At first frightened, Phil soon realizes that his time trap paradoxically affords him perfect freedom."[13] He drives his car without worrying about wrecking it and even causes a police car to wreck. He talks about all the things he was brought up not to do, and then does them, including robbing an armored car and driving his car on the railroad track. "I'm not going to live by their rules any more!" he proudly declares. Phil even comes to the point of finally kidnapping the groundhog and driving over a cliff with it, dying in the flames to escape from the cycle of *chronos*. But he just comes back the next morning to the same alarm clock at 6:00 A.M. He commits suicide in various ways, playing out the illusion of escape. But all to no avail. Richard Corliss offers a vivid description of this situation: ". . . he is trapped in time. . . . Yet he can't die, he can't escape. He can only change.[14]

One of the recent commentators on Galatians describes the underlying issue in language that could almost serve as a guide to this film. Richard Longenecker writes: "What Paul seems to have in mind here in speaking about sowing to the flesh are the libertine tendencies of his Galatian converts that he has alluded to earlier in this section: quarrelsomeness (5:15, 16), conceit (5:26), envy (5:26), living aloof from the needs of others (6:1-2; perhaps also 6:6), and pride (6:3-4). Such things not only reflect a misuse of Christian freedom (cf. 5:13) but also have disastrous results both personally and corporately, for 'destruction' is their final end."[15] Each one of these features of what Paul calls "life according to the flesh" matches the way Bill Murray plays the newscaster in *Groundhog Day*.

- He is quarrelsome with his producer and cameraman and refers to a fellow broadcaster as "Hairdo."
- He is stupidly conceited, referring to himself as the "talent" on the news team without recognizing the menial connotation of this expression in the newscasting realm. His conceit also leads him to view the townspeople as "hicks."
- He is envious of the success of others who are able to move up in the profession and do not have to return to Punxsutawney year after year.
- He lives aloof from others, passing people on the streets of Punxsutawney whose troubles do not touch him at all. He passes the same beggar every morning for months of repetition before he discovers the man's story.
- His pride leads him to treat everyone else with contempt, from his colleagues on the film crew to the insurance agent he meets on the street.

To use Paul's language, he has been sowing to the flesh, and the film simply depicts its consequences.

Nowhere are the illusions more deadly than in the love affair Phil Connors tries to carry on with Rita, played by Andie MacDowell. Although attracted to her, Phil actually looks down on her as a subordinate member of the film crew; he has contempt for her love of poetry and her honorable standards of conduct. He tries to seduce her and fails time after time, even after he contrives to fix the van so they can't leave town and learns to respond to her toast to "world peace" by saying, "I like to say a prayer and drink to world peace." After Rita discovers that he has set her up for a romantic evening by studying her reactions, they begin to discuss what love is. In response to his statement that he loves her, Rita replies with a moral perception that seems rooted in the Pauline tradition: "You don't even know me. . . . Is this what love is for you?" Rita asks, implying that he thinks of love as a form of seduction. "I could never love anyone like you, Phil, because you never love anyone but yourself." When Phil persists in the attempt at this false kind of love, she slaps him, again and again and again. Like many American males, Phil has a difficult time figuring out the difference between genuine love and the desire to seduce someone, to manipulate and shamefully possess a partner. To use the ancient categories, it is the difference between *agapē*, genuinely caring love, and *eros*, seductive love, driven by the desire to achieve pleasure and gain prestige by controlling others. The latter is expressed in the Sonny & Cher tune playing on the radio every morning when Phil wakes up: "I Got You, Babe," a triumphal song of possessive *eros*. By contrast Paul advocates *agapē*, which is motivated by the Spirit of Christ, who gave himself for the shamed. The issue here is not sexual desire as such, which Paul views as a good and holy impulse (see 1 Cor 7:7), but the tendency to subordinate others to one's own ends, shamefully using them in the pursuit of satisfaction and honor.

"Reaping Corruption" as a Step toward Redemption

We have seen that Phil's obsession with gaining honor for himself and heaping dishonor on others locks him into *chronos*, into a deadly repetition of futility. As Paul argues, there is an element of divine order and judgment in this cycle of deed and consequence: "The one who sows to his own flesh will from the flesh reap corruption, but the one who sows to the Spirit will from the Spirit reap eternal life" (Gal 6:8). Most commentators feel that "corruption" is used here in the sense of an eschatological judgment of "eternal damnation"[16] As commentator Ronald Fung explains, "Paul has chiefly the eschatological harvest in mind: 'corruption' refers to physical death and disintegration, from which, for those who sow to the flesh, there is no rising to eternal life."[17] While the certainty of final judgment is a recurrent feature of Pauline thought, in other letters Paul argues that such corruption is a present experience of futility (Rom 1:22; 8:20-21) and alienation from the saved community (1 Cor 5:5). By detailing this experience, Paul hopes that his hearers will grasp their situation and turn toward the truth. Salvation is understood as escaping from the "wrath to come" (1 Thess 1:9), because Christ has exposed and absorbed such alienation, for those who accept the gospel. The purpose of Paul's warning in Galatians is to bring the congregation to its senses before it is too late. He very much wants them to avoid the kind of final judgment that continued mocking of God and reliance on the arrogant impulses of the flesh will produce.

In *Groundhog Day* the spiral of "corruption" is a present experience that Phil Connors undergoes, but there are hints that a reckoning lies ahead. In the first stage of his "reaping corruption," Phil responds to the futile repetition of Groundhog Day by the juvenile strategy of living as if there were no consequences. After pigging out on food while Rita looks on with disgust, he hears her citing the lines of Sir Walter Scott describing future judgment:

> The wretch, concentred all in self,
> Living, shall forfeit fair renown,
> And, doubly dying, shall go down
> To the vile dust, from whence he sprung,
> Unwept, unhonour'd, and unsung.

He contemptuously laughs at this warning and moves into the second stage of the spiral of corruption, seducing several of the young women in Punxsutawney with false promises of love and marriage while failing to conquer Rita. He then moves into a third stage of amoral cynicism and suicidal self-destruction. After failing to bring the deadly cycle of futile repetition to a halt by kidnapping the groundhog and dying with him in the flames, Phil tries a variety of other forms of suicide. He electrocutes himself by dropping a toaster into his bathwater and the next day leaps from a high building to a certain death on the pavement below. There are brief references later in the film to five or six additional suicides, none of which provides release from the cycle of futility.

The final stage in Connors's cycle of "corruption" is a mocking of God, reminiscent of Paul's warning in Galatians. He tells Rita that since he keeps coming back from death, "I'm a god . . . I am immortal." Rita replies with scorn, "Because you survived a car wreck?" In view of her twelve years in a good Catholic school, Rita denies that Phil or anyone else can rightfully claim to be God. This conversation merely brings to clear expression a pretension visible throughout the film. In the scene of weather forecasting that opens the film, Phil pretends to blow on the projection of cloud formations to produce the illusion that he is causing their movement. A few scenes later, he snarls in response to a mildly critical comment from a coworker, "I *make* the weather." Reviewer Jonathan Romney captures this motif by commenting that "time will be out of joint until he realizes that actually it's the weather that makes him."[18] In fact, he has six weeks of deadly repetition to undergo, until winter is finally over.

As Paul had hoped for the Galatians, the clear depiction of consequences ultimately leads Phil Connors to stop his headlong dash into "corruption." After telling Rita about the futile suicide attempts, he says in despair, "I wake up and it's still February 2, and there's nothing I can do about it. . . . The worst part is that tomorrow you will have forgotten all about this and will think I'm a jerk again." "No," she assures him. Then, for the first time in the film, he speaks an honest word about himself: "It's all right. I *am* a jerk." She replies in a nonaccusatory spirit: "No, you're not." Although lacking in the precision and explicitness of Paul's doctrine of unconditional grace overcoming shame, this scene is the key to Phil's transformation. To use Paul's terminology, "reaping corruption" has led Phil to an honest acknowledgment of his shameful status so that he is finally able to grasp the message of grace.

Rita goes on to address the question of repetition, wishing sometimes she had a thousand lifetimes: "I don't know, Phil. Maybe it's not a curse; just depends on how you look at it." It has been a nice day, she says, and "maybe, if it's not too boring, we could do it again sometime." He replies, "I hope so." He is finally beginning to realize that the corruption he has been experiencing is derived from how he "looks at it," how he relates to the passage of time and the people he meets along the way. For the first time, he stops trying to seduce Rita. When she wakes up at 3:00 A.M. in his bedroom after dropping off to sleep while he was reading poetry, he says it is okay. "I promise I won't touch you." He had just finished reading Joyce Kilmer's "Trees" when she fell asleep, the poem being a symbol of his acknowledgment that he can no longer play god with the weather or anything else.

Phil gently pulls the covers over Rita and lets her sleep. As she sleeps, he says quietly, "What I wanted to say was, I think you are the kindest, sweetest, prettiest person I ever met in my life. I've never seen anyone as nice and beautiful as you are." He kisses her gently on the cheek. "The first time I saw you, something happened to me. I never told you, but I knew that I wanted to hold you. . . . I don't deserve someone like you. But if I ever could, I swear I would love you for the rest of my life."

It is only when he gives up the illusion of godly powers and discovers that love is unconditional that he can begin, in Paul's words, "working for the good of all."

The "Harvest" of "Working for the Good of All"

Impelled by Rita's love, Phil Connors finally gives up on the cycle of manipulation by means of the flesh and begins to help other people. He discovers that "self-centeredness is actually less rewarding than generosity," in Stanley Kauffmann's words.[19] At first he gives the beggar a tip, then a meal, then rescues him from freezing on a bitterly cold night. He learns to run fast enough to save a boy falling from an apple tree; he learns the Heimlich maneuver so he can rescue a man choking on a fishbone; he fixes a flat tire for some vulnerable older women; he helps a squabbling couple to find a resolution; he helps a man out with his sore back. These episodes led several reviewers to refer to a certain optimistic do-goodism in *Groundhog Day*. Audrey Farolino writes, "The movie's premise is rather Kafkaesque, but its message is more Capraesque: Even if you're stuck in the same place with the same people doing the same things every day, you can find salvation of a sort through little acts of kindness and selflessness."[20]

Although it is possible to contend that Phil Connors "seems to become a better person more out of boredom than anything else,"[21] viewing the film through the lens of Galatians allows us to suggest that Phil has finally grasped the true nature of love and the need to stop playing god, which is the ultimate form of living according to the flesh.

The links to Galatians are obvious: "Doing what is good" in Gal 6:9 is "identical with the concepts of the 'fruit of the Spirit' (5:22-23) and of 'following the Spirit' (5:25; cf. 5:16)."[22] The admonition not to grow "weary" in doing good reflects Paul's fear that the enthusiasm for life in the Spirit was waning, that the Galatian converts "were beginning to revert from an outgoing type of Christian faith that seeks the welfare of others to a selfish, self-contained religious stance that has little concern for others."[23] The social context for this kind of "doing good" is emphasized in 6:10: "Therefore, while we have time, let us do good to all, especially to those of the household of faith." This wording makes it clear that the primary responsibility of these early Christians was local. Most of them had very limited means and time. The primary arena of responsibility was to care for the members in their small households of faith.[24] This needs to be understood within the framework of early Christian communalism and cooperation within the house and tenement churches, the small "families of faith" that marked the early church.[25] Early Christians were to seek the welfare of others in good times as well as bad, countering the despair of a cyclical life that goes nowhere. The "eternal life" of 6:8 began in the present moment for the Galatian

Christians, because Christ had freed them from the treadmills of the flesh.

Paul's idea that "we shall reap a harvest if we do not give up" is partially embodied in a vocational sense by Phil's discovery of mature broadcasting skills at the end of the film. After repeatedly blowing off the assignment to cover Groundhog Day, providing revoltingly cynical and boring commentaries, he begins to reap a harvest of genuine eloquence after coming to terms with the "corruption" of the flesh. With the townspeople crowding about, he tells the television audience:

> When Chekhov saw the long winter, he saw a winter bleak and dark and bereft of hope. Yet we know that winter is just another step in the cycle of life. But standing here among the people of Punxsutawney and basking in the warmth of their hearths and hearts, I couldn't imagine a better fate than a long and lustrous winter. From Punxsutawney, it's Phil Connors. So long.

The crowd applauds and Larry the cameraman says with amazement, "Man, you touched me." Rita says admiringly, "You surprised me; I didn't know you were so versatile." Phil's soliloquy comes to terms with *chronos* and accepts its promise under the aegis of grace. Its promise is reminiscent of the divine assurance given to the children of Noah in connection with the promise never again to destroy every living creature. When my wife and I were students in Germany, we frequently read these words concerning the reliability of nature's cycles, painted with charming artistry on the walls of farmhouses:

> As long as the earth endures,
>> seedtime and harvest, cold and heat,
> summer and winter, day and night,
>> shall not cease. (Gen 8:22)

Phil not only accepts this kind of promise that time will bring its harvest but also finds therein his own mature gifts as a newscaster. He finally makes sense of Groundhog Day as a promise not only that winter will pass away in due season but also that in the loving "hearths and hearts" of friends, a "lustrous winter" can be a source of delight.

At the end of the romantic comedy, Rita is impressed with Phil's good deeds and vocational versatility. She decides that he is an appealing partner. At the bachelor auction, Phil gets the highest bid because the community appreciates what he has done. Rita finally takes out her checkbook, adds up how much she has left in her account, and bids $339.88. They go out together, and Phil makes a beautiful portrait of her in the ice, saying, "No matter what happens tomorrow, for the rest of my life, I'm happy now, because I love you." She replies, "I'm happy too." They kiss tenderly, with mutual cherishing.

The next morning the alarm goes off at 6:00 again, and her arm reaches across to turn it off. Phil gets up to look out the window, and amazingly, there is a clean white snow on the ground. He jumps back in bed and kisses her, and Rita says, "Oh Phil, why weren't you like this last night. You just fell asleep." It is obvious that his obsession of seduction has been broken. He now speaks with the new orientation of doing good for all: "Is there anything I can do for you today?" She replies playfully, "I probably can think of something."

Conclusion

Paul's exhortation in Gal 6:9-10 emphasizes that each Christian group, enlivened by the Spirit, has "time" to fulfill their lives, to "live here" in the present. The echo of *Groundhog Day* is particularly clear in the wordplay on the word "time" (*kairos*) in verses 9 and 10.[26] At the "proper *time*" we will reap the harvest. "So then, as we have *time*, let us do good to all people, and especially to those of the household of faith."

I regret that this echo of the word "time" does not show up in our modern translations, but it was clearly visible in the original Greek text, and it provides the resource to understand the deepest meaning of the film — and of the daily routines of modern life. Our times may seem to be the same day after day, stuck in *chronos*, but if we look around, there are fresh opportunities to love every day we live. New people cross our paths; new problems arise for us to solve; new challenges face us as times change in the fast-moving worlds of work and social responsibility. New ways can be found to deal with routine tasks. This realization correlates closely with the "deeper message" of *Groundhog Day,* perceived by Richard Corliss: "It says that most folks' lives are like Phil's on Groundhog Day: a repetition, with the tiniest variations, of ritual pleasures and annoyances. Routine is the metronome marking most of our time on earth. Phil's gift is to see the routine and seize the day."[27]

In the light of Galatians, however, the key issue is not seizing the day in an opportunistic manner but rather overcoming the prideful illusions that the times and seasons can be brought under human control, that others can be mastered and seduced to suit our own rhythm and ego needs. If the film offers a "life lesson, a story of self-discovery and change,"[28] then that lesson centers on the need to turn away from the illusions of the flesh. Unfortunately, the lesson remains on the fairy-tale level in *Groundhog Day.* The lovers come down the steps of the bed and breakfast at the end of the film, and Phil, gazing at the fresh snow, says, "It's so beautiful. Let's live here." A false note is struck as their station wagon is seen making tracks through the freshly fallen snow, indicating the promise of a new life in Punxsutawney for a couple who will live here happily ever after. Especially for Phil and Rita, whose matured vocations require the broadcasting facilities of Pittsburgh, this ending is wide of the mark. Given the cultural appeal of an idyllic life in an isolated town or safe suburb, this is one more illusion of the flesh.

The reference in Gal 6:8 to the Spirit indicates a more serious possibility of living in the *kairos* of fulfilled time. The Spirit leads followers of Christ off the treadmill while we maintain our daily routines of work and family care. Christ frees us from our culturally shaped compulsions to embrace selfish love, to escape the complexities of vocation and mutual responsibilities. Thus Paul calls the Galatian Christians to discover new forms of "reaping a harvest," "doing what is right," and "working for the good of all . . . while we have time." Both in the film and in Paul's mind, this is the most important indicator that someone is, in fact, unstuck in time. But to use an allusion in Matthew Giunti's review in the *Christian Century*, the continued unwillingness of the American public to "roll up its sleeves and take a crack at a few of the country's enduring social problems"[29] indicates that most of us remain stuck. Is it really possible now for us to recapture the meaning of our national motto, "The New Order of the Ages"? Can we shake loose from our illusions and mature toward the promise that will surely come to fulfillment "in its own time"?

7. *Babe* Takes the Lead in Honoring the Lowly

[Let] the love be genuine,
  abhorring the evil,
    cleaving to the good;
  [having] affection for one another with brotherly love,
    taking the lead in honoring one another. . . .
  sharing in the needs of the saints,
  pursuing hospitality to strangers. . . .
being of the same mind toward one another,
  not setting your minds on exalted things,
but being drawn toward lowly people,
  "not being wise-minded in yourselves" . . .
Do not be conquered by what is evil,
  but conquer the evil with the good.

Romans 12:9-10, 13, 16, 21

Introduction

In January of 1996, Richard Brookhiser published an article in *The Atlantic Monthly* that relates to the issue of civility in the context of honor and shame. In the section on "Politeness as Politics," Brookhiser describes the "Rules of Civility and Decent Behavior in Company and Conversation," which George Washington copied out by hand at the age of sixteen, and which seemed to guide him throughout his career.[1] These 110 rules are from an English translation of a French Jesuit writing of 1595 intended to replace the courtly manners that restricted honor to aristocrats. A combination of stoic and Christian egalitarianism surfaces in these rules, which guided Washington throughout his life.

These "Rules of Civility" are strikingly similar to the ethos of Romans 12. For instance, Rule 1 is: "Every action done in company ought to be done with some sign of respect to those that are present," whether they be of aristocratic or ordinary rank.[2] Rule 36: "Treat [artificers and persons of low degree] with affability and courtesy, without arrogance." Rule 32 announces "a principle of accepting honor only with reluctance and modesty."[3] Rule 63 warns: "A man ought not to value himself or his achievements or rare qualities of wit, much less of his riches, virtue or kindred."[4] In general, Brookhiser writes, these rules "were outlining and absorbing a system of courtesy appropriate to equals and near equals."[5] Washington's adherence to these democratic manners throughout his public career evoked Parson Weems's comment that it was "no wonder every body honoured *him* who honoured every body."[6]

It is clear that honor and shame lie at the center of the issue, which involves "taking the lead in honoring one another . . . being drawn toward lowly people" and not being "wise minded in yourselves," to use the words from Romans 12. It is ironic that Washington, a young Protestant in a predominantly Protestant nation, was guided by a Roman Catholic tract, which served as a conduit for biblical egalitarianism in an era when the most radical Protestants were little concerned with manners. This remains the case, at least officially, for most "mainline" Protestant groups: manners are not a subject in typical Protestant courses in Christian ethics, nor are they a regular topic of debate in the American Society of Christian Ethics.

In 1995 a cinematic echo of these themes sounded from a most unlikely source, *Babe*,[7] an Australian film with a story line set in some modern-day country of the British Commonwealth. This live-action, barnyard story is a fable with extraordinary human relevance. Babe is a piglet who was picked up and placed in a sack as "only a runt" after his mother had been trucked off to that "other world" of pig happiness, from which no grown pig had ever returned. Arthur Hoggett, a sheep farmer (played by James Cromwell), is walking through the fair and decides to take a chance at guessing the weight of the runt. He wins the pig, and Babe is subsequently adopted by Fly, the mother Border collie on the Hoggett farm. "He's going to sleep with us until he finds his feet," she announces to her skeptical mate, Rex.

After some adventures growing up in the farmyard, Babe breaks the rules and goes outside to discover that "something is definitely wrong" in the sheep pasture. Some rustlers are trying to make off with the flock. Babe returns to alert the dog Rex and Mr. Hoggett, saving part of the flock. The family laughs at Mr. Hoggett's "watchpig," but shortly thereafter Mr. Hoggett looks with amazement as Babe succeeds in getting some chickens to gather in different colored groups in the farmyard, as obedient as can be. He decides to teach Babe the tricks of sheepherding. Fly explains that the key is "attitude. They just have to know who's boss." When Babe tries to "dominate" the sheep by running around and trying to bark like a dog, they just laugh at him. But then Babe speaks to them with a civil tone, and, amazingly, the sheep walk calmly out of the fold two by two in a stately row.

Farmer Hoggett decides to train Babe for the National Grand Challenge Sheepdog Trials. When they arrive, Babe speaks to the sheep with respect, while Fly uses the ordinary domineering tone of a sheepdog. "All right, blockheads, pay attention over here," she says as the sheep shy away in terror. "Now, you pay attention to what this pig has to say to you, or I'll come in there and rip ya to shreds!" They just veer off and refuse to communicate. Only when Babe discovers the sheep's password do they decide to respond to his requests. The crowd laughs in derision as Babe is led out to the competition, but Mr. Hoggett is undeterred. The sheep obediently file through the course, in pairs, in response to Babe's instructions. The sportscaster is speechless as the crowd goes silent in amazement. At the end of a perfect performance of sheepherding, the

106

crowd breaks into wild applause. Through a lowly pig treating the lowlier sheep with civil respect, a miracle occurs that affects everyone in the story.

Can this film and Romans 12 provide guidance in this difficult era at the end of the century when civility and good manners are increasingly held in contempt by Americans? Do they throw light on the deeper dimensions and motivations of civility in a time when simple admonitions to behave well are no longer effective?

"Beastliness" and the Challenge of Genuine Love

In the 1990s there have been many studies calling attention to the rise of a new "beastliness" in American social relations. As J. Budziszewski observes, "Good manners seem to be taking it in the chops lately. . . . Discourtesy, ingratitude, boorishness, and indecorum are now so much expected in public life that one begins to make sport of them."[8] In *The Triumph of Meanness*, Nicolaus Mills provides an extensive analysis of a tendency to make "meanness and denigration central to mainstream political writing."[9] He goes on to describe talk shows that provoke guests to say derogatory things to each other, news programs that allow analysts rudely to interrupt each other, the rise of hostilities between the sexes and the races, and the popularity of rap's incitement to violence and contempt. Meg Greenfield criticizes "the new verbal incivility," describing it as "a continuous low, nasty, combative whine that has become the accepted background music of our daily lives." It is a form of cowardice: "it does not have the guts," she writes, "to confront the opponent's argument; instead it attempts to discredit and destroy the opponent, to cast doubt on his moral standing to be in the argument at all. . . . And we ourselves, not to mention our saintly political leaders in both parties, could do a lot to change it for the better if we wished."[10]

The weakness of these efforts to reinstitute civil manners is that the argumentative basis has become increasingly questionable. How can we argue for polite, courtly manners in a democratic society? If "ladies" are not to be treated with deference, for example, and if the infirm are all to be "mainstreamed" and treated like everyone else, then who is left as the object of polite behavior? Why not treat everyone equally as dirt, showing as much disrespect for those in authority as for the powerless?

In the face of this question, Judith Martin writes her breezy *Miss Manners Rescues Civilization,* suggesting that there is "a national crisis that calls for Miss Manners. . . . What ought to stop people from shouting epithets, flaunting obscenity, desecrating national symbols and otherwise upsetting their fellow citizens is etiquette."[11] It is to be enforced through wise childrearing, house rules, and ostracizing violators. She has a clear grasp of the central role of "a perceived lack of respect. . . . Being treated respectfully is not one of our Constitutional rights, nor is treating others respectfully a legal obligation. Only manners require it. Yet dissin' — showing real or apparent disrespect — is cited as the motive in an amazing number of murders."[12] Budziszewski offers a somewhat more formidable "intellectual defense" on the ground that "good manners not only rehearse the ideal of virtue but anticipate and celebrate it." Yet he provides no basis for adhering to virtue itself. Nicolaus Mills concludes his critique of "meanness" by suggesting the need for egalitarian visions; but he holds no hope that such "utopianism" can "spare us from the pessimism of our own culture, in which meanness and spite seem so deeply entrenched that we imagine them playing an even greater role in our future."[13]

 It is ironic, in view of this recent rise of American "beastliness," that an Australian pig becomes a prime example of democratic manners, refusing to discriminate between worthy and unworthy creatures. As Terrence Rafferty observes,

> Babe looks at his new surroundings with an unprejudiced, child-like eye, and sweetly fails to recognize the prevailing differences in status among the species. He's polite to all the creatures, even the despised sheep. . . . Babe's salvation is that he really doesn't know his place; he has no idea that a pig's only purpose, as far as its human overseers are concerned, is to be eaten.[14]

So, despite the good humor and the brilliant animatronic effects of this film, it hardly offers a cogent basis for modern manners. But the correlation with Saint Paul's treatment of manners may offer a promising resource.

The passage in which Paul discusses these issues in Romans 12 opens with a succinct maxim that serves as a thesis for the entire section: "[Let] the love be genuine." This wording shows that Paul assumes the presence of "the love" among his Roman audience. The Pauline ethic, therefore, addresses the fundamental weakness in contemporary approaches to civility: the ethic he espouses rests on the prior gift of God's loving action to each person. Since God's love for the shameful was expressed in the life, death, and resurrection of Christ, the recipients of "the mercies of God" (Rom 12:1) are called to pass it on to fellow humans. The use of the definite article in "the love" indicates that Paul refers not to love in general but to the specifically Christian form of love already manifest in the Roman churches.[15] The social context of the early Christian "love feast" probably provided the primary resonance of this term for the Roman Christians.[16] It is the nature of such love, poured into the heart (Rom 5:5) of each beloved member of the community (Rom 1:7), that it be both spontaneous and undiscriminatingly generous. Hence, Paul urges that their "love" should be "genuine" in distinguishing between "evil" and "good" (Rom 12:21). Congregational involvement in making such distinctions links this passage very closely with 12:1-2, where the term *to agathon* ("the good") is also used.[17] The highly emotional verbs "abhorring"[18] and "cleaving"[19] in 12:9 imply a passionate commitment to the objective good of the fellow members of one's congregation.

What contemporary readers might find puzzling, however, is that so many of the ways to abhor evil and cleave to the good are related to the seemingly minor arena of manners.

Honoring One Another with Brotherly Affection

Halvor Moxnes makes some intriguing suggestions about Rom 12:10, which I translate "having affection for one another with brotherly love, taking the lead in honoring one another." Moxnes has shown that by linking recognition with the egalitarian theme of brotherly love, Paul resists the cultural tendency to grant honor "on the basis of status or merits. There is to be no connection between service performed in leadership and honour and recognition above others. Honour is to be awarded solely on the basis of 'brotherly love.'"[20] The congregational focus of the ethical admonition is expressed by the phrase "for one another" in this verse. That "brotherly love" would normally be perceived to include each other within a congregation would seem to be so self-evident[21] as to make this admonition unnecessary, but the peculiar historical circumstances in Rome demanded the emphatic inclusion. The competing house and tenement churches were not in fact viewing each other as equal brothers, as the evidence in Romans 14–15 reveals. The use of the term "affection" in 12:10 augments this appeal with a concept widely used in Hellenistic ethics:[22] the unconditional solicitude typical for family and friendship is to be extended into the Christian community, particularly including persons in other house and tenement churches previously held in contempt. Family affection is to replace the harsh "judgment" (Rom 14:3-4, 10) and "contempt" (Rom 14:3, 10) that had poisoned relations between congregations.

The real puzzle in Rom 12:10 is how to translate *proēgoumenoi*, rendered above as "taking the lead."[23] This straightforward option may not have been considered before because the audience situation has usually not been taken sufficiently into account at this point. The translation used in the heading of this chapter, "taking the lead in honoring one another," fits the basic meaning of the verb[24] and meets the requirement of the accusative *allēlous* ("for another") in the context of *timē* ("honor").[25] It takes account of the social context of honor that marked the ancient world, in which public recognition was the essential basis of personal identity.[26] This translation matches the Hebraic idiom mentioned by Otto Michel, namely, the virtue of taking the lead in greeting others.[27] This translation also matches the congregational situation in Rome, in that members of competing groups were refusing to accept each other. Romans 14–15 reveals that discriminations on the basis of cultural traditions of honor and shame were still being made among Christian groups. If each group would now "take the lead" in showing honor to their competitors, the imbalance in honor due to social stratification and group competition would be transformed in a way that matched "genuine love."[28]

The film *Babe* seems to be an almost perfect embodiment of these ideas. Babe's success derives from his treating the sheep "with brotherly love," so to speak. As Richard Schickel notes, the sheep "take a shine to him because Babe speaks politely to them and treats them with respect."[29] But this sense of brotherhood has already been extended to Babe by Farmer Hoggett and the dog family before the pig's herding talent develops. When Hoggett first looks at Babe, he picks up the pig, as the narrator (Roscoe Lee Browne) explains: "The pig and the farmer regarded each other, and for a fleeting moment something passed between them, a faint sense of some common destiny." The men at the fair say it is the first time the pig has not "screamed its head off" when being picked up. The first words Babe says to Fly, the mother dog, come in response to the mother's declaration that pigs are almost as stupid as sheep. "Excuse me, no we're not." This polite statement, respectfully but firmly given, sets the tone for the later development. In time, the pups accept Babe as one of the family, but Mrs. Hoggett feeds him slop and tells him with glee that he is going to grow up to be a "big fat pork chop." This kind of disparity should also be felt throughout the reading of Romans 12: while the Christian groups in Rome are urged to honor one another with brotherly affection, the outside world will continue to treat them as slaves or hirelings, as sexual objects and faceless things always to be exploited but never honored.

The matter of giving honor to others whom the world holds in contempt explicitly surfaces when Babe meets the matriarchal ewe, who insists, "I'll not be called a common sheep, thank you kindly. I'm a Border Lester ewe. The name's Maa." Babe learns to treat all of the sheep with respect, which is the key to their cooperation and Babe's success as a "sheeppig." When Babe arrives at the sheepdog competition, his courteous speaking to the sheep in the stockade is rendered plausible by actress Christine Cavanaugh: "Excuse me, sheep. Hello, hello, good morning to you all!" One of the sheep turns around to face Babe, who says, "Oh boy, I've never met a sheep with such a strong, dark face. Are they feeding you well?" At first, the only reply is a sullen, inarticulate baa. Then Babe comes back at it: "It must have been terrible weather for you, out in the field with all this rain we've been havin.'" Still no answer, except for baa. The sheep are here at the competition as objects to be herded by dogs; in this contemptible status, they refuse to communicate.

It is only after Babe cites the sheep's password that they are willing to cooperate. They go through their paces in exemplary fashion in the competition, to the utter amazement of the entire audience. Babe responds appreciatively to their cooperation, "Ah, beautifully done. I can't tell you how grateful I am to you all. Now for one last favor, if the three ladies with collars would kindly walk out of the ring, I'd be very much obliged." They walk out of the ring quietly and stand to face the other three sheep inside the ring. Then Mr. Hoggett opens the small sheep pen, and the six sheep file in with soldierly precision.

The stands erupt with applause, and even Mrs. Hoggett, who had earlier fainted at the sight of her zany husband with his sheep-pig, breaks into joyful tears. The crowd dances and applauds, as much for their own transformed shame as for the pig and his boss, who stand silently at the end of the film, unaffected by the expression of public honor. The animals at the Hoggett farm mount their own celebration. The delight of brotherly love and the impact of honoring the lowly have rarely been portrayed in a more appealing manner.

Being on the Same Level with Lowly People

Paul's interest in overcoming social discrimination based on Mediterranean systems of honor and shame is particularly visible in Rom 12:16. I translate it as "being of the same mind toward one another, not setting your minds on exalted things, but being drawn toward lowly people, 'not being wise-minded in yourselves.'" As in 12:3, we find here three distinct sayings with the same component: "mind." The thematic progression is usually disguised by translators' preferences for graceful English expressions. Walter T. Wilson has shown that the progression is marked by an opening maxim (verse 16a) followed by a two-part explanation (verse 16b-c), and concluding with a "direct application to the audience."[30] There are close parallels in other Pauline letters, which indicates that the campaign against honorific discrimination is a major theme in Pauline thought. The expression "be of the same mind toward one another" is found with slight variatians in 2 Cor 13:11; Phil 2:2; 4:2; and Rom 15:5.

To be "of the same mind toward one another" does not imply agreeing on particulars or achieving a consensus on general points that overcomes disagreements.[31] It implies rather the admission of mental equality that might allow people to work with each other. As one commentator has put it, the attack is against "every sort of spiritual aristocracy" within the church.[32] If love is to be genuine, it must eschew any claim of possessing superior insight or status, lest competition between believers and their congregations be encouraged to assume destructive dimensions. The admonition not to "set the mind on exalted things"[33] and the exhortation not to be "wise-minded in yourselves" carry forward the same impulse.[34] Paul is demanding here that love (12:9) be allowed to draw one into association with the less enlightened. Superiority is replaced by equality, condescension by solidarity.

A distinction between "exalted things," embodied by the dominant animals on the Hoggett farm along with Mr. and Mrs. Hoggett, and the "lowly" is evident throughout the film. "Pigs are definitely stupid" is the caption shown when Babe is brought home, to the disapproving view of the sheepdogs. That the creatures at the top have the right to dominate others is the premise of the farm, accepted if not welcomed by all. When Babe first meets Maa the ewe, Maa mistakes the pig for a "wolf," her term for a dog. Maa complains about their arrogant behavior and expresses the hope that Babe will not be "like them wolves. Treat you like dirt . . . bite at you. Some wolves be so bad, they run a sheep down and tear it to pieces." Babe replies, "I would never do that."

After Babe first hears of the bad behavior of dogs, and yet is welcomed by Fly into her family, the pig's moral resolution is described by the narrator of the film: "The pig promised himself that he would never think badly of any creature, ever again." The cooperative consequences of "being of the same mind toward one another" have rarely been so eloquently depicted. On the first day that Babe is invited to join the dogs in the sheepfold, he witnesses the sheep being cowed into obedience. When Babe tries to act like a domineering dog, only to have the sheep roar with laughter, Fly explains: "You're treating them like equals. They're sheep. They're inferior." Babe responds, "Oh, no they're not." Fly explains that if the sheep ever doubt the dog's superiority, they "will walk all over you." But Maa explains, "All a nice little pig like you need do is ask." With this encouragement of his prior inclination toward civility, Babe tries a polite approach. Farmer Hoggett is astounded when the sheep calmly march out of the pen. The sheepdogs are apoplectic that success in the difficult task of sheepherding could be gained by simple courtesy rather than by terror. Babe tells the sheep, "Thanks very much; it was very kind of you." They reply, "It was a pleasure."

In a later episode, Babe discovers wild dogs tearing up and killing the sheep. Babe runs and butts the killer dog off its feet, saving the flock. But Maa is mortally wounded and Babe shares the tears of the other sheep with his lament "Ma — a — Ba — a." It is an unmistakable imitation of the sheep's sorrow, the final embodiment of "being of the same mind toward one another."

Avoiding Conceit

To be "wise-minded in oneself," which in the Hellenistic categories of the first century would have implied the self-sufficiency of a mind that believes itself superior, is essentially destructive to community. The wording of Paul's admonition in Rom 12:16c is adapted from Prov 3:7 by changing the singular to plural and dropping the antithesis about fearing God: "Do not be wise in yourself, but fear God and refrain from all evil." The effect of the minor alterations is to relate the citation more closely to the congregational situation

114

in Rome so as to address the superiority claims of congregations and ethnic groups.[35]

The connection between conceit and community is specified by the antithesis between setting the mind on "exalted things"[36] and associating with "lowly people" (Rom 12:16b).[37] The latter clearly refers to low social status: "It refers to somebody or something that lacks honor, but instead has shame. . . ."[38] Only by repudiating the sense of superiority held by those of higher social status is it possible to achieve genuine solidarity. If the overall argument of Romans is accepted by the recipients, they will see that all persons are in fact "lowly" because all have sinned and fallen short of the glory of God (Rom 3:9).

At first glance, Babe seems to be involved in the conceit that he is really a sheepdog. Mrs. Hoggett thinks it is silly to have a "pig that thinks it's a dog." But, though accused early on of having a confused identity and thinking he is a sheepdog, Babe introduces himself halfway through the story as a "sheeppig," indicating now that he knows exactly who he is.

The animal on the Hoggett farm that comes closest to conceit is Rex, the famous sheepdog whose pups are greatly in demand. He looks on with disdain as Fly and her pups welcome Babe, and he's particularly offended when Farmer Hoggett invites Babe to join them in the task of sheepherding. Rex looks on with contempt as Babe tries to bend the sheep to his will, and then he reminds Fly: "You and I have descended from the great sheepdogs. We carry the bloodlines of the ancient Bahoo. We stand for something. But today I watched with shame as all this was betrayed." She replies, "Rex, dear, he's just a little pig." But Rex stalks off grumbling, "All the greater the insult."

Fly later tells Babe that "for a sheepdog there is no prouder moment" than to be a champion in a competition. She explains that Rex could have been a champion, but had lost his hearing trying to save sheep in a flood when they were too "stupid" to follow his instructions to save themselves. "The plain truth is," Fly insists, "except for the stupidity of sheep, Rex would have been the champion of champions."

Rex is shamed by Babe's success, and he attacks Fly when she tries to console him. When Mr. Hoggett tries to intervene, Rex bites him as well. After the vet arrives to sedate and chain the menacing sheepdog, Babe becomes the main sheepherder. In time, Rex's loyalty to Mr. Hoggett leads to a softening of his anger. He comes along to the sheepdog competition and provides the decisive aid in Babe's success. Since none of the sheep is willing to communicate with Babe, Rex runs back to the Hoggett farm and, for the first time, addresses the sheep in civil speech. He explains Babe's dilemma and asks for their help. They consult with each other and offer to give him the "password," if Rex will make a "solemn promise" to "treat us civil." "You gotta treat us nice, like." Rex says he'll try to be civil, promising not to bite anymore and not to let the password be "used against any sheep, anywhere." They give him the password, conveying the secret of sheep identity and group loyalty:

> Baa, Ram, Ewe,
> Baa, Ram, Ewe,
>> to your breed, your fleece, your clan be true
>> Sheep be true,
> Baa, Ram, Ewe.

Rex returns and gives the password just in time to enable Babe to break through the iron resolve of noncommunication on the part of the sheep in the competition. So the message here is that even the conceit of "wolves" can be transformed, that they can learn the essential value of civility.

That humans also require transformation is central to the film. For example, the rules committee spends its time considering whether to disallow Babe as a contestant, because as one of the officials complains, "It's preposterous. We'll be the laughingstock of every sheepdog association in every civilized country in the world." The fear of shame is the underside of conceit for humans as well as for sheepdogs.

Overcoming Evil with Good

The issue of victory over evil surfaces both in Romans and in *Babe*. The opening narration of the film raises the matter of changing how creatures are treated:

> This is a tale about an unprejudiced heart, and how it changed our valley forever. There was a time a few years ago when pigs were afforded no respect, except from other pigs. They lived their whole lives in a cruel and sunless world.

The expression "unprejudiced heart" appears to include both Mr. Hoggett and Babe, but the transformation includes everyone in the valley, implying that a new "respect" had been achieved. All of the creatures — including Rex, the people in the stands, the proud officials of the National Grand Challenge, and even Mrs. Hoggett — all share in applauding the victory of the humble pig. But there is a curious element in this celebration: Babe and his boss stand silently to receive it, and they appear completely unaffected by it. The farm animals who have been watching on TV join in their own celebration, including the three musical mice who have carried the story at each phase in Disney fashion. The narrator informs us that no one in the stands knew what to say, but Mr. Hoggett did: "That'll do, pig. That'll do." Babe looks up to his master with contentment. It is as if the reward for victory is intrinsic in the performance itself; both the farmer and his pig are content simply to have done the job well. Neither of them needs the honor of public applause, because their need for honor has somehow already been met.

There is a remarkable parallel to this detail in the final verse of Rom 12:9-21. Paul writes "not being wise-minded in yourselves," but omits the final line of this well-known proverb ("and the Lord will reward you"). In place of a promised reward, the concluding maxim of 12:21 reinterprets the saying from Proverbs that wraps up the passage as a whole: "Do not be conquered by what is evil, but conquer the evil with the good." The implication is that, by avoiding arrogance, the Roman Christians will overcome evil with good. The omission of a reward would clearly have been felt as a

117

correction by an audience acquainted with the usual approach to ethics. In this respect, Romans 12 is distinguished from Hellenistic-Jewish texts of the time.[39] In place of the promise of rewards from heaven, Romans offers a transformative ethic motivated by a reward already received, namely, the grace of God conveyed by the gospel that restores right relationships everywhere.

The idea of grace preceding ideal performance is powerfully embodied in the story of *Babe*. When Mrs. Hoggett leaves on the bus for a three-day conference, Mr. Hoggett feels free to invite both Fly and Babe into the house to get out of the rain. The cat is as outraged as Mrs. Hoggett would have been. After being tossed out of the house into the rain because she scratched Babe's nose, Cat insinuates herself and lifts up the tissue of shame: "I probably shouldn't say this, but I'm not sure you realize how much the other animals are laughing at you for this sheepdog business." She goes on to explain that "pigs don't have a purpose, like ducks don't have a purpose" except to be made into "pork" and "bacon. . . . They only call them pigs when they're alive." The cat concludes with false solicitude, "Oh, I haven't upset you, have I?"

Babe runs off into the stormy night to ask Fly whether even Boss Hoggett eats pork, and hearing that he does, he flees in despair. When Hoggett takes the dogs to search all over for Babe, he echoes the good shepherd seeking the lost sheep in the biblical parable. They find Babe chilled in the swamp and tenderly carry him home. The vet prescribes medicine and warm liquids, but Babe refuses to eat or to respond to Fly's reassurance that the "Boss needs you." He refuses to drink from the bottle even while being held in the arms of Mr. Hoggett. But then the boss sings a song to him:

> If I had words, to make a day for you,
>> I'd sing you a morning, golden and true,
> I would make this day last for all time,
>> then fill the light deep in moon shine.

Despite the fact that this mortal eats meat, and that therefore the lives of every animal on the farm have short limits, this master of Hoggett Farm cares for each creature with a profound and passionate love. He cares enough to struggle for the preservation of life, even of a pig. This exhibition of what Paul would call "abhorring the evil" and "cleaving to the good" causes a change. Babe begins to drink from the bottle and finds the will to live again, as the farmer rises to dance and leap in front of the fire. All of the farm animals are gazing in at the window at this astounding scene. Babe returns to the kitchen, hungry again and content to live. Evil is conquered here not by admonitions or by moral examples but by addressing shame at its deepest level, providing an answer to the question whether someone finally cares for a creature or not.

The verb "conquer" that is used twice in Rom 12:21 has a significant cultural resonance with honor. It was widely employed in the celebrations of the Greek goddess Nike and of the Roman goddess Victoria.[40] The imperial authorities celebrated Victoria in monuments, coins, public inscriptions, triumphal parades, public games, and other propaganda as the key to world peace: "Pax ["peace"] was thus the blessed condition brought about by Augustus' labor. It rested upon Victoria; and Augustan propaganda constantly and intimately linked the imperial virtues of Pax and Victoria. Pax could only be achieved through Victoria; and the promise of permanent Pax lay entirely in the guarantee of perpetual Victoria. Victory was thus the essential prerequisite for peace."[41] A subtle but profound interaction with the Roman cultural context thus surfaces in the wording of Rom 12:21, where Paul trumpets a new kind of triumph over evil: by civility and hospitality rather than by force.[42]

As the "culminating exclamation"[43] at the end of a discourse on "genuine love," Rom 12:21 places the Christian ethic within a transformative framework that is universal in scope but local in operation. Even a drink of water given to a thirsty person or a civil word spoken to a slave becomes a means of expressing the love of Christ and thus extending the realm of divine righteousness. Given the beleaguered and marginalized circumstances of the Roman Christians, it is no exaggeration to name this verse "the bravest statement in the world."[44]

Conclusion

Romans and *Babe* are agreed that the kind of civility that can conquer meanness and prejudice does not rest on a new law but on the mercy of the master. It is heaven's marking of the sparrow's falling that is crucial here, in full recognition that both the life and death of finite creatures are in God's hands. Hoggett's singing and dancing also fit the description of the joy in heaven over a single lost creature brought back to the fold. This is crucial both for the film and for the present moment: how can we remain civil in a harsh world unless we know the divine Master loves us, that Christ dances at the banquet in our behalf? When we at last discover that our lives are infinitely worthy in God's sight, then we shall have the resources as well as the motivation to treat others with seemingly gratuitous honor. What is needed now is a new ethic of civility, based not on patronizing manners but on the kind of solidarity found in *Babe* and Romans. Can we join the Master in dancing at the prospect of us stupid pigs honoring even more stupid sheep as the epitome of this triumph of good over evil? If so, we may hear the words of the parable, "Well done, good and faithful servant, enter into the joy of your master!" Or to use the language down on the farm, "That'll do, pig. That'll do."

THE SHAMEFUL GOSPEL AND THE PROBLEM OF REDEMPTION

8. The Blood of Christ
   at the *Edge of the City*

Therefore, having been set right by faith, let us have
peace with God through our lord Jesus Christ,
   through whom we also have received access by faith to
this grace in which we have stood;
let us also boast in the hope of the glory of God;
   not only that, but let us also boast in the afflictions,
knowing that the affliction produces perseverance,
   and perseverance, confirmation,
      and confirmation, hope,
         and hope does not humiliate,
      because the love of God has been poured into our hearts
         through the Holy Spirit given to us.
"For to what purpose, while we were still weak, did
Christ die at the right time for the ungodly?
   Scarcely even for a righteous person will someone die;
      for in behalf of a good person perhaps someone might
         dare to die."
But God demonstrates to us his own love in that while
we were yet sinners Christ died for us.
   Even more certainly, therefore, having been made
righteous now in his blood, shall we be saved by him
      from the wrath.

> For if as enemies we were reconciled to God through the
>   death of his son,
>   the more certainly as reconciled shall we be saved by his
>   life.
> Not only that, but let us also boast in God through our
>   Lord Jesus Christ,
>   through whom we now have received the reconciliation.

Romans 5:1-11

Introduction

Old-fashioned Christians used to sing and preach a good deal about the "blood of Christ." The "Old Rugged Cross" was one of the favorite hymns in the churches where I grew up. For various reasons it is not as popular among current mainline Christians, in part because some of the traditional theories of the atonement no longer seem credible. As some Christians become more and more liberal, it seems that the theme of the blood of Christ is left to their more evangelical competitors.

I would like to follow Paul's reasoning in the fifth chapter of Romans to discover why the blood of Christ was so important for him, and to find a new way to understand its relevance today. A basic distinction needs to be made at the outset, however. While our traditional theologies and understandings of Jesus' death focus attention on individual forgiveness of sins, this passage — like most of Paul's letters — focuses on the deeper and broader dimensions of the human dilemma: the problems of weakness, alienation, and suffering. We see this in the references to "peace with God," to "reconciliation" with God, to "boasting," and to "affliction." Paul's approach is grounded in the effectiveness of Christ's death in behalf of the vulnerable and undeserving.

After reviewing what this passage indicates is wrong with the human race, I want to explore how this was related to the blood of Christ. I also want to touch on Paul's reversal of boasting, which has more to do with who we are than with what we have done.

Along the way I want to bring this text into conversation with a film about redemption through blood, *Edge of the City*.[1] This low-budget film, made for television under the title *A Man Is Ten Feet Tall*, appeared for a short time in 1957.[2] It has been shown sporadically since that time. The film features Sidney Poitier as the friend who gives his life for Axel Nordmann, a neurotic army deserter on the lam played by John Cassavetes. In Arthur S. Barron's summary of the plot, Axel

> gets a job in a New York freight yard by 'kicking back' part of his pay to a brutal boss. The deserter is befriended by a warm and sympathetic Negro foreman. Under the impact of this friendship he thaws out and moves toward maturity. In a vicious freight-hook fight, however, the Negro is killed by the bully. After a period of cowardly indecision, the deserter finally goes after the murderer and drags him to the police.[3]

This film has been cited as the first instance in American cinematic history for a black person to appear simply as a friend of a white protagonist.[4] However, this feature of the story eliminated the possibility of national distribution in the pre-civil-rights period of the 1950s. Thus a film that presents one of the most compelling Christ figures in American cinema, elaborating the profound theme of redemption through self-sacrificial blood, remains an unrecognized and largely unavailable classic. It is the only film I know that rises to the level of a potential dialogue partner with the proclamation of the blood of Christ in Romans 5.

The Necessity of Christ's Death

What is so wrong with humans that Christ had to die? The usual answer to this question makes little sense: he had to die to provide forgiveness for the sinful deeds that humans commit. One difficulty is that there is no reference to forgiveness in this passage in Romans, and very few such references in the rest of Paul's letters. In addition, since the God of Israel's faith was forgiving, and since there were institutions of forgiveness in temple and synagogue prior to Jesus' time, one can hardly make a case that the Jewish religion was lacking in this regard. So I would like to examine the four expressions Paul uses in verses 6-10 to describe the human dilemma, to build the case on this evidence rather than on the traditional viewpoint.

The first expression is in Rom 5:6: *"While we were still weak,"* Christ died for us. Weakness is not used here in the sense of being unable to do the law and thus being inclined to mistakes and sins, as the traditional teaching has suggested. Commentators have been puzzled by Paul's seemingly untheological[5] and overly "mild"[6] choice of the term *weak* in this sentence, but it would have resonated powerfully within the honor-shame framework of the audience in Rome. Weakness relates to human vulnerability and affliction, which Paul elaborates in Rom 5:3-4. His argument correlates with what recent psychologists have suggested, that humans feel vulnerable at a very early age, when already as infants they discover they are outside the womb and unable to cope for themselves. The terror and pain are heightened if loving care is not provided in a reliable manner. The feeling of not being loved at this basic level evokes primal shame. This is the springboard for later actions to cover up shame or to escape its pain, which further relates to the boasting theme in Romans 5. Some of us boast to cover up our vulnerability; some of us, to show we are more worthy than others. But most of the members of the early church in Rome were laborers, slaves, and homeless immigrants from the most marginal social circumstances.[7] Their weakness consisted in having little to boast about, and thus facing a chronic, collective shortfall in group self-esteem. In a basic sense, most boasting derives from weakness in one form or another: some seek to cover up painful circumstances, and others feel they are losers with nothing to boast about to bring them honor. The annals of group conflict from the beginning of recorded history reveal an infinite variety of strategies to overcome shameful weakness.

In *Edge of the City*, John Cassavetes plays the role of Axel Nordmann from Gary, Indiana, a man on the run because of his shame and weakness. He had joined the army in the hope of finding something to boast about so his family would love him. "I figured I could do something good" by joining the army, he says, ". . . if I made sergeant, I could come home. The thing is . . . a guy's gotta do something before someone can love him." But after being bullied as a nobody, Axel deserted. He gets a job on a railway loading dock where his weakness is exploited by a foreman who demands a kickback from his salary. He is befriended by Tommy Tyler, played by Sidney Poitier. TT is another foremen on the dock, one who does not take kickbacks or bully his gang. He is a "simple, well-adjusted extrovert with an innate genius for psychiatry," in Robert Hatch's somewhat sarcastic description.[8] In fact, the source of TT's uncanny goodness and psychological acumen remains obscure throughout the film. When Axel tells him that he had joined the army to accomplish something so people would love him, Tommy replies "Where did you get a crazy idea like that? . . . you're wrong." I think the best way to explain this behavior is to recognize that Tyler is playing a kind of Christ role in the film, struggling for the dignity of his young friend and ultimately dying in an effort to protect him from the murderous bully, Charlie Malek.

The matter of human weakness in Paul's thought is directly related to Jesus' death. His ministry to the weak and dishonorable members of society was bitterly controversial (Matt 9:10-11; 12:9-14). In the words of John Riches, Jesus had opposed "the belief that God's justice required that he should destroy the wicked. . . . This can be seen most clearly in his linking of his proclamation of the Kingdom of God with his meals with tax-collectors and sinners."[9] He was friendly to women of ill repute (Luke 7:36-50), to rough fishermen as well as to hated government agents (Matt 8:5-13; Luke 19:1-10). He opposed the contempt with which the weak and vulnerable members of society were treated (Mark 9:42; Matt 5:22; 18:10-14). His effort to overcome hostility toward outsiders culminated in the cleansing of the Gentile court of the temple, which led directly to his death (Mark 11:17-18).[10] He conveyed the boundless love of God to the weak and the lost (Matt 18:14), and he challenged the presumptions of the strong (23:1-36), ending up by being crucified between two thieves. In a very real sense, the urban underclass of first-century Rome could easily understand that the blood of Christ flowed on their behalf, because most of them were also weak and exploited by their superiors.

The second term used to describe the human dilemma is in the reference to Christ dying *"for the ungodly"* or *"impious"* (Rom 5:6). At first glance this terminology would seem to have no bearing on those who take their responsibilities to God seriously. But the word "impiety" should be interpreted in the light of Rom 1:18-25, which shows that humans tend to be so obsessed with their own honor and the status of their groups that they make gods of and for themselves. We see a great exhibition of this on Superbowl Sunday every year: one reason this annual football championship is such a huge national story, drawing an audience of millions and fiercely affecting the self-identity of states or cities whose teams are playing, is that we all want to be number one. If we can't achieve it individually, then at least we want our teams or nation or group to surpass others. Failing that, we still want to know who is superior, to have an icon to study if not to worship. Thus, impiety for Paul is not a matter of lacking religion. Rather, impiety follows a religion — whether secular or traditional — that is self-serving and thus idolatrous. Paul has in mind the aggressive ungodliness of those who "suppress the truth" (Rom 1:18) about their own shame while seeking honorable status that competes with the status of God. In fact, only God is truly super; only God is finally worthy of honor; only God deserves to be number one. When we seek this for ourselves or our group, we are usurping the position of God. As Paul writes in Rom 1:25, people tend to "worship and serve the creature rather than the creator."

It was the death and resurrection of Christ that had finally led Paul to understand that the competition to be more righteous than others, to gain honor and public respect through religious activities, was really a form of impiety. He had opposed the Jesus-movement because it challenged this system of religious superiority. Only after he understood the gospel could he grasp the shocking truth that his piety had been an assault on the honor of God, that he had in fact been impious, despite his extraordinary adherence to the law. The blood of Christ exposed this basic human dilemma.

The third reference to the human situation in our passage comes in the statement *"while we were yet sinners Christ died for us"* (Rom 5:8). In a basic sense, the status of sinner has a double connotation: it refers to the strategy of covering up shame through seeking godly honors and lying about our true situation; and it refers to the evil actions that flow from such a deception. But note that it is the actions of humans in a collective sense that are in view here: Paul refers to "sinners" in the plural and includes himself among the "us," which should lead interpreters to think of the behavior of groups rather than isolated individuals. Romans 1:18 refers to sin as "suppression of the truth" about who we are and who God is. Since human weaknesses and the vulnerability of our groups are too painful to bear, we try to cover them up. Our groups devise claims of superior status and virtue that are far from the truth. Later in the first chapter of Romans, Paul describes the social perversions that result from such chronic dishonesty: the shamed seek to shame others; the injured seek to injure others to show their superiority and gain self-respect. Hence guilty deeds arise from shameful status, making all groups of humans sinners, a status which each group desperately seeks to disguise.

Axel Nordmann is involved in the most basic form of human cover-up, denying who he is. As a deserter from the army, he is using an assumed name, Axel North. Later in the film, it turns out that he had been using yet another name in the army. As a weak and impressionable teenager, he had accidentally killed his popular elder brother in a car accident. This led to a complete alienation from his parents, especially from his father, an upstanding policeman from Gary. The alienation is complete when Axel deserts the army and begins running. The opening of the film shows him running through the loading dock area, barely making it through a closing gate. He is a kind of prodigal son, unable even to communicate with his family. But in this case, his crime, desertion from the army, clearly derives from his shame. In contrast to the usual Christian paradigm of individual sin and forgiveness, in which evil deeds lead to shame, this is a story of original shame resulting in evil actions. The crime is an acting out of much deeper pain of shameful status that is unavoidable. This story resonates at a profound level with the honor-shame paradigms of the ancient world out of which our biblical texts arose.

Jesus frequently explained his ministry as directed toward the "lost" in the sense of being outcasts of society. He had a particular affinity for lepers, Gentiles, women, and persons in menial occupations whom other, holy people kept at arms length. But it was not until the crucifixion that the full dimensions of his campaign to overcome shameful status became clear. On Calvary human running and covering up and boasting and shaming led to the death of this man who took the side of the shamed. This death demonstrated the final measure of redemptive love that is capable of curing the shameful void from which evil actions spring.

Like Tommy Tyler in the film, Jesus dealt with outcasts simply by accepting them. TT shares his food with Axel, and then takes him to the neighborhood where he lives and begins to share his life with him. Later, when the evil supervisor finds out who Axel really is, threatening to expose him to the authorities if he does not return to the kickback scheme, he is inclined to begin running again. TT convinces him to stay and face the consequences: "You're in trouble. But you got a couple things mixed up. First of all, it's important to me what happens to you. Don't you understand that? And I'm your friend." It was this kind of friendship to outsiders that got Jesus crucified, just as it gets Tommy Tyler killed at the conclusion of this powerful film.

The fourth expression Paul uses to describe the human dilemma is this verse: *As enemies we were reconciled to God through the death of his son*" (Rom 5:10). As Stanley Porter observes, "Paul apparently equates being a sinner with being an enemy of God."[11] The cross reveals all humans as God's enemies, as those who crucify the Christ to avoid the exposure of their own shame, to retain their status of honor in religion and politics.

This is the opposite of one of the traditional doctrines of the atonement, which supposed that God was the one who needed to be reconciled, paid off by the blood of an innocent victim in order to overlook the sins of the guilty. Although widely believed, this explanation of Christ's death gets things completely backward, if our text is to be taken seriously. Instead, the cross exposes the enmity of the human race against God while at the same time offering unconditional reconciliation. The blood of Christ says, "The fight is over, so you can come home again."

In *Edge of the City*, Axel is reconciled by the death of his friend. TT takes Axel's place when Malek attacks him with a meat hook and fights Malek to a standstill. With Malek's hook pinned to the ground, TT has a chance to kill the extortionist. But he doesn't want to kill this enemy, this man who was a "lower form" of human. He lets Malek go, saying, "This doesn't make any sense." But the minute he turns his back, Malek pins him to the chain-link fence and impales him with the meat hook. Like Christ fixed on the cruel cross, TT is fatally wounded. As TT lies dying, both he and Axel say, "It was my fight." The truth is that TT stood in for Axel; his death saved the young man's life, leading to reconciliation with his family and to his emergence as a man capable of standing "ten feet tall."

Axel goes back to his room and then goes to the pay phone to complete a call to his mother for the first time since deserting the army. She is alone in the house. Axel says, "Mom, are you all right? . . . I want to come home." His dad walks in then and hears from his wife that Axel wants to come home. He says, "I don't care what you've done. We want you to come home. It's from now on that counts. . . . We miss you. You're all we've got. Please son, talk to me, say something. You can curse me or yell at me if you want to." Axel replies, "You really want me?" The blood of Tyler in effect says to him, "The fight is over, so you can come home again. You can be reconciled to those you have injured, even if unintentionally; you can be reconciled to who and what you are."

The New Form of Boasting

The story of the redemption of Axel Nordmann by the death of his friend and protector Tommy Tyler also ties in with the theme of boasting, which runs through the text of Romans 5. Paul urges that we should "boast in the hope of the glory of God" (Rom 5:2). The glory is what was lost in the garden of Eden and in every person's replication of the fall, as we deal with our vulnerability and seek glory for ourselves. We either want to boast in the glory we have achieved, or we want to run away because no glory seems possible.

But now, in Christ, we boast in the hope given to us through the death of Christ, a hope that by grace we shall all participate in glory, that we shall find our proper task that God intends for us to do. For Paul, this is a "hope" rather than an accomplishment, because he is convinced that none of us can ever achieve enough to boast. By contrast, human boasting is so dishonest and distorted that it loses all semblance of glory.

In an early scene of *Edge of the City*, Tommy Tyler is enjoying his lunch break and the glorious sight at the end of a pier, overlooking New York City across the bay. "This is freedom!" he says to Axel. After talking over the situation on the loading dock, Tommy urges the necessity of making a choice between working for decent people and working for people like Malek. The language he uses recalls Paul's reference to God's original design that humans should reflect the "glory of God." Tyler explains, "There are the men and then there are the lower forms. . . . You go with the men and you are ten feet tall. You go with the lower forms and you are down in the slime." He later comments about Malek: "Of all the lower forms, he gets down under everybody."

As the story develops, Axel begins to gain a sense of his own worth and his potential glory, so to speak. After dinner at the Tyler apartment with Mrs. Tyler and a friend they have invited as Axel's date, the men enjoy cigars and wine, pretending it is high-quality stuff. TT says, "Now you are about seven and a half feet tall. Only have two and a half to go." Axel says, "No, we're just making believe." TT replies, "No, *you are.*" But it takes the death of his friend finally to lead Axel to a proper sense of what it means to be a human. At the end of the film, there is a genuine "hope of the glory of God," as Axel comes to terms with his vulnerability and begins to take responsibility.

The climactic turn toward genuine human responsibility in *Edge of the City* is closely related to Paul's admonition that Christians should "boast in afflictions" (Rom 5:3). People instinctively flee from afflictions rather than boasting about them because afflictions elicit shame, which is to be avoided at all cost. Axel is running away from his shameful afflictions throughout the entire story until the end. Although he has seen the fight in which his friend is killed,

Axel refuses to cooperate with the police out of fear of retaliation by Malek and exposure of is desertion from the army.

After the murder, he stops by TT's house to speak with his wife, Lucy, who weeps with him. She has not been told what really happened on the loading dock and assumes that TT died as a result of an accident. When she asks how it occurred, Axel evades the question out of fear of afflictions: "It happened, that's all." When she insists on hearing what happened, he acknowledges that there was a fight and that he can't say with whom because of the consequences. Knowing that Tommy would never kill someone, she now knows that he was murdered. She is distraught that this man whom they had befriended would evade his responsibility like this. "You're running away without telling the police!" He replies, "Lucy, you just don't understand," that is, about the afflictions that will come if Axel testifies. But she won't let him off the hook: "You're just like everyone else. Take your white man's money and get out of here." He flees only to be stopped by his girlfriend, who begs him, "Please don't run away."

So Axel decides to face his afflictions and responsibilities. He goes to find Malek and says, "I'm going to take you in to the cops." The extortionist attacks Axel, brutally beating him. But Axel rises again and catches Malek from behind, choking him into submission. The closing scene of this powerful film shows Axel dragging the murderer off to the police. It is a potent modern embodiment of Paul's belief that affliction produces perseverance,

> and perseverance, confirmation,
> and confirmation, hope,
>   and hope does not humiliate. (Rom 5:4-5)

But the basis of Paul's hope is more clear and secure than any modern film can embody:

>   and hope does not humiliate,
> because the love of God has been poured into our hearts
> through the Holy Spirit given to us. (Rom 3:5)

At the end of the passage, Paul returns to this theme of a new form of boasting, not in our own accomplishments but in Christ, who sets us free from our escapist tendencies. "Let us boast in God through our Lord Jesus Christ," Paul writes (Rom 5:11). In place of boasting in our godly status, our accomplishments, our personal glory or the glory of our group, we now boast in the God who triumphed through weakness, who uncovers and overcomes our enmity by the blood of the cross. And so our salvation takes the form of reconciliation. It produces a new identity leading to peace with God.

Peace with God

There is a translation problem that must be resolved before we can move on to the interpretation of Rom 5:1. Although many interpreters and the committees that determine the standard Greek texts of our day believe the context of 5:1 favors the indicative translation, *"We have* peace with God," the more strongly attested subjunctive form should be accepted. It should be translated as a hortatory subjunctive: *"Let us have* peace with God."[12] This formulation provides an echo for the term "reconciliation" in 5:11.[13] Peace with God involves peace with all persons, enemies and competitors alike. If the hostile competition with God is exposed at its core, at the vulnerable, afflicted center of shame, then we can afford to act differently toward our enemies. In Axel's case, it leads him not to kill Malek but to bring him to proper justice for the murder of his friend. The important thing is that he has to take responsibility, at a risk to himself and in full acknowledgment of his weaknesses and vulnerability. He acts in behalf of peace, knowing that in reporting the murder to the authorities, he will have to face the penalty for deserting the army. But peace with God and the world can come only by facing the truth about who we are as well as what we have done. What impels Axel is the sacrificial death of his friend, the one who enabled him to rise to his full potential as a man "ten feet tall."

This film provides access to one of the most profound aspects of the Christian faith. It helps us to begin thinking about the atonement without assuming some alleged unavailability of forgiveness or the need to assuage divine wrath by the blood of an innocent victim. It provides the imaginative resources to understand a highly abstract text in Romans that underlies much of the later development of the doctrine of the atonement. By exposing shameful human realities, it leads us to understand how Christ died for weak people like us, how we have so frequently made ourselves God's enemies, and how the blood of Christ leads us toward reconciliation. Some of us have been running away from our true selves, and others of us are fleeing from afflictions; all of us remain uncomfortable with our vulnerability and weakness; we try to accomplish something in life so people will love us, not realizing that this motivation just leads us into forms of boasting and hiding that make our situation more dishonest and more difficult to bear. We take refuge in our group identity as members of an allegedly superior nation, or an allegedly righteous church, but our uneasy feeling of vulnerability remains. The Spirit is inviting us shameful deserters to come home again and to face mature responsibilities as we hear the admonition with ears made sensitive by *Edge of the City:* "Let us have peace with God through our Lord Jesus Christ!"

9. The Gospel Free of Charge: Bondage and *The Firm*

For if I preach the gospel, there is no ground for
boasting,
for a necessity is laid upon me, and woe is me if I do
not preach the gospel!
For if I do this of my own will, I have a reward;
but if not of my own will, I am entrusted with a
stewardship.
What then is my reward?
That in preaching I may offer the gospel free of charge,
in order not to exploit my right in the gospel.
For though I am free from all,
I enslaved myself to all,
in order that I might win the more.
To the Jews I became a Jew,
in order that I might win Jews.
To those under the law I became one under the law,
though I myself am not under the law,
in order that I might win those under the law.
To those outside the law I became one outside the law,
though I am not free from God's law but am under the
law of Christ,
in order that I might win those outside the law.

To the weak I became weak,
    in order that I might win the weak.
I have become all things to all people,
    in order that I might by all means save some.
I do all things for the sake of the gospel,
    in order that I might become a coparticipant in it.

1 Corinthians 9:16-23[1]

Introduction

This passage from 1 Corinthians is surprising at every turn. Paul has been preaching the gospel to the Corinthians free of charge, and now he is forced to defend himself. It seems the opposite of the usual problem that church leaders are advised to treat with great caution. Ordinarily the trouble for ministers comes when they demand higher and higher salaries. Jim Bakker went to a federal prison because he went too far in this direction. But Paul gets into trouble because he makes no such demand.

What Paul fears may be comparable to the dilemma of the young lawyer played by Tom Cruise in *The Firm*.[2] He falls into bondage the moment he takes the keys to the Mercedes convertible offered as an employment bonus by a law firm. This prospective graduate of Harvard Law School is shown at the beginning of the film being interviewed by various prestigious law firms, with salary bids that get higher and higher. He receives an astounding bid from a Memphis law firm, along with the down payment for a great house. They even pay off his entire student loan. Soon after Mitch and his wife Abbie settle down down in Memphis, they hear of two members of the law firm being killed by an accident in the Cayman Islands. Abbie, played by Jeanne Tripplehorn, wonders why the wife of the law firm member they were visiting at the time of hearing the accident seemed scared. Soon they find out that no fewer than four members of the law firm have died of strange accidents in the past few years. They discover that the workload is so heavy that there is virtually no time for family life. Piece by piece they find

137

that the fabulous payment implies a form of bondage that ultimately threatens life itself. A member of the Department of Justice later informs Mitch that no lawyer had ever left the firm alive, because it functioned secretly as the legal representative of the Chicago Mafia.

Paul's Refusal to Enter into Bondage for Money

Paul's preference to preach the gospel *"free of charge"* was probably based on the prevalence of organizations like this firm in Greco-Roman culture. It was a patron-client society, in which most people were under the protection and influence of movers and shakers at the top. To accept money from a rich patron meant to become that person's client. It was typical for clients to show up at the front door of their patron's house at around 9:00 A.M. to accompany him or her into the forum, where business would be conducted. The power and prestige of patrons and patronesses was reflected in the size and competence of their entourage. This system of patronage was integral to the concepts of honor and shame in the Greco-Roman world.

Recent studies of this patronage system have gone a long way toward explaining Paul's peculiar behavior.[3] From his earliest letters — to the Thessalonians — Paul refers to himself as a self-employed handworker, supporting himself rather than accepting money from the churches he was founding. "We worked night and day," he tells the Thessalonians, "so that we might not burden any of you while we proclaimed to you the gospel of God" (1 Thess 2:9). This forced him into a precarious situation, as studies of the economic level of handworkers have shown.[4] He was often without food or shelter and had to restrict himself to the workshop as the primary arena of his evangelistic work, because of the long hours of labor required to survive. He evidently continued that practice in Corinth, preferring not to enter into dependency relations with the well-to-do patrons of house churches.

The wisdom of his practice became evident when these house churches turned into competitive factions, boasting that the evangelist sponsored by their patron was superior to the others: "I belong to Cephas!" or "I belong to Apollos!" they boasted (1 Cor 1:12). Competitive claims of honorable status threatened to splinter the church. Since Paul was not a client of any of the house churches, he was free to respond to the church conflicts in Corinth at a creative level.

As chapter 9 of 1 Corinthians reveals, however, Paul's wise strategy caused difficulties as the conflict developed. Agitators began to suggest that Paul's refusal to accept money was an admission that he was not really qualified to be an apostle. If Peter and Apollos were willing to accept Corinthian money, why wasn't Paul? Didn't this indicate that he lacked apostolic stature? Was this not an admission of inferior honor? He had, after all, not been one of Jesus' disciples, as Peter had been.

An important cultural premise made this charge seem plausible: to do something worthwhile in the Greco-Roman world demanded recompense, either in money or public recognition.[5] If you were not paid, your efforts were worthless. In effect, you were being treated like a slave. In a society in which two-thirds of the population were either slaves or former slaves, this premise was psychologically compelling. To be free meant to be properly recompensed. This is the underlying reason why Paul's discussion of the salary issue in 1 Corinthians 9 opens with the rhetorical question, "Am I not free?"[6]

In a strange way, many of us today feel the same about compensation. If we do not receive the raise we expect, we feel hurt. We feel as if all the hard work we have done is unappreciated. The same thing can happen with a perceived lack of public recognition or with a grade lower than we feel we deserve. We all know from personal experience how worked up people can get over wage and salary levels. The hurt can even lead people to feel that they are being treated like slaves. It is a strange syndrome: free people living in a free society that has presumably abandoned the traditional systems of honor and shame, yet feeling that they are being treated like dishonorable slaves.

We discover in reflecting on this passage that the expectation of recompense is related to the fear of humiliating bondage. We are acting as slaves whenever we feel slighted and injured because of a perceived lack of recompense, in whatever form it is expected to come. Although remuneration can become an issue of justice, we are thinking as slaves whenever it gets tangled up with our sense of self-worth. We are also responding as slaves if we can be bought, induced to act in a manner that is against our better judgment, whether the payoff is in the form of honor, or prestige, or even the keys to a slick new Mercedes.

How the Gospel Triumphs over Bondage

The gospel strikes to the heart of these injured feelings. Paul can say "I am free from everything" (1 Cor 9:19) because of the grace of God shown in the Christ event. Grace sets people free because it comes to them whether they deserve it or not, whether they have performed up to expectation or not, indeed, even when they have made themselves God's enemies. The gospel shatters the central premise of the honor-shame system. The heart of the gospel concerns the death and resurrection of Christ: the one truly free person was put to death by people like us who are in bondage to the cycle of honorable recompense. Jesus was free to love those who did not love him back, to accept people who were beyond the pale of honor in their society. His freedom threatened the carefully polished character armor of those who best measured up to society's standards. Even in his death, Jesus refused to act on the principle of recompense. "Abba, forgive them," he said of the soldiers crucifying him, "for they do not know what they are doing" (Luke 23:34).

Before his conversion, Paul had rejected this free-wheeling Jesus and his disciples. As far as he was concerned, this gospel of freedom threatened the entire system of religion, ethics, and public responsibility. He had persecuted the Jesus movement in the synagogues of Damascus. But then, in the words of 1 Cor 9:1, he "saw Jesus our Lord." This vision altered Paul's entire worldview. If Jesus — the one fully shamed for solidarity with the shamed of society — was really resurrected, then the gospel of freedom must be true. The systems of recompense on which the entire ancient culture rested were suddenly revealed as forms of bondage. If "Jesus means freedom," to use the memorable title of Ernst Käsemann's book,[7] we his disciples are no longer slaves to the law, slaves to the expectations of others, slaves to some system of tit-for-tat.

Our text from 1 Corinthians sets forth this revolutionary outlook in surprising detail. "If I preach the gospel, there is no ground for boasting." That is, there is no basis for gaining prestige and status. If the gospel sets us free from bondage to the various firms of this world, then boasting, which is driven by the desire for status, is no longer necessary. Paul's compulsion to preach is the pressure of the gospel itself: "a necessity is laid upon me, and woe is me if I do not preach the gospel!" Grace captures us and leads us to pass grace on to others. The necessity of the gospel mission is inherent in the gospel itself, and it has nothing whatsoever to do with rewards of any kind. "If I do this of my own will," Paul explains, "I have a reward; but if not of my own will, I am entrusted with a stewardship." There is a stewardship of grace that is fundamentally different from the usual stewardships of reward. For grace produces freedom, which is its own reward. So Paul can ask, "What then is my reward? That in preaching I may offer the gospel free of charge!" The reward here is freedom itself, which derives from grace. Paul does not *have* to be any person's slave, to submit to the client role in any of the Corinthian house churches, to be burdened with the necessity to perform and conform. Thus he is free to preach the gospel free of charge, to embody it in his own motivations, and to revel in its freedom.[8]

In contrast to John Grisham's best-selling novel, the film version of *The Firm* offers a vision of redemption and freedom reminiscent of themes in 1 Corinthians 9.[9] "I think I may have found a way out," Mitch tells Abbie halfway through the film, "not out exactly; it's more like a way through. . . . I know it's weird, but if we follow the law, it might just save us." Shedding the attitude of slavery to the firm, Mitch sets about gathering material for the Justice Department to indict the firm for mail fraud in overcharging clients, while at the same time gathering a dossier of secret copies of files to protect himself from the Mob, promising to abide by the legal rules of lawyer-client confidentiality. He uses the reward

141

money to set up his brother and secretary in the safety of a remote Caribbean island, because they have cooperated in the dangerous plot against the firm and the mob.

The federal agent handling the case is astounded that Mitch turns out to be someone who has freed himself from the profit motive: "You didn't win a thing." Mitch replies, "O yeah I did. I won my life back. You don't run me and they don't run me. . . . I discovered the law again. You actually made me think about it. . . ." Mitch is beginning to recover the ideal of the law as a system of justice and freedom for all.[10] On one level, this is a story of a slave who outwits his masters and discovers the meaning of his vocation. But something happens in the closing scene of the film to bring it near to the theme of 1 Corinthians.[11]

When Maggie returns home at the end of the film, Mitch asks her, "Did I lose you?" He had betrayed his love by allowing himself to be seduced by the firm, both figuratively and literally. But in his actions to free himself and his family from the evil tentacles of the firm, he had shown himself faithful to his commitment of love. So Maggie replies: "I've loved you all my life. Even before we met. Part of it wasn't even you. It was just a promise of you. But these last days, you kept your promise. How could you lose me?" Both Maggie and Mitch recognize at the end that they are ultimately redeemed by faithful love, by what Paul would call "grace." The closing scene shows Mitch and Abbie heading off in the same old jalopy they drove down from Boston. They're returning now to find a "small unknown loft . . . with a lot of potential." They won't have the huge salary and the Mercedes, but this time they will start out in the law business as free and honest people.

Although panned by some critics,[12] this film rings true to the experience of Christian freedom that many have known. This is a freedom that transforms our vocational motives, freeing us from the bondage to recompense. It allows us to discover the deeper satisfactions inherent in our daily work, leading us to honest service. It awakens vocational energies that are a joy to exercise. Yet the allure of various forms of recompense still follows us like a shadow, beckoning us back into narrow, familiar confines of feeling and behavior. What would happen if we were to perform our life-work "free of charge"? What new relationships would such freedom produce?

Freedom and a Healthy Basis of Multiculturalism

Paul describes the social consequences of genuine freedom in a way that provides one source of inspiration for what we now call "multiculturalism."

> For though I am free from all,
>   I enslaved myself to all,
>   in order that I might win the more. . . .
>   I have become all things to all people,
>   in order that I might by all means save some.
>
> (1 Cor 9:19, 22)

What Paul describes here is more than a mental paradox: being "free from all . . . enslaved to all." Grace frees Paul from the necessity to impose his standards on others. He can meet them on their own turf with the stunning news that God loves them unconditionally just as they are. Paul no longer has the compulsion to perform according to the principles of recompense and honor. He does not need to discriminate against persons of allegedly inferior culture or class. Thus he is able to meet people in a disinterested way, respecting who they are and thus acting against the discriminatory prejudices of his age. Although she does not explain the links with the systems of honor and patronage, Barbara Ward has a clear grasp of the eschatological egalitarianism of Paul's thought:

> Life at the turn of the ages means self-enslavement to everyone: Jews and Greeks and members of the church, whether Jew or Greek. God's call in Christ, which grants freedom, wisdom, and power, is to radical identification with the other.[13]

This means that those who have been treated as inferiors can now accept the invitation to equality in Christ. This text from 1 Corinthians provides one of the unacknowledged sources of the distinctive form of social tolerance that marks the multicultural movement. It stems from a civil religion shaped by the biblical legacy of equality and freedom for all. A significant measure of moral sensitivity to the deep issues of social discrimination and prejudice lies at the heart of this. To refer to others with racial epithets is to shame and dehumanize them; to hold other people's cultures in contempt is fundamentally inconsistent with an egalitarian society. This larger concern for social justice and equality is broadly supported by Paul's effort to treat the "weak" and the "strong" alike, to stand with both "Greeks" and "Jews." In David Sterritt's view, this kind of moral commitment is largely missing in the cinematic version of *The Firm*:

> The end of the story is satisfying in a Hollywoodish way, complete with fast-moving climax and victorious conclusion. But it portrays Mitch as more interested in salvaging his professional future than in cleaning up all the evil he's encountered; and it encourages us to accept his shortcuts as a reasonable compromise. While this isn't bad enough to be called an inexcusable ethical failing in the movie, it suggests that 'The Firm' resembles the law firm in its willingness to hedge on moral issues.[14]

Although I admire Mitch's newfound commitment to the law because it ideally treats all persons equally, this film does not develop the radical implications of freedom as Paul does. At this point therefore, our dialogue must be between Paul and current efforts to enforce civility.

I am struck by how different Paul's motivation is from that of most forms of current multiculturalism. He placed himself in a kind of self-imposed indebtedness to the values of the people he served,[15] whereas the rules of current political correctness demand that we should force others to conform to *our* standard of multiculturalism. Whereas Paul was free in Christ to accept people as they were, respecting their cultural and theological diversity, the impulse of some advocates of multiculturalism is to assault every error in speech or thought, to shame miscreants into conformity. Whereas his commitment to respect cultural and theological differences derived from his freedom from the law of Moses, the tendency of political correctness is to erect and enforce a new, linguistic legalism. The anger that current liberals feel toward conservatives, and that conservatives feel toward liberals, is a clear indication that the rules of recompense are still operative. The result is that ideological multiculturalism seems to be driving Americans farther and farther apart, separating us into hostile circles, each attempting to force others into conformity. By trying to achieve cultural tolerance through the ancient systems of recompense, of blame, shame, reward and punishment, we find ourselves drifting into deeper conflicts and new forms of tribalism. The campuses of America are marked by hostile walls and loud demonstrations against each other's sins of imperialism or hegemony or political incorrectness. In this discord of competing systems of recompense, freedom is severely impaired.

Conclusion

Our reflections on the interplay between the gospel and *The Firm* invite us to consider a new approach to vocational motivation as well as a new form of multiculturalism. These new possibilities are based on the gospel of grace that can release people from the imprisonment of shame. Paul's approach to social tolerance, as explicitly related to the cross event, poses a challenge to contemporary liberals: "In the gospel the only real freedom is *crucified* freedom," as Barbara Hall explains.[16] Grounded in the love of Christ, whose shameful death overcomes shameful status for all, Paul was willing to renounce his freedom in order to find "a radical self-identification with others."[17] This transformed both his vocational aims and his social relations.

Is it really possible to achieve this kind of self-identification without having gained a prior freedom from the law? Can the universal tendency toward boasting that lies at the core of social discrimination be exposed and healed by anything but a gospel of unqualified love? Can the stewardship of grace be recovered so that each of us may be set free from bondage to recompense? Can we find courage to struggle for this new kind of freedom, despite all the contrary pressures of our society?

A powerful answer is found in George Matheson's hymn, written a century ago. It counters the current illusion that freedom is available in some absolute form, detached from obedience to the Lord who alone can set us free. It offers encouragement in the struggle for freedom, both for ourselves and others. And it suggests an alternative to the American illusion that a lordly financial compensation will make us masters of our fate:

Make me a captive, Lord, and then I shall be free.
    Force me to render up my sword, and I shall conqueror be.
I sink in life's alarms when by myself I stand;
    imprison me within thine arms, and strong shall be my hand.

My heart is weak and poor, until it master find;
    it has no spring of action sure, it varies with the wind.
It cannot freely move til thou hast wrought its chain;
    enslave it with thy matchless love, and deathless it shall
        reign.[18]

10. Shame and the Other Gospel in *Unforgiven*

> You know the story of my past life in Judaism, how I furiously persecuted the church of God and harried it, and how in Judaism I surpassed many of my own age in zeal for the traditions of my religion. But the God who had set me apart from my very birth called me by his grace, and when he chose to reveal his son to me, that I might preach him to the Gentiles. . . . Personally I was completely unknown to the churches of Judea; they merely heard that "our former persecutor is now preaching the faith he once harried," which made them praise God for me.
>
> Galatians 1:13-16, 22-24

Introduction

In Galatians Paul describes himself as one who used to be a remorseless zealot, involved in violent persecution of the church. His story is similar in structure and motivation to the violent redemption tales that have dominated American entertainment since the 1930s. In these stories, selfless superheroes take the law into their own hands to redeem the innocent. *Unforgiven* is a recent embodiment of this story, hailed by reviewers as anti-heroic but actually conforming in most regards to the typical pattern that John Shelton Lawrence and I have identified as "the American monomyth." The full paradigm of this type of story is as follows:

> A community in a harmonious paradise is threatened by evil: normal institutions fail to contend with this threat: a selfless superhero emerges to renounce temptations and carry out the redemptive task: aided by fate, his decisive victory restores the community to its paradisal condition: the superhero then recedes into obscurity.[1]

In *Unforgiven*,[2] one of the prostitutes in Big Whiskey, Wyoming is cut up by two cowboys. Since the sheriff will not punish this crime except for requiring the cowboys to give some horses to the saloonkeeper whose income will now be diminished, the prostitutes offer a reward for anyone who will provide vigilante justice. A young man who has been living out the fantasy of the western gunman names himself the "Schofield Kid" and recruits a retired gunman and his partner to kill the two cowboys who abused the "lady." Will Munny, played by Clint Eastwood, is the superhero who kills the first cowboy. After his partner is caught, tortured, and killed by the sheriff, Munny goes to the saloon where a posse is gathered and shoots the sheriff and five of his deputies. Having redeemed the prostitutes, Munny rides out alone and disappears.

Unforgiven develops some significant twists in the story of the American monomyth. The most important is that governmental law enforcement, rather than the desperado, is the evil corrupting the community. In targeting a wicked political and economic system as needing violent redemption, this film is similar to the novel *The Turner Diaries*, which appears to have been an important motivation in the Oklahoma City bombing of 1995. Another twist is that the macho dimension of the American monomyth is mocked throughout this film. The prostitute is cut up because she laughs at a cowboy's lack of manliness, thus precipitating the murderous rampage; the motivations and abilities of the redeemer figures fall ludicrously short of the macho ideal; and the violence of macho redemption is displayed in shocking detail. Yet the outcome of the dramatic action in *Unforgiven* remains true to the type of story we find in St. Paul's violent actions prior to his conversion. This story of "regeneration through violence"[3] offers, in effect, another gospel: in its present guise it invites the public to solve its problems by shooting down its sheriffs and placing truck bombs in front of its federal buildings. To explore this issue, I would like to begin by describing the religious motivation that lies behind the gospel of violent zeal.

The Other Gospel of Violent Zeal

Paul's campaign against the church shows that he was part of the holy war tradition. He had been a violent member of a radical branch of the Pharisee party, sincerely and unreservedly devoted to the cause of ushering in the messianic age through conformity to the Jewish law.[4] His record prior to conversion was plain: "as to the law, a Pharisee; as to zeal, a persecutor of the church; as to righteousness under the law, blameless" (Phil 3:5-6). He had conformed to the values of his religious tradition out of competition for honor, claiming at one point to have "surpassed many of my own age in zeal for the traditions of my religion" (Gal 1:14).[5] There was no doubt about his sincerity or his ability to pursue the high cause: he persecuted heretics such as the Christians without reservation (Gal 1:13). His behavior fits the pattern of zealous war and officially sponsored lynchings in the first century; some segments of the revolutionary movement believed that passionate zeal for God required absolute repudiation of any other earthly king and hence called for resistance against Roman rule.[6] Following the example of Phinehas (cf. Num 25:7-13) and the Maccabees, these passionate religionists "showed the same readiness to take the law into their own hands and even to use violent means to preserve the integrity of God's law and his sanctuary, often sacrificing their own lives in the process."[7] In this context zeal was "an eschatological intensification of the Torah," requiring violence against transgressors and expecting divine intervention in an apocalyptic framework.[8] David Rhoads concludes that, although splintered into various factions, the revolutionaries "fought with the common hope that God would bring a decisive victory. . . . the Jews believed they could count on God's decisive aid because they were supporting their commitment to him by aggressive military actions."[9]

Jesus had rejected such zeal, calling instead for love and understanding of the enemy and submission to Rome.[10] He died in place of the zealot Barabbas, having refused to play the role of the militant messiah and to call for the legion of warrior angels when captured, or later to respond to the messianic taunts to come down from the cross. His resurrection meant that God had confirmed that this nonviolent one was indeed the promised messiah, and that the method of bringing the messiah through zealous violence was obsolete. After his conversion, Paul turned away from this zealous fanaticism toward a strategy of conversion through the gospel of love.

Unforgiven conforms in decisive ways to the plot of the American monomyth, which derived from the zealous strand of the biblical tradition. As *The Captain America Complex* and *The American Monomyth* have shown,[11] this story form crystallized in the 1930s out of the earlier forms of the cowboy western and the Indian captivity narrative. These seventeenth- through nineteenth-century tales adapted the biblical holy war tradition of the servants of God defeating God's enemies. But it was not until the twentieth century that the heroes became super, renouncing marriage and other temptations to become invulnerable to the bullets of their adversaries.

Unforgiven is a corrupted form of this story, in which paradise is sullied by the abuse of prostitutes, and in which the gunfighter is engaged by the desire for reward money. There is no veneer of religious justification in this film: "No church is seen in Big Whiskey, nor God mentioned."[12] The story of William Munny is typical of monomythic heroes, however, in his double identity. He had earlier been a gunman, but renounced this life after his marriage to Claudia Feathers. But she had died of smallpox and left Munny to raise their two children on an impoverished farm in Kansas. When their hogs die, Munny is forced by economic circumstances to consider the invitation to earn the reward by killing the two cowboys. His renunciation of the temptations of sex, whisky, and swearing holds true to the monomythic paradigm until the moment he discovers that the brutal sheriff and his deputies have killed his innocent friend, Ned Logan, played by Morgan Freeman.

Munny takes a swig of whisky and returns to town, dropping the empty bottle in the rain. He passes Ned's body displayed in a casket in front of the saloon with the sign, "This is what happens to assassins around here." The scene is now set for violent retribution on a corrupt government that tolerates the mutilation of women and the torturing and shaming of prisoners.

When Will Munny comes into the saloon with his shotgun, Sheriff Little Bill Daggett, played by the Academy Award–winning actor Gene Hackman, is briefing the posse for the next day's hunt. The humiliated prostitutes are looking on as their redemption unfolds. Munny asks who owns the establishment, and then shoots the owner down with one barrel. When the sheriff calls him a cowardly son of a bitch for shooting down "an unarmed man," Will replies, "He should have armed himself if he was going to decorate his saloon with my friend." Will admits that he had been a vicious killer and says, "I'm here to kill you, Little Bill, for what you done to Ned." His shotgun misfires, but he shoots Bill and five deputies with his pistol without missing a shot, lets the others clear out the back, and takes a final swig of whisky from the bar. He leaves the saloon and escapes a town full of armed men. A deputy has a final chance to shoot the killer, but he shies away as Munny rides off and says: "You'd better bury Ned right" and not abuse any more prostitutes. Delilah and Alice come out to watch their redeemer ride off in the rain, with the other whores behind them. The camera pans to the scarred face of the abused Delilah, which is radiant with satisfaction as she admiringly watches her superhero ride off into obscurity, completing the mythic cycle.[13]

The printed soliloquy at the end of *Unforgiven* confirms the disappearance of the superhero, lifting up the irony of redemption through disreputable violence: "William Munny had long since disappeared with the children . . . some said to San Francisco where it was rumored he prospered in dry goods."

To a broad segment of the American public that embraces movies like this, awarding them top honors at Academy Award ceremonies, this "other gospel" is highly appealing. This film received the 1992 Academy Award for Best Picture, Best Director, Best Supporting Actor, and numerous other awards. Part of the current appeal is that the film seems ambivalent about idealizing the western hero. In John G. Cawelti's words, "As if to remind us of the falsity of the gunfighter myth, *Unforgiven* provides us with a dime-novel hero accompanied by his writer. English Bob is, in good postmodernist fashion, ambivalently deconstructed by the sadistic sheriff Little Bill, who reduces him to a pathetic victim. On the other hand, in the film's violent climax, Will Munny actually improves on dime-novel shoot-outs by escalating the body count. . . ."[14]

When this kind of violent ideology gets embodied in events like the Oklahoma City bombing, which was also directed against governmental agents perceived to be brutal and corrupt, we become aware of the threat it poses. The correlation with Galatians offers a resource for understanding the misguided idealism shaped by painful experiences of shame and honor that might lead people to model their behavior after this superheroic ideal.

Zealous Violence as a Response to Shameful Humiliation

The language Paul employs to describe his motivations and actions helps us to grasp the powerful mechanisms of honor and shame that lie behind zealous violence. The competition for honor typical of the Greco-Roman world is visible in Gal 1:14, where Paul claims "in Judaism I surpassed many of my own age in zeal for the traditions of my religion." The competition in zeal is competition in adhering to the highest ideals of the society, ideals worth killing or dying for. In Paul's case, if the "traditions of my religion" were to be maintained, the Christians had to be put down. They accepted sinners and polluting Gentiles into their fellowship, violating the standards of Israel's holiness. Their love feasts violated kosher food laws, and their worship was centered on Jesus, whom Paul's Pharisaic party believed to be a false messiah who had corrupted Israel and had been deservedly executed by the authorities. Their shameful behavior and devotion to one who had died the shameful death of crucifixion enraged the zealous Saul of Tarsus, who acknowledged that before his conversion he had "furiously persecuted the church of God and harried it" (Gal 1:13).

The violence in *Unforgiven* is the response to shameful humiliation, which at some deeper level is related to the motivation of zealous retribution on the part of a person like Saul. The issue of violating societal standards surfaces when Munny is invited by the Schofield Kid to go north to "kill a couple of no-good cowboys." "For what?" "For cuttin' up a lady. They cut her eyes out, cut her ears off. Hell, they even cut her teats." Munny looks off in the distance with disgust and says, "Jesus." Later, when he is recruiting Ned to join him on the zealous campaign, Munny relates how the cowboys cut up a woman, and Ned is horrified. Ned acknowledges the zealous logic: "Well, guess they got it comin'. Course, you know, Will, if Claudia was alive, you wouldn't be doin' this." In order for Munny and his partner to enact the required violent retribution, they have to renounce wifely standards. They must do so in order to rescue the damsels in distress, a stock motif in the cowboy western that derives from the Indian captivity narratives of colonial America, in which innocent women are kidnapped by malevolent Indians.

The issue of shame also surfaces in the motivation of the cowboys who mutilated the prostitute Delilah. Aside from this brutal action against an offending prostitute, they are described by the sheriff as not being "tramps, or loafers, or bad men. They was just hard-working boys that was foolish." The cowboy Quick Mike had reacted violently when Delilah, played by Anna Thompson, "giggled at his teensy little pecker." This threat to the macho image initiates the dramatic development of the film, because when the sheriff fails to punish the crime, the prostitutes decide to put up the bounty money for private retribution. The saloon owner, Skinny Dubois, had shown the sheriff his contract with Delilah, whom he brought out from Boston, to prove his contention that the cowboys had damaged his property. "Nobody's gonna pay good money for a cut-up whore." The sheriff decides the culprit should bring in five ponies for Skinny, and his accomplice is to bring in two. So the sheriff ends up not whipping the culprits. The leading prostitute, Strawberry Alice (played by Frances Fisher), says "That ain't fair, Little Bill." The whores talk it over and decide they have to do something to prove that "we ain't horses." Prostitution is dishonorable enough, but to be treated as no better than animals is too painful to tolerate. Since only the death of these cowboys can alleviate their shame, they begin to pool their money for bounty hunters.

The issue of overcoming shame also plays a role in shaping the action of William Munny and his partner, Ned Logan. At first glance, it appears gratuitous that the film repeats the scene of Munny falling on his face into the filthy mud of his hog yard while trying to separate sick hogs. While attempting to be a responsible parent to his two children in the absence of his wife, Munny is depicted as utterly humiliated by circumstances. A humorous accent on this motif is his repeated failure to mount his plow horse to ride off to the redemptive task. Then, in the saloon at Big Whiskey, the sick Munny is brutally beaten by Sheriff Daggett and thrown out into the muddy street on his face in the rain.

This ritual humiliation of the superhero replicates scenes in earlier Clint Eastwood cowboy westerns:[15] the prelude to the inevitable, violent resolution in which the restored superhero recovers strength and kills the villainous torturers. But it is the public shaming of his friend Ned that provokes the bloody retribution that kills the wicked sheriff and his deputies. After the cleansing violence, Munny issues a final warning to the town about not shaming the members of the community: "You'd better not cut up or otherwise harm no whore, or I'll come back and kill every one of you sons of bitches." The protection of the weakest and most shameful members of society is the moral imperative that ultimately justifies the violence against hard-hearted representatives of the government. Undergirded by the American monomyth, which requires a hero with a secret identity to redeem an otherwise helpless society, this is the classic American story of regeneration through violence, with the underlying issue of shame articulated clearly and honestly.

Corrupt Authorities That Require Violent Redemption

The ultimate target for first-century Jewish zealotry was the Roman government; before his conversion, Paul was likely on the side of the Shammai movement of Pharisaism[16] and was therefore sympathetic with the zealot movement and hostile toward the Gentile world that was dominating Israel. His conversion led him to a reluctant acceptance of governmental authority and legitimacy, as articulated in Rom 13:1-7. While he remained critical of "the rulers of this age" who "crucified the Lord of glory" (1 Cor 2:8), Paul evidently recognized the need for governmental law enforcement. Rather than expecting redemption to come through the violent cleansing of the political system, he turned to the moral transformation of small groups. At the core of this new approach was a redefinition of shameful boundaries between Greeks and Jews, epitomized by Paul's call to preach his Jewish gospel "to the Gentiles" (Gal 1:17).

The development of hostility against a corrupt government is an important motif in monomythic entertainment of the last several decades, from the *Rambo*[17] films to *Unforgiven*, where the sheriff is a former criminal, a brutal man who treads on American ideals of equality before the law even as he takes vengeance on British Bob's contempt for the American Independence Day.

The impact of this tradition of political zeal on the country was brought much closer to home on April 19, 1995 with the truck bombing of the federal building in Oklahoma City. Timothy McVeigh has now been convicted of this crime, but since the prosecution decided not to explore the ideology that motivated this act, which might appear to violate his First Amendment rights, the country is left to piece this motivation together out of fragments of evidence.[18] On the evidence available to the general public, it seems likely that McVeigh's association with the Michigan Militia and other right-wing, paramilitary groups points toward the kind of zealous violence that Paul had once espoused. These groups are convinced that an international conspiracy involving Jewish bankers and the United Nations is taking over the United States government and depriving them of an allegedly constitutional right to bear arms.[19]

Carl Raschke of the Department of Religious Studies at Denver University, who has specialized in the study of apocalyptic and paramilitary groups in this country, writes that "there are thousands of people out there who are angry at the federal government and have been talking about a holy war."[20] Two of these state militia groups issued newsletters prior to the bombing in an effort to prevent the execution of the neo-Nazi leader Richard Snell on April 19, 1995 in Arkansas, recalling the conflagration in Waco on April 19, 1993. These newsletters referred to the Battle of Concord on April 19, 1775 as the beginning of a revolution that threw off governmental tyranny. McVeigh himself has referred to the Waco incident in interviews after his trial.

Just as the Jewish zealots in Paul's day were following the heroic examples of figures like Phinehas and the Maccabbees, contemporary militias and neo-Nazis are inspired by the scenes of violence in popular culture. Richard Snell admitted that the actions of his group in killing a black state trooper from Arkansas were modeled after the novel *The Turner Diaries*, written by William Pierce, the head of a hate group called the National Alliance.[21] Prior to detonating a nuclear weapon that destroys the wicked Pentagon, the hero of the novel, Earl Turner, leaves a truck filled with fertilizer and diesel oil in front of the FBI headquarters in Washington. The subsequent explosion kills 700 employees. One of the early accounts in the *Chicago Tribune* noted the coincidence in timing: "The blast takes place at 9:15 a.m. The Oklahoma City bomb went off at 9:04 a.m."[22] Subsequent news accounts revealed that McVeigh sold copies of *The Turner Diaries* as he made the rounds of gun shows, and that it played a decisive role in the plans of other groups to attack federal installations. The *Chicago Tribune* reported that Jennifer McVeigh testified about a letter from her brother that advised her "to read the 'Turner Diaries,' a racist and anti-Semitic novel about a revolution against the federal government — a book prosecutors claim was McVeigh's blueprint for the bombing."[23]

There are many widely popular films that embody a zealous ideology similar to *The Turner Diaries*. For example, in *High Plains Drifter* Clint Eastwood plays the abused hero who returns to burn down an entire wicked town after killing its evil sheriff. In *Pale Rider*

Eastwood plays the avenging minister who rescues innocent miners by blowing up the buildings of their wicked oppressor and by shooting down the malevolent federal marshal and his gunmen. In *Rambo: First Blood, Part I,* Sylvester Stallone plays the role of a Vietnam veteran abused by his home town in Oregon. He slays the wicked governmental agents and then burns the entire town.

In all of these films the community is restored by zealous violence, which destroys corrupt governmental agents so that innocent citizens can live in peace and freedom once again. Stallone plays a similar role in *Copland,* wiping out the police who are corrupting New York City. It now appears quite likely that it was this widely popular story form, embodied in some of our most popular films, as well as in *The Turner Diaries,* that inspired McVeigh. Evidently, he was living out the fantasy of being like Luke Skywalker, the hero of *Star Wars* who destroys nazi storm troopers and their allies, or like Earl Turner, the heroic bomber and martyr who restores American democracy through mass murder.

The Divided Heart and the Possibility of Conversion

Is there a fundamental flaw, a fatal inconsistency, in characters like Timothy McVeigh and their mythical counterparts, Luke Skywalker, Earl Turner, and William Munny? Is the Saul who furiously persecuted the church really the same person as the Paul who now preaches "the faith he once harried"? Is there a contradiction within the persecutor that needs to be resolved before a more human form of human interaction becomes possible? Or is this a question of two gospels restoring honor by different means?

Most interpreters have opted for the theory of a divided mind. In the case of *Unforgiven,* leading reviewers perceive the story of "a divided soul, a genuine tragic hero" split between the urges of pitiless violence and familial responsibility.[24] Richard Grenier contends that this film "was a repudiation and dismantling of the whole legendary, masculine character type of which, for this generation, Eastwood himself had become the leading icon."[25] In his earlier life, Munny had apparently been involved in the civil war in Missouri, where he earned the reputation of being the "meanest goddamn son of a bitch alive," in the words of the Schofield Kid. But William Munny the hog farmer from Kansas is depicted as a model father, loyal to his children, and reluctant to return to his former life. In Christopher Frayling's sarcastic assessment, "It is made clear that Munny has become a sensitive single parent to his two children, dislikes cruelty to horses as well as to women, and has generally turned New Age."26 But David Denby offers a more discerning description of Munny's inner conflict:

> . . . he needs the money, but he also needs the approval of his dead wife, who persuaded him eleven years earlier to give up drinking and killing and settle down. The wife's loving admonitions still play inside his head — he talks stiffly about "the error of my ways," as if she were haunting him. Grimacing as he struggles with his horse . . . we can see what's working on him — he's ashamed of himself. Munny's wife has destroyed any pleasure he might take in getting back into the saddle as an outlaw.27

The conflict is finally resolved after Ned Logan is killed, when Munny takes his first swig of whisky, which he had renounced since his marriage. "Rather than debilitating him, alcohol seems almost to accentuate the steely clarity of his recovery. . . . The artificial constraints imposed by his wife's 'goodness' are swept away. He awakens to his own innate destructiveness — a perverse cure indeed."28 In this film it is the nonviolent persona that is false and has to be repudiated to achieve redemption.

In the final duel scene in Big Whiskey's tavern, Munny acknowledges that he is the one who has "killed women and children . . . just about anything that walks or crawls at one time or another." After remorselessly shooting Little Bill and the last wounded deputy at point-blank range, Munny leaves the saloon and warns that if he sees anyone outside, "I'm going to kill him. If anyone takes a shot at me, I'm going to kill his wife, all his friends, burn his damned house down."

The juxtaposition between the violent redeemer and his public reputation in the minds of decent people is lifted up in the caption that closes the film: "And there was nothing on the [grave] marker to explain to Mrs. Feathers why her only daughter had married a known thief and murderer, a man of notoriously vicious and intemperate disposition." This echoes the caption that opens the film, which refers to Munny's mother-in-law as one who found it "heartbreaking" that her lovely daughter would have married "William Munny, a known thief and murderer, a man of notoriously vicious and intemperate disposition."

The title of the movie seems to resonate with this motif: the man who must remain "unforgiven" by society is really its redeemer. Although the traditional facade of the white hat and the high moral quality of the redeemer is abandoned in the 1990s version of the American monomyth, the plot remains intact. One would never mistake William Munny for the Lone Ranger, but the story line remains the same. Intemperate violence that cleanses shame is the current version of Barry Goldwater's refrain of a generation ago: "Extremism in the defense of liberty is no crime."

An important element of "the Werther invitation"[29] is visible in the story of the Schofield Kid's attempt to live out the myths of the western gunfighters as well as in the celebration of those myths by the writer Beauchamp, who accompanies English Bob, the archetypal bounty hunter drawn to Big Whiskey by news of the prostitutes' reward. The fact that the myth proves false in both of these characters lends credence to the idea that *Unforgiven* wishes to critique the myth system. Clint Eastwood thinks his film has eliminated the last remnants of glamour in gunfighting. At the time of the Academy Awards ceremony, he told a reporter: "This story preaches that it isn't glamorous to take up the gun. It is not glamorous to kill people, it's not beautiful, and I think that's very current on people's minds today."[30] This apologia deals only with the surface texture of *Unforgiven* while overlooking its conformity with the plot of the American monomyth. Although the film insists that "the gunslingers of the old West" like Munny were "very, very bad men,"[31] they are nevertheless made essential for the redemption of the community. Those who take up the unpopular task of violent redemption are depicted as true heroes, secretly admired by all despite the feelings of mothers-in-law. Munny is converted by the call to duty when he hears about the abuse of the "lady" in Big Whisky. Thus I believe that Harry Brod is right to reject the widespread assessment that *Unforgiven* "demythologizes people who indulge in violent behavior."[32] In place of the divided heart of traditional tragedy, what we have here is the classic double identity of the American superhero. Instead of conversion, there is merely a changing from the costume and behavior of Clark Kent to that of Superman.

Conclusion

The question is not so much whether conversion in response to a gospel is possible, but which kind of gospel and conversion we should prefer. The culturally endorsed stories of regeneration through violence, when linked with experiences of shameful humiliation, can lead us individually and collectively into violent campaigns against perceived sources of oppression. But it is also clear that such stories require suppression of the truth on a grand scale. Pat Dowell has pointed out that the screenplay of *Unforgiven*

> . . . advances the story by a series of lies. The tale of the atrocity that takes Will and Ned after the bounty is false in its details. Its perpetrator has lied about the prostitute's provocation — she didn't steal his money, she laughed at his 'teensy pecker.' The prostitutes lie to potential bounty hunters about how much money they have and how badly the victim was hurt. All along the way there are lies, from the self-aggrandizements of wannabe bad men like the Scofield Kid and gunman English Bob . . . to the myth that Little Bill Daggett protects the common good.[33]

Dowell wonders whether Will Munny's statement of his transformation from reckless frontier killer to responsible parent and citizen, "I ain't like that any more," is the "biggest lie of all" given the difficulty in telling "the good guys from the bad guys."[34] Since the story line conforms to the scheme of regeneration through violence that leads from the preconversion persecution of Paul down through the materials of the American monomyth, I would say that the most massive lie is that such violence will produce an honorable peace, despite all the mythic allure.

Unforgiven makes it clear that the dynamics of honor and shame provide the motivating power to reenact such stories of violent zeal. As Judy Coode observes, "You can be a Real Man and preach that killing is bad, but *to prove yourself,* pull that trigger."[35] That act alone is capable of restoring honor, for oneself and one's society. Although the mythic logic is compelling, Americans remain uncomfortable with its enactment, as shown especially in condemnations of bombings performed by "terrorists." Given the seriousness of the challenge and the profound appeal of such stories, it is time our churches and universities entered into discussion of both of these gospels. The distinctively Christian story of regeneration through sacrificial love is unlikely to develop its full potential for our society until it is juxtaposed with the other gospel of regeneration through violence that dominates American popular culture. When the two models of redemption are held up before us, side by side in our catechism classes and college curricula, it should become clear that either choice will eliminate the other. Our culture cannot continue to affirm both options, because *Unforgiven's* gospel has repeatedly demonstrated the capacity to incite people to burn the whole "damned house down" in a vain effort to achieve triumph over shame.

11. A Problematic Hope for the Shamed in *The Shawshank Redemption*

> For in this hope were we saved.
> But hope that is seen is not hope,
> for who hopes for what they see?
> But if we hope in what we do not see,
> we await [it] with perseverance.

Romans 8:24-25

Introduction

There is a distinctive emphasis on hope in Paul's letters. In Chapter 8, we briefly discussed the key line in Rom 5:5: "Hope does not humiliate." That is, hope sustains the hopeful person, not because the object of hope will always be achieved but "because the love of God has been poured into our hearts through the Holy Spirit given to us." The contrast with classical Greco-Roman culture is palpable at this point: hope was viewed in that culture as a weakling's resort, a refusal to face the difficult fate that life inevitably imposes. Hope in that context was cowardly and thus shameful. But for Paul it was the new relationship with God that makes the difference, because the Spirit of God conveys a grace that assures

162

the believer of a new relationship of honorable sonship, as Romans sets forth. When the burden of overcoming shame is no longer merely a matter of future luck, hope itself can become more resilient and realistic. Hence Paul can admonish the Roman Christians

> Let us also boast in the afflictions,
> > knowing that the affliction produces perseverance,
> > > and perseverance produces character,
> > > > and character produces hope. . . .
>
> > > > > > > (Rom 5:3-4)

Paul's approach to hope has been adapted in the American civil religion,[1] with its optimism about a better tomorrow, an optimism whose decline lies at the center of the current malaise. In contrast to earlier citizens, who were in closer touch with the biblical legacy, hope for most contemporary Americans is no longer linked with "perseverance" and "character." For early Americans, this hope was grounded on scriptural promises such as those we find in Rom 5:1-5; 8:20-23; 10:14-17, promises that retain the link with divine justice and a realistic appraisal of the fragility of life and of the continued effect of evil.

Although panned by many critics,[2] *The Shawshank Redemption*[3] has been celebrated "for the way it evokes the power of hope."[4] The film is of particular interest, because its hope of deliverance is so clearly derived from the Bible, albeit in the ironic form of a small rock hammer hidden inside its pages. Andy Defreyne, played by Tim Robbins, is a banker from Maine who was wrongly convicted of the murder of his wife and her lover and sentenced to life imprisonment. Shawshank Prison is a brutal institution that dehumanizes and murders its inmates. Its warden is a corrupt, Bible-thumping hypocrite who siphons off prison funds and receives bribes for the labor of prisoners. By persistent, intelligent effort over a twenty-year period, Defreyne manages to escape by gradually hammering a hole in the concrete wall of his cell. Having created a fictional partner to launder the warden's ill-gotten funds during his years as the prison bookkeeper, Andy boldly shows up at the bank after his escape from prison. He presents the fictional identity papers and empties the bank account. Then he gives his evidence of prison corruption and murders to the local newspaper. The brutal captain, Byron Hadley, is charged with murder and Warden Norden shoots himself before he can be arrested. In the meantime, Andy disappears into Mexico. He is later reunited with his prison friend Red Redding, played by Morgan Freeman, who joins him on the Mexican beach where Andy is building a small resort as a future livelihood and refuge.

The link between the Bible and the hope of escape did not originate with *The Shawshank Redemption*. In *Escape from Alcatraz*, a Bible also serves to hide the means of escape. The larger frame of this link is the distinctively American crime story in which an innocent person is falsely accused and ultimately redeemed: shameful status is wrongfully imposed but ultimately overcome. But is this kind of escape adequate to portray the human situation?

Hope in the Context of Ongoing Vulnerability

Romans 8:24-25 speaks of being saved "in this hope," which presupposes a situation of ongoing vulnerability for those who have been redeemed. Romans 5:3 urges that believers actually "boast in our sufferings," because the new relationship with Christ that overcomes shameful status gives the power to persevere. "Peace with God" (Rom 5:1) should continue to be sought in the here and now, in the midst of ongoing adversity. We need to keep the social situation of the Roman Christians in mind when interpreting these verses, so that hope does not focus on mere change of circumstance, guaranteeing peace through overcoming adversity. The slaves and former slaves who made up the bulk of the Roman churches could not entirely overcome exploitation by their masters and patrons. Some of the Roman Christians had been forced into exile by the Edict of Claudius less than a decade prior to the writing of Romans, so their return after the death of Claudius still posed burdens that would have to be borne.

In the case of current American culture, of course, hope has a much less realistic definition than in Romans. It is largely the hope of a better tomorrow, when adversity does not overwhelm us.

It is essentially the hope for happy endings. In the case of prison stories, hope consists of escaping and finding a "second chance" through assuming a new identity. In Romans, the current situation of vulnerability — living in the midst of socially shameful circumstances — is expected to continue. Hope "does not disappoint," not because of a successful escape from current adversity or the sudden achievement of honorable status, but because shame has been overcome in the present moment by God's love poured into the heart in the context of the new community.

In *The Shawshank Redemption*, several of the inmates are redeemed by a hope that at first seems so illusory as to be dangerous. For six years after his wrongful imprisonment, Andy Defreyne continues to write the state legislature requesting that they supply more materials for the meager prison library. Finally, boxes of used books and records arrive in the warden's office. When the box of records is opened, Andy places Mozart's *Marriage of Figaro* on the record player in the warden's office so that the love duet is broadcast through the entire prison. The prisoners stand in stunned silence in the exercise yard; they have never heard anything so hauntingly beautiful. Many years later, Red reflects that it was so lovely it made your heart ache: "Those voices soared higher than any dared to dream . . . and for a moment every last inmate at Shawshank felt he was free." Defying the order that he turn off the record, Andy locks the warden's door and turns up the volume. After emerging from solitary punishment in "the hole" two weeks later, Andy tells his buddies that prisoners need such music "so we don't forget that there are places outside not made of stone and there is something inside that they can't get to, can't touch, is yours — hope." His friend Red, who is the narrator of the movie, replies, "Hope is a dangerous thing. Hope can drive a man insane. It's got no use on the inside [of prison]." This is a sentiment that Greco-Roman authors would have heartily endorsed, but one that Paul counters in Romans.

The Shawshank Redemption places the issue of "hope" in its starkest light, allowing us to reflect on the viability of Paul's message for persons living on the edge of despair, in the most shameful bondage. Does the hope of freedom really sustain life? Or does it weaken resolve and hasten death?

Hope and the "Institutional Man"

Red fears hope because it drives people insane, especially when it remains unfulfilled for a long time. It prevents people from facing current circumstances. Even when freedom comes, hope proves empty — because after years in prison inmates become "institutionalized." The skepticism articulated by Red resonates with the negative view of hope in some strands of the Greco-Roman culture of Paul's day. As Rudolf Bultmann observed, hope was often viewed as deceptive and corrupting, so that Cynic philosophers flatly rejected it, while Stoic and Epicurean philosophers offered warnings about falling prey to empty promises.[5]

The institutionalization that throttles hope in *The Shawshank Redemption* begins with a kind of obscene initiation when the prisoners first arrive. The hardened inmates jeer and take bets about which of the new prisoners will break down first. The first night in Shawshank sets the tone for the kind of imprisonment they are going to experience, which is particularly shocking to those arriving for the first time. The first night is always the worst, because the shock of institutionalization is so severe. When the officers lock everyone in, the prisoners begin to try to break the new prisoners, for example, by threatening them with inmates who will rape them. It is an awful scene in which inmates participate in the brutal institutionalization of each other. When one of the fresh inmates blubbers and cries, Captain Hadley beats him with nightstick and boots until he is unconscious. The trustees take him to the infirmary, where he dies later that night. The first clue the audience has that Andy will resist this institutionalization comes when he asks his fellow prisoners the name of this murdered inmate. They respond with contemptuous amazement, with something like, "Who cares, what does it matter, who gives a damn what his name is? He's dead." They have entirely internalized the message of institutionalization: their lives and names are worthless; their shame is complete.

This is an issue close to the center of Paul's message: how to provide marginalized people a new self-identity different from the shameful societal identity imposed on them as slaves and outcasts.

The confines of institutionalization are identified with the law of Moses, which Paul insists does not have the capacity to redeem. His realistic appraisal of the ongoing effect of the demeaning institutional forces of Greco-Roman culture is visible in Romans 8, which admits the destructive impact of "principalities and powers" but denies that any of them can "separate us from the love of Christ." Whether prisoners or slaves, marginalized women or orphans, Christians can derive an honorable self-identity and group-identity from this loving relationship with Christ. Therefore they do not need to conform their souls and hearts to the corrupt and tyrannical social institutions around them.

The impact of institutionalization surfaces in the film in connection with the parole of Brooks, an older prisoner at Shawshank. When he gets his parole paper, he threatens to kill a fellow prisoner because, after fifty years in prison, he is afraid of getting out. "These walls are funny," says Red. "First you hate 'em. Then you get used to 'em. Enough time passes, it gets so you depend on them. Institutionalized. . . . They send you here for life. That's exactly what they take."

After his parole, Brooks writes the guys in the prison about "how fast things move on the outside . . . cars are everywhere. The world went and got itself into a big damn hurry." He works bagging groceries, which is hard at his age, and lives in a halfway house. He feeds the birds and has trouble sleeping at night, waking up scared, having trouble remembering where is. He thinks of getting a gun and sticking up a store to get back in prison. Then he carves his name on the ceiling of the halfway house and hangs himself.

Later in the film, Red reveals that he fears the same fate. "Do you think you will ever get out of here?" Andy asks Red. If he does get out, Andy says, he will go to Mexico on the Pacific coast, "because the ocean has no memory." He wants to open up a little hotel on the beach, fix up a boat, and take guests out charter fishing. He could use a man like Red who knows how to get things done. Red replies that he couldn't make it on the outside: "I'm an institutional man now, just like Brooks was." Don't think about Mexico, he advises, because "it's down there and you're in here." Despite this resistance, Andy tells Red that if he ever gets out, he should find a hayfield near Buxton, with a long rock wall marked by an oak tree on the north end. It is the spot where Andy had once gone for a picnic with his wife, proposing to her. "Promise me Red, if you ever get out, find that spot." There will be a black, volcanic rock that seems out of place, but something will be buried under it. This is the hidden substance of hope for an institutional man, though it is a hope that Red has no intention of ever pursuing.

The theme of the "institutional" men imprisoned by stone walls is juxtaposed throughout the film with the image of birds that have the capacity to fly away in freedom. The birds seem to symbolize the definition of redemption as escape from bondage. Brooks has a bird under his coat in prison that he cares for day after day, letting the bird fly free only when he is paroled. After his parole, it seems that the only creatures Brooks can relate to are the birds in the park. This motif is carried through when birds soar as the magnificent Mozart opera is being played over the loudspeaker system, articulating the hope of freedom. Field birds are also heard chirping when Red ultimately finds the stone wall near Buxton. This occurs near the end of the film, when Red has been paroled after more than forty years in prison. And there are seagulls in the final scene on the Mexican beach, when the two friends unite in freedom.

The embodiment of hope comes after Andy makes his remarkable escape from Shawshank. Red is paroled and leaves the prison without shaking any hands. He takes the bus up to the halfway house where Brooks committed suicide, sees his carving on the ceiling, and begins bagging groceries. He faces the truth that he, like Brooks, cannot make it on the outside; he begins to think of breaking his parole, because he lives in fear all the time. He is stopped by the promise he made to Andy.

Hitching a ride to Buxton, Red finds the stone wall with the great tree at the end of it. There is a dark rock that seems out of place, and underneath it is a metal box with an envelope inside a plastic sack, with a stash of money and a letter to Red, reminding him, "Hope is a good thing, maybe the best of things, and a good thing never dies. . . . Your friend, Andy." So he carves his own name in the ceiling next to Brooks's and takes a bus to the ocean.

He is excited, as only a free man can feel. He walks down the beach toward Andy, who is renovating his boat. The seagulls are heard as the two friends meet while the camera backs off for a panoramic view of the ocean without memory.

The metal box under the rock in Buxton is the most eloquent metaphor I have found in contemporary cinema for the "hope" that "we await with perseverance." It provides a new birth for an "institutional man." It helps us gain a fresh understanding of Paul's theme of freedom from the law, the principalities, and the powers. But does Romans throw any light on the film?

Affliction, Perseverance, Character, and Hope

The climax in Rom 5:3-5 assumes that affliction is a normal part of life, even for the converted. Paul contends that affliction is not meaningless. Although caused by the ongoing pressure of the principalities and powers, it can have a transforming effect on believers whose shame has been replaced by a new relationship with Christ and with the community of the once shamed. Believers are enabled to "boast in the afflictions" because they know that "affliction produces perseverance, and perseverance produces character, and character produces hope." Such boasting flies in the face of everyday experience as understood in the ancient setting, in which affliction was either the punishment of the gods or a sign of their uncaring attitude toward humankind. Most humans, it was thought, are the playthings of fate, which means that their individual lives are without any significance. They could be pitilessly snuffed out at the whim of the gods without leaving a mark. Paul's argument assumes that such shameful nothingness has already been overcome by Christ, and therefore that believers should retain hope in the final triumph of God over the wicked institutional forces surrounding them. Since believers are beloved by Christ, they are able to take a completely different attitude toward suffering. Now affliction can become a resource for human maturation.

"Affliction produces perseverance," Paul writes. When sustained by hope and preserved from the contamination of fateful nothing-

ness, believers can find that affliction develops their resistance, strengthens their muscles, stiffens their backbone of resolve. They become tough yet resilient in a new and more mature fashion than could ever have been possible before their new life in Christ.

The idea of hope allowing affliction to produce perseverance is embodied throughout *The Shawshank Redemption*. While most of the prisoners are broken by affliction, Andy retains hope and resolutely sets his mind to overcome his situation. He gathers a rock collection, carefully carving stone chess pieces, while steadily and secretly chipping a hole in the concrete wall with his tiny rock hammer. His perseverance is almost geologic, wearing down resistance by tiny blows, hour after hour, day after day. He also perseveres in requesting book donations for the prison library, in filling out tax returns for prison guards, in keeping books for the warden, and in teaching literacy to other inmates.

"Perseverance produces character," Paul writes. A new kind of character was gradually being formed in the early Christian communities, which refused to acknowledge the power of fate and resolutely resisted meaninglessness and hopelessness. In place of the raging but ultimately helpless victims their society presumed they should be, these early Christians were developing responsible, resilient character that dared to reshape everyday life on the pattern of love. An internalized standard of conduct and a hopeful outlook on life were being formed in each believer, because the reinforcement of the sacramental meal and the constant rehearsing of the significance of Christ's death for others prevented the kind of defeatism that grim circumstances usually produces. Their character was being transformed daily by the imprint of the character of the loving, responsible Christ.

In typical American prison stories, "perseverance" is featured but "character" is missing, because there is nothing wrong with the victim of the false conviction that results in imprisonment. These stories harbor the vision of an innocent victim; he requires no forgiveness because there has been no sin, no growth in character because there is no character flaw. This is very different from the plot development in detective stories that assume the flawed character of the perpetrator, and place the detective in the position of relentlessly and cleverly pursuing this character flaw along with other clues until guilt is exposed and punishment can be applied. The classic escape films set in the European frame of imagination assume the guilt of the escapee: *Les Miserables* and *Papillion* feature prisoners properly convicted of crimes they actually committed who find ways to escape, whether through the Parisian sewers or through the swamps of Devil's Island. Since the sewer and swamp recur in *The Shawshank Redemption,* it appears that the American cinematic imagination requires wading through the debris of shame before realizing hope.

Although *The Shawshank Redemption* works with these motifs, the results are quite different from what Paul envisioned. For most of the inmates, the affliction of Shawshank Prison simply confirms the bad character that got them into prison in the first place. Many inmates devote themselves to a continued life of crime, exploiting and raping fellow prisoners and heaping shameful abuse on those who have not yet learned to be institutional men. They continue to deny the secrets of the heart as well as the crimes they have committed. As Red sarcastically remarks, "I'm the only guilty one in here." The typical expression of dishonest character is the inmates' rationalization that they were convicted only because "my lawyer screwed me."

Consistent with his remarkable perseverance in prison, Andy's character remains steady and resilient through most of the film. He courageously refuses the seductions of the rapists, resisting beating after beating without submission. He holds to his convictions despite consequences, especially when he plays Mozart over the loudspeaker. Of all the prisoners, he seems least affected by the wickedness of the environment: he accepts its dehumanizing presence without letting it touch his deepest core. Yet in the end his character too is corrupted.[6] He becomes involved in the crooked schemes of the warden, acknowledging at one point that he entered prison as an honest man, that it took prison to make him a crook. But in the end he manages to turn tables on the wicked warden, stealing all of his ill-gotten gains while exposing him. When he ends up escaping with the "river of dirty money flowing through this place," the filmmakers render his escape palatable to the audience by emphasizing how wicked and hypocritical the warden is and by underlining how desperate, corrupt, and hopeless the prison conditions are. That something good comes out of this ill-gotten wealth should not disguise the fact that Andy has developed a manipulative, dishonest character.

One episode that conforms to the scheme of affliction producing good character occurs when the warden comes in to solitary and claims that Andy's protégé, Tommy, was shot while trying to escape. Tommy was a potential witness whose testimony might have resulted in Andy's freedom. His cellmate in another prison had confessed to the murders for which Andy was falsely convicted. His hopes shattered by Tommy's death, Andy says for the first time that he wants to get out of the money-laundering scheme. Threatening to turn Andy over to the sodomites and to burn the library, the warden imposes another period in solitary confinement. When Andy gets out of solitary, he admits to Red, apparently for the first time, that his wife had said he was a hard man to know, a closed book. He acknowledges that he did not know how to show love to her, and feels that he drove her away into another man's arms, and thereby to her death. Red says that that makes him a bad husband, but not a murderer. This scene signals the emergence of a changed character, one that acknowledges complicity in the tragic murder of his wife. And it comes only after Andy has spent two months in the hole, the ultimate form of affliction that Shawshank Prison is able to apply.

"Character produces hope," Paul writes. At first glance this seems to be a mere repetition. The previous verse urges that Christians should "boast in the hope of the glory of God," suggesting that hope sets off the cycle involving affliction, perseverance, character, and now — hope? What Paul has in mind is that mature hope requires the foundation of the new character, formed in the image of Christ. This character is not merely or even primarily individualistic; it is found in the early Christian communities in which members are formed and reshaped by their common life, and thus rendered capable of resisting and even transforming the circumstances of their everyday life in the slums of Rome. It is under the adverse pressure of such circumstances that mature hope arises,

sustained by the community's mutual support and by its daily rehearsal of the death and resurrection of Christ.

One of the puzzles of *The Shawshank Redemption* is "what creates and sustains Andy's hope and what enables him to infect some with it but not others."[7] A small part of the answer is visible when one reflects on the notion that character produces hope. This is captured in the story of Red, the most responsible and mature character in the film. This dignified man is steady, nonretaliatory, humane and realistic, despite the fact that he steadfastly renounces the kind of hope that sustains Andy. Toward the end of the film, after Andy has made his escape, the parole board meets again and Red is asked this time to sit down for an interview. After forty years and several such interviews, Red admits he has no idea what rehabilitation means. He says he regrets what he did, looks back on the stupid kid who committed that terrible crime, and now would talk some sense to him. For the first time Red provides an honest assessment of his former self. His character has now reformed to the point that the parole board feels it is safe to let him back onto the streets. After finding these streets hard to take for someone who has been an institutional man for forty years, he goes to a gunshop and considers buying a weapon, a purchase that would guarantee his return to Shawshank. Instead, he buys a compass in order to find that rock at the north end of the stone wall. His promise to Andy, which his character will now not allow him to break, has led to his own freedom. The choice of this compass over a gun is a fitting metaphor for the discovery and triumph of hope at the end of the story.

Finally, Paul insists, *"hope does not humiliate, because the love of God has been poured into our hearts through the Holy Spirit given to us."* The key question with regard to hope is whether it will ever be fulfilled; if not, the ultimate humiliation occurs, because the triumph of fate over hope will then have been proven. Life will then be shown to be meaningless. Since hope is directed against shame and humiliation, if it proves illusory, humiliation has no further defense. In Paul's worldview, the future triumph of Christ at the end of time is the ultimate guarantor of hope. But the interim guarantor that protects the heart against humiliation is the "love of God," which continues its detoxifying effect no matter what tribulations ensue. Even if the lives of believers end in tragedy, they will not be humiliated, because the crucified one will be at their side, suffering along with them and helping them to bear their burdens.

That hope does not humiliate, in the sense of disappointing happy expectations, is the main theme of *The Shawshank Redemption,* which features the one person who steadily follows the logic of his hope, regains his freedom, and brings his best friend along as well. The theme of humiliation is developed in other ways throughout the film by the way the prisoners are brutalized by each other and by the prison staff. But humiliation is also seen to be a crucial factor in their crimes, most clearly in Andy's discovery of why his wife and her lover had been shot years before. Tommy's cellmate, Blatch, had told him of having followed a golf pro home, "him and this tasty bitch he was with," who was married to a "hotshot banker." Blatch shot them after the robbery because the golf pro treated him "like dirt." Without the love of Christ that can heal the shame of being treated with contempt, violent retaliation is an all too typical reaction.

Baptism and the Rebirth of the Shamed

It is remarkable in a film so overtly hostile to religion that the metaphor of baptism recurs at two decisive points.[8] A brief recapitulation of the biblical tradition will aid in understanding these details. In Romans 6 baptism is described as the death of the old person. Persons scarred by institutionalization and restricted in dehumanizing ways by the law are washed clean, given a fresh start by sharing in the death of the redeemer. The shameful self is overcome by its inclusion in the shameful death of Christ.

The first baptismal episode in *The Shawshank Redemption* is the hosing down of fresh inmates to turn them into institutional men. They are forced to discard their clothes, brutally hosed down with cold water from a firehose, covered with delousing powder, and given prison garments. Their old self is washed away by a dehumanizing initiation similar to that given to the inmates of the Nazi concentration camps. If their old self is not dead, it will be killed in prison. The man who dares to ask when they will eat after this initiation is brutally beaten; no freedom of speech is allowed for institutionalized men.

The second baptism takes place on the night of Andy's escape when he crawls through 500 yards of sewer and then runs down a creek in the storm. As he stands exultantly under the rain that washes the sewer debris off his body, there is a clear echo of the baptism theme. It is Red who later articulates the theme of a transforming baptismal most cogently: Andy "crawled through 500 yards of shit and came out at the other end as fresh and clean as a newborn baby." As far as his friends in prison are concerned, this transformation is genuine and admirable. Andy becomes the subject of endless later conversation among the inmates, the symbol of their hope for freedom and a retention of their own humanity. But is it a baptism that makes Andy into "an instrument of righteousness" matching Paul's vision (Rom 6:13)?

Conclusion

Despite their similarities, we must ask whether St. Paul's or Andy's story of redemption is more satisfactory in the end. This story of an educated yuppie with a flair for financial manipulation who outwits his captors and escapes alone, with a friend to keep him company, seems uncomfortably similar to the escapist trends in current American society. Is the original story of Christ suffering in behalf of prisoners, the ill, the outsiders, the lame, the halt, and the blind not more satisfactory? Is it not healthier for our society to harbor hopes of redemption that include both rich and poor, both the intelligent and the slow? Moreover, it seems more realistic, in view of Brooks's fate, to acknowledge that a hope that overlooks ambiguity is bound to be deadly. Even after we are paroled from our various forms of bondage, fears and insecurities will remain to haunt us. And while the Pacific ocean has no memory, Mexico certainly does. The escapist vision of an idyllic life there, without any Mexicans in sight or any awareness of their story of institutionalized bondage, seems to be a sad example of ethnocentric American imagination.[9]

Is it not healthier for our culture and for our individual imaginations, which nourish our hopes and dreams, to keep these biblical and cinematic stories in a lively conversation with each other? Should not the blood of Christ, the freedom of the gospel, and the supremacy of love help to inform and shape our hope of redemption? Have we no need to confront the secrets of the heart and resist the deceptions of the flesh, even on a Pacific beach? I say yes, because there remains a substantial truth in Andy's words: "Hope is a good thing . . . and a good thing never dies."

EPILOGUE

12. The Great Code of Scripture: From Shawshank Prison to the Carolina Tides

But what does [scripture] say?
  "The word is near you,
    on your lips and in your heart,"
  that is, the word of faith that we proclaim,
because if you confess "with your lips" the Lord Jesus,
  and have faith "in your heart" that God raised him
      from the dead,
    you shall be saved.
For [a person] has faith in [the] heart toward
      righteousness,
  and confesses by lip toward salvation.
For the scripture says,
  All "who have faith in him will not be put to shame."
For there is no distinction between Jews or Greeks.
  The same one is Lord of all,
[bestowing] riches upon all who call upon him.
  For "all who call upon the name of the Lord will be
    saved."

Romans 10:8-13

179

Introduction

This passage is a classic instance of Paul's interpretation of scripture to make his point about the promise of the gospel. In Rom 10:5 he cites "Moses" as the author of citations from Lev 18:5 and Deut 30:11-14, which he interprets in a typical Rabbinic fashion.[1] In 10:11 he adapts a citation from Isaiah, again altering it by the addition of a word at the beginning of the sentence. The quotation marks in the caption above indicate the scope of his citations, showing that he reinterprets these Old Testament passages in the light of his commitment to Christ's triumph over shame. Now he claims that none of the groups that place their faith in Christ "will be put to shame" (Rom 10:11). This verse resonates with the theme we have been tracing through the ten films of this book. They offer resources to take shame seriously and to move the understanding of the center of Paul's thought beyond the traditional paradigm of individual sin and forgiveness. But how plausible can this be when the films we discuss seem largely hostile to the Bible and its message?

The Dilemma of Scripture

It is highly relevant for our project of interpreting the interplay between scripture and cinema that a film like *The Shawshank Redemption* treats the Bible as an instrument of oppression. When Andy arrives at Shawshank Prison along with other recently convicted felons, they are briefed by the warden, who says he believes in two things — discipline and the Bible. He adds: "Trust in the Lord, and your ass belongs to me." The warden repeatedly cites scripture to justify the brutality and exploitation that mark the prison. When the warden shakes down Andy's cell early in the film, he hands back the Bible, and says "I hate to deprive you of this; salvation lies within."

An even greater irony is the safe in the warden's office hidden behind a plaque with the biblical slogan, "Judgment cometh and right soon!" As Andy places the records and receipts of the prison scams in the safe every night, it is obvious that this slogan simply disguises the record of ill-gotten lucre. It violates every tenet of the biblical accounts of divine judgment. That Andy has grasped this disparity is evident in his jousting with the warden in citing scripture, showing that he has indeed virtually memorized it. Andy cites Mark 13:35, which refers to the master returning when least expected to demand an accounting from his servants, a clear reference to the expectation that the dishonest secrets will be exposed. The warden replies with an evasive citation from John about "those who are in me will not walk in darkness," implying that his piety will prevent exposure. Although the Bible is changed in the film and in a stream of our Christian tradition into an instrument of corrupt oppression, there remains a certainty that this safe will one day be opened and judgment will indeed come. Despite all attempts to co-opt its message, the biblical assurance of judgment prevails.

There is no doubt that the central religious symbol in *The Shawshank Redemption* is the Bible itself. It is a carved-out space inside Andy Defreyne's Bible that hides the little rock hammer with which he prepares his escape. The top page of the carved-out space for the rock hammer is clearly visible to the observant film viewer: it is the title page of the book of Exodus, the biblical story of escape from bondage. After escaping, Andy leaves this Bible for the hypocritical warden, writing a final message on its front page that the warden had spouted, which now has a completely different bearing: "Salvation lies within." A new form of salvation is clearly being offered in this film, one that replaces the intervention of Yahweh at the Exodus and of Christ on the cross. Salvation now comes through the little rock hammer in the hands of an intelligent and determined person who refuses to give up hope in his own capacity to achieve freedom against all the odds.

We see in this and other films the unexamined results of a process of secular derivation that remains critical of biblical religion while continuing to use its redemptive language. Michael Medved is sensitive to some aspects of this issue, pointing to the warden's use of the Bible as "a particularly blatant example of the sort of anti-religious stereotype that's gratuitously insulting at the same time it's dramatically unconvincing."[2] This overlooks the grain of truth in *The Shawshank Redemption*. Those of us who have developed an understanding of the tragic course of Christian civilization must recognize a substantial truth in this critique. After centuries of turning the religion of shameful inmates into a religion of jailors who delight in creating institutionalized people, can we still say that truth lies within the covers of this book? Is the Bible only useful now as a place to hide the tools with which we each must fashion freedom for ourselves? Or can the original power of Christ's shameful death in behalf of the shamed, of the baptism of the shamed that draws believers into the shameful death of Christ, and of the granting of a new identity as God's free sons and daughters, be conveyed to current audiences? Would we be better off abandoning any attachment to the biblical origins of our culture and turning our attention to the secular media alone?

Grace and the Great Code

For the most part, contemporary films are either neutral or overtly hostile to traditional religion. Of the ten films discussed in this book, only two afford any direct role for the community shaped by the Bible, *Babette's Feast* and *Forrest Gump*. While the other films interact more or less directly with biblical ideas, they do not reflect awareness of the proximity. Yet the Bible remains the wellspring of imagination for all of Western culture. As Northrop Frye showed, the Bible provides the "Great Code" of our literary tradition, providing its leading metaphors, language, rhetorical tendencies, typologies, and myths.[3] What Frye identifies as the "central myth of the Bible . . . the myth of deliverance"[4] has a particular bearing on the realm of cinema, because the "primary and model form" of the various types of redemptive stories "is the deliverance from Egypt,"[5] a story of release from shameful bondage. Speaking of the American scene, Randall Stewart claimed that "the Bible has been the greatest single influence on our literature. Our writers, almost without exception, have been steeped in biblical imagery, phrasing, and cadences."[6] My impression is that a similar claim could be made about the cinema.

The language and metaphors of the Bible still retain their power in some of our most secular artifacts, as evident in the themes of shame, grace, conversion, love, and hope adapted in these ten films. We have encountered a kind of exodus from bondage in *The Shawshank Redemption*, with the intervention of Yahweh at the Red Sea replaced by a tiny hammer. In *Unforgiven* we found a story of the violent conquest of evil that was ultimately derived from the Old Testament, but filtered through generations of American imagination. We have reflected on several varieties of the story of redemption, adapted from biblical paradigms, in *The Prince of Tides*, *Groundhog Day*, *Edge of the City*, *The Shawshank Redemption*, and *The Firm*. In *Babe* we encountered an embodiment of classic biblical admonitions about honoring the lowly because such redemption has established a radical kind of equality.

The preoccupation with issues of honor and shame that we found in these films does not match the dominant interpretive tradition as accurately as it reflects the Bible itself. While the Bible frequently depicts divine grace as rescuing people from shameful captivity, bringing down the proud and exalting the lowly, and welcoming outsiders into the messianic banquet, the dominant interpretive tradition concentrates on formulas and ceremonies of individual guilt and forgiveness. How is it possible that secular artifacts like movies offer a grasp of a side of the Great Code that traditional theologians have overlooked? A brief examination of the caption at the head of this chapter suggests an answer.

Confessing the Lord Jesus

The references to confessing Jesus as Lord in Rom 10:9 and to having "faith" in the gospel that leads to righteousness in 10:10 sound like the stereotypical formulas of dogmatic Christianity: "If you confess 'with your lips' the Lord Jesus, and have faith 'in your heart' that God raised him from the dead, you shall be saved." These verses have been so frequently cited by stern preachers, so often echoed on religious billboards, that their liberating link to triumph over shame has become opaque. In a profound subversion of the original message of redeeming grace, they now convey the message that making the right confession with the right words is the ultimate method of gaining honor. In the threatening rhetoric of some preachers, any failure to employ the proper formula of "confessing Christ as savior and Lord" casts one in the situation of final shame. In the most extreme form of this subversion, religious extremists follow the pre-Christian Saul in persecuting nonconformists. They can be as remorseless as Will Munny in *Unforgiven,* as hypocritical as Warden Norden in *The Shawshank Redemption.*

What this dogmatic approach overlooks is that *the shamed, crucified one* is confessed here to be the Lord, and that it was precisely the demand for religious and moral conformity that led to his death. In his crucifixion the entire realm of gaining honor through meeting the conditions of approved behavior and belief was overthrown. Just as in *Edge of the City,* the decisive factor is not our having "accomplished something so someone can love us," but the death of the shamed one on our behalf. And the salvation gained thereby is not a guaranteed place in heaven, but a new life aimed "toward righteousness" (Rom 10:10). Those committed to divine righteousness will inevitably be led into more and more dangerous forms of affliction as they attempt to face their responsibilities, just as in the stories of the Apostle Paul and of Axel Nordman in *Edge of the City.* They will set about doing "good to all persons" as in Galatians and in *Groundhog Day.* They will be compelled to follow the dictates of love as in 1 Corinthians 13 and in *Forrest Gump.* They will be inspired by 1 Corinthians 11 and by *Babette's Feast* to invite unworthy outsiders into their banquets. They will abandon the route of letters authenticating their orthodoxy and charisma in order to follow the logic of 2 Corinthians 3 and of *Mr. Holland's Opus* by helping the shamed to find their voices.

Our reflections on the interplay between these movies and biblical texts help to sharpen the distinctions that should be made in the interpretation of "confession" and "faith" in the passage used as the caption for this chapter. To "confess" the "Lord Jesus" is not to make a dogmatic claim about his status but to reveal one's own identity. A "confession" in this biblical sense is a "slogan of identification" that marks someone "as belonging to Jesus."[7] Since

Jesus was the crucified one, the confession of Rom 10:9 claims solidarity in shame. It binds the speaker to someone else in final loyalty.[8] To refer to Jesus as Lord ". . . denotes an attitude of subserviency and sense of belongingness or devotion to the one so named."[9] This kind of confession designates to whom the speaker is committed but does not determine what attitude others should take. In contrast to the later development of formulaic "confessions" in the Christian tradition, Paul had no intention of making this confession into a claim of honorable status that raises the speaker above others, using required language that others must employ to avoid peril. To "confess" in this context is also far removed from the traditional connotation in our culture, in which "confession of sins/guilt" is the dominant usage.

To "have faith 'in your heart' that God raised [Jesus] from the dead" (Rom 10:9) reflects the same distinctions found in the use of "confess." If the resurrection of Christ really occurred, it confirms that the shamefully crucified one is the divinely authenticated Lord. But no universal claim about the facticity of the resurrection is intended here. The faith is "in your heart," therefore indicating that a "deeply motivating belief . . . is in view and not merely a recitation of creedal form."[10] To have such a belief is not to make any claim of superiority. It is rather evidence of having abandoned the traditional systems of earning honor and avoiding shame, because this Lord has the marks of the shameful cross on his resurrected body. The key question, therefore, is what is "in your heart."

The Condition of the Heart

The threefold reference to "heart" in Rom 10:8-10 shows that for Paul faith is more than a head trip. It is more than a set of beliefs. It is related to the condition of the heart, that motivating center of mind, emotion, experience, and purpose. This is a realm ordinarily dominated by shameful secrets that faith in Christ crucified has the power to expose. As this text proclaims, the redeeming "'word is near you, on your lips and in your heart,' that is, the word of faith that we proclaim" (Rom 10:8). Paul knows that the Romans have been living out this faith, that it is deeply anchored in their converted hearts, and thus that they will recognize its consistency with the "word of faith" that the letter to the Romans proclaims. He gives priority here to the message fastened deeply in the heart; it is already "near" them.

I think the message of triumph over shame in many recent films is somewhat comparable to what Paul had in mind. Informed by a culture whose early shaping was on the pattern of the Great Code, and particularly sensitive to the issues of honor and shame, these films may comprise the most significant "preparation for the gospel" in our time. They are "near" to us at the emotional level, where shame and honor are guarded, and where traditional religion is usually unable to penetrate. In the privacy of the theater we are enabled to gaze at shamed faces in ways that could be genuinely transforming.

We have explored this process of redemptive exposure in connection with *The Prince of Tides*. We were challenged by Paul's vision of other people as the letters written "on our heart" in connection with *Mr. Holland's Opus*. We saw the process of a heart overcoming its illusions and redirecting its energies toward the service of others in *Groundhog Day*. We encountered a compelling embodiment of "an unprejudiced heart" in *Babe,* as the contours of civility and honoring the lowly were explored in connection with Romans 12. The crucial indication that a heart has really been transformed by the gospel of grace is whether it now has room for the shamed. Since it is really the heart of a community that is in view here, the litmus test is whether the welcome of grace includes those against whom society discriminates.

No Distinction between Jews or Greeks

In Rom 10:12 Paul reiterates his conviction that Christ has erased the boundaries of honor and shame: "For there is no distinction between Jews or Greeks. The same one is Lord of all, [bestowing] riches upon all who call upon him." The social distinctions that marked the Greco-Roman world have been eliminated by Christ, whose crucifixion and resurrection revealed that he is "Lord of all." His shameful death on behalf of the shamed, which exposed the pretensions of those whom the world honors, was shown through the resurrection to have revolutionary social consequences. As Franz Leenhardt remarks, "All, whoever they may be, must renounce all claim to their own righteousness. . . ."[11] Social discrimination is now illegitimate. The "riches" of divine favor, which traditional religion has always believed would be bestowed only on the honorable, is now bestowed impartially "upon all who call upon him." It is not that such a "call," "confession," and "faith" qualify a particular individual or community for the blessings. It is rather that only those willing to accept solidarity with the shamed are in a position to receive such blessings. To "call upon" this particular Lord is to acknowledge and traverse the abyss of national, familial, and personal shame and in the words of *The Shawshank Redemption,* to come out "at the other end as fresh and clean as a newborn baby."

The theme of "no distinction" is carried out in each of the films treated in this book. In *Babette's Feast* the unworthy are invited to the banquet. The interaction between the film and the love feast in Corinth stimulates us to reflect on the potential of potluck meals celebrated as the Lord's Supper to overcome shameful discrimination in its various forms. The shameful secrets in *The Prince of Tides* are overcome by exposure in the context of unconditional regard, allowing a grace that accepts each person and family to have its redemptive effect. In *Edge of the City* a black family can therefore be allowed to provide redemptive welcome for a white misfit, even in the imagination of 1957, long before anyone thought of political correctness. Forrest Gump can be depicted as having Bubba Blue as his best friend in the army, despite the black pigment of his skin. The relations between discriminated species can be transformed into the civility of equality and grace in *Babe,* which places pigs and sheep on an equal level with sophisticated and dominant dogs. The need for the violent resolution of shame as embodied in *Unforgiven* therefore disappears.

No One Put to Shame

In Rom 10:11 Paul quotes Isa 28:16 about believers not being put to shame, but adds the word "all" to the beginning: "All 'who have faith in him will not be put to shame.'" Although this is difficult to translate, its inclusivity is unmistakable. With this one word, "all," the smear of shame is removed from the entire human race. Whether Jew or Greek, barbarian or Roman, slave or free, male or female, no persons or groups "who have faith in him will be put to shame." But as we noted above, such faith is not self-honorific. The right confession and properly defined faith do not earn this triumph of not being "put to shame," despite centuries of twisted, self-serving theology. To "call on the name" of this Lord (Rom 10:13) is to abandon any claim of already possessing honor and to take one's place alongside the dishonored shepherd and his disheveled flock. It is not the formulation of this faith that is decisive but a reliance on the kind of grace that "makes no conditions and singles out none of us in particular . . . takes us all to its bosom and proclaims general amnesty," to use the words of the general in *Babette's Feast*. To return to Paul's wording, "All who call upon the name of the Lord will be saved."

Does this include even the wolves, echoing the Isaianic prophecy of the messianic peace, that "the wolf shall live with the lamb" (Isa 11:6)? The story of Rex in *Babe* says so. Does it include crooked lawyers like Mitch and Andy? *The Firm* and *The Shawshank Redemption* say so. Does it include twisted, religious fanatics? *Babette's Feast* says yes. Does it include imbeciles and victims of AIDS? *Forrest Gump* affirms both. Or do all such shameful people need to be shot down in the Big Whiskey saloon, as *Unforgiven* suggests?

Many of these and other films, in their own ways, "call upon the name of the Lord" (Rom 10:13) in modern idiom and images. Eschewing the language of traditional confessions of faith, they hold to a deeper and more fundamental vision of grace triumphing over shame. For, as Paul says, the crucified one bestows "riches upon all who call upon him" (Rom 10:12), riches more satisfying than the truffles and turtle that Babette prepares, or the fare that makes Axel and TT feel "ten feet tall." If we were to grasp the deeper message of Paul and these films, the riches of grace would extend past the pigs and the sheep and the dogs to ourselves, and even, in time, to the lower forms like Malek, the wolf at the *Edge of the City*. If we could take this message of triumph over shame to heart while confessing the crucified one with our lips, we might find that it would, in the words of *Babe*'s narrator, "change our valley forever."

Notes

Notes to Chapter 1

1. Cited by John Easton, "Reel Scholarship," *University of Chicago Magazine*, April 1997, 26.

2. The material in this first section is adapted from Robert Jewett, *Saint Paul at the Movies: The Apostle's Dialogue with American Culture* (Louisville: Westminster John Knox, 1993), 7-12.

3. E. A. Judge, "The Conflict of Educational Aims in New Testament Thought," *Journal of Christian Education* 9 (1966): 39.

4. In "Conflict of Educational Aims," Judge cites Tacitus, *Annals* 4.38.20, "Disregard of fame leads to one's virtues being disregarded."

5. Judge, "Conflict of Educational Aims," 38-39; he cites Sallust, *Bellum Jugurthinum* 85.26, "Reticence would only cause people to mistake modesty for a guilty conscience."

6. E. A. Judge, "Roman Literary Memorials," *Proceedings of the Ninth Congress of the Australian Universities' Language and Literature* (Melbourne, 1964): 28.

7. Judge, "Roman Literary Memorials."

8. Ulrich Knoche, "Der römische Ruhmesgedanke," *Philologus* 89 (1934): 102-34. Reprint in H. Oppermann, ed., *Römische Wertbegriffe* (Darmstadt: Wissenschaftliche Buchgesellschaft, 1983), 420-45 (quotation from p. 424).

9. See Hans Drexler, *"Honos," Romanitas* 3 (1961): 135-57. Reprint in Oppermann, ed., *Römische Wertbegriffe*, 446-67, esp. 455.

10. See particularly Halvor Moxnes, " 'He Saw That the City Was Full of Idols' (Acts 17:16): Visualizing the World of the First Christians," in D. Hellholm, H. Moxnes, and T. K. Seim, eds., *Mighty Minorities? Minorities in Early Christianity — Positions and Strategies: Essays in Honour of Jacob Jervell on*

His 70th Birthday, 21 May 1995 (Oslo: Scandinavian University Press, 1995), 107-31, especially the section on "Cities as Culture — Honour and Shame," 114-18.

11. Philo, *Embassy to Gaius.* 145-54.

12. *Acts of Augustus* 6.34.

13. Dieter Georgi, *Theocracy in Paul's Praxis and Theology,* trans. David E. Green (Minneapolis: Fortress, 1991), 86.

14. Everett Ferguson, *Backgrounds of Early Christianity,* 2d ed. (Grand Rapids: Eerdmans, 1993), 197.

15. Georgi, *Theocracy,* 87.

16. See especially J. Rufus Fears, "The Cult of Jupiter and Roman Imperial Ideology" and "The Theology of Victory at Rome: Approaches and Problems," in *Aufstieg und Niedergang der Römischen Welt,* II.17.2, ed. H. Temporini (Berlin: de Gruyter, 1981), 1-141 and 737-826, respectively.

17. Velleius Paterculus, *History of Rome* 2.131.1.

18. Cicero, *De Natura Deorum* 2.3.8., cited by Burkhard Gladigow, "Roman Religion," in *The Anchor Bible Dictionary,* vol. 5 (New York: Doubleday, 1992), 815, with reference to the Roman claim to be the "most religious of mortals."

19. James D. G. Dunn, *Romans 1–8,* Word Biblical Commentary 38a (Dallas: Word, 1988), 145.

20. Dunn, *Romans 1–8,* 159.

21. Dunn, *Romans 1–8,* 160.

22. See Walter Bauer, *A Greek-English Lexicon of the New Testament and Other Early Christian Literature,* ed. William F. Arndt and F. Wilbur Gingrich, 2d ed. (Chicago: University of Chicago Press, 1979), 849, s.v. *hystereō.*

23. Fréderic Godet, *Commentary on St. Paul's Epistle to the Romans,* trans. A. Cusin; rev. and ed. T. W. Chambers (New York: Funk & Wagnals, 1883; reprint, Grand Rapids: Kregel, 1977), 148.

24. 2 Cor 11:5; see Chapters 7-9 in Jewett, *Saint Paul at the Movies,* for a discussion of the conflict with the Corinthian superapostles.

25. Dunn, *Romans 1–8,* 168.

26. Richard B. Hays, "Justification," in *The Anchor Bible Dictionary,* vol. 3 (New York: Doubleday, 1992), 1131; see Peter Stuhlmacher, *Paul's Letter to the Romans: A Commentary,* trans. S. J. Hafemann (Louisville: Westminster John Knox, 1994), 31.

27. Halvor Moxnes, "Honour and Righteousness in Romans," *Journal for the Study of the New Testament* 32 (1988): 71. Unfortunately Moxnes goes on to claim that "It is the particular boasting of the Jew, not something which is common to Jews and Gentiles, which Paul attacks. . . . Paul sees a direct connection between boasting and the Jewish Law. . . ." This overlooks the clear implication of the earlier argument of Romans, which makes it plain that all humans are involved in seeking honor that belongs to God alone, and that they all thereby forfeit their share of the "glory of God."

28. See Ulrich Heckel's discussion of the pejorative use of "Gentile" in "Das Bild der Heiden und die Identität der Christen bei Paulus," in R. Feldme-

ier and U. Heckel, eds., *Die Heiden: Juden, Christen und das Problem des Fremden,* Wissenschaftliche Untersuchungen zum Neuen Testament 70 (Tübingen: Mohr Siebeck, 1994), 269-96, esp. 270-72.

29. Yves Albert Dauge, *Le Barbare: Recherches sur la conception romaine de la barbarie et de la civilisation,* Collection Latomus 176 (Brussels: Latomus, 1981), 393-810, showing that the term "barbarian" in Roman materials serves to depict outsiders as irrational, ferocious, warlike, alienated, chaotic, and in all respects the opposite of the civilized Roman.

30. Ernst Käsemann, *Commentary on Romans,* trans. Geoffrey W. Bromiley (Grand Rapids: Eerdmans, 1980), 20.

31. See James C. Walters, *Ethnic Issues in Paul's Letter to the Romans* (Valley Forge, Penn.: Trinity Press International, 1993), 68-79.

32. See the provocative study by Gregory M. Corrigan, "Paul's Shame for the Gospel," *Biblical Theology Bulletin* 16 (1986): 23-27 and Steve Mason, "'For I Am Not Ashamed of the Gospel' (Rom. 1.16: The Gospel and the First Readers of Romans)," in L. Anne Jervis and Peter Richardson, eds., *Gospel in Paul: Studies on Corinthians, Galatians, and Romans for Richard N. Longenecker,* Journal for the Study of the New Testament — Supplement Series 108 (Sheffield: Sheffield Academic Press, 1994), 254-87.

33. See Raymond Pickett, *The Cross in Corinth: The Social Significance of the Death of Jesus,* Journal for the Study of the New Testament — Supplement Series 143 (Sheffield: Sheffield Academic Press, 1997), 97-107; Alexandra R. Brown, *The Cross and Human Transformation: Paul's Apocalyptic Word in 1 Corinthians* (Minneapolis: Fortress, 1995), 75-148.

34. Joel Marcus, "The Circumcision and Uncircumcision in Rome," *New Testament Studies* 35 (1989): 78.

35. See David D. Gilmore, ed., *Honor and Shame and the Unity of the Mediterranean* (Washington D.C.: American Anthropological Association, 1987); Bruce J. Malina, *The New Testament World: Insights from Cultural Anthropology* (Atlanta: John Knox, 1981), 25-50; idem, *Christian Origins and Cultural Anthropology: Practical Models for Biblical Interpretation* (Atlanta: John Knox, 1986); Jerome H. Neyrey, *Paul in Other Words: A Cultural Reading of His Letters* (Louisville: Westminster John Knox, 1990); Victor H. Matthews and Don C. Benjamin, eds., *Honor and Shame in the World of the Bible,* Semeia 68 (Atlanta: Scholars Press, 1996); Robert Atkins, "Pauline Theology and Shame Affect: Reading a Social Location," *Listening* 31 (1996): 137-51.

36. Malina, *New Testament World,* 27.

37. Malina, *New Testament World,* 29.

38. Malina, *New Testament World,* 32.

39. Malina, *New Testament World,* 55.

40. Bruce J. Malina and Jerome H. Neyrey, *Portraits of Paul: An Archaeology of Ancient Personality* (Louisville: Westminster John Knox, 1996).

41. David Arthur deSilva, *Despising Shame: Honor Discourse and Community Maintenance in the Epistle to the Hebrews,* Society of Biblical Literature Dissertation Series 152 (Atlanta: Scholars Press, 1995); idem, "'Worthy of His King-

dom': Honor Discourse and Social Engineering in 1 Thessalonians," *Journal for the Study of the New Testament* 64 (1996): 49-79.

42. Arthur J. Dewey, "A Matter of Honor: A Social-historical Analysis of 2 Corinthians 10," *Harvard Theological Review* 78 (1985): 209-17.

43. John H. Elliott, "Disgraced Yet Graced: The Gospel According to 1 Peter in the Key of Honor and Shame," *Biblical Theological Bulletin* 25 (1995): 166-78.

44. Moxnes, "Honour and Righteousness in Romans," 63.

45. Moxnes, "Honour and Righteousness in Romans," 62.

46. Romans 1:24, 26; 2:7, 10, 23; 9:21; 12:10.

47. Romans 1:16, 27; 5:5; 6:21; 9:33; 10:11.

48. Romans 1:21, 23; 2:7, 10; 3:7, 23; 4:20; 5:2; 6:4; 8:18, 21, 30; 9:4, 23; 11:30, 36; 15:6, 7, 9; 16:27.

49. Romans 2:29; 13:3; 15:11.

50. Romans 2:17, 23; 3:27; 4:2; 5:2, 3, 11; 15:17.

51. Moxnes, "Honour and Righteousness in Romans," 64.

Notes to Chapter 2

1. See Peter Lampe, "The Corinthian Eucharistic Dinner Party: Exegesis of a Cultural Context (1 Cor 11:17-34)," *Affirmation* 4 (1991): 1-15; Robert Jewett, "Tenement Churches and Communal Meals in the Early Church: The Implications of a Form-Critical Analysis of 2 Thessalonians 3:10," *Biblical Research* 38 (1993): 23-43; idem, "Tenement Churches and Pauline Love Feasts," *Quarterly Review* 14 (1994): 43-58; and idem, *Paul the Apostle to America: Cultural Trends and Pauline Scholarship* (Louisville: Westminster John Knox, 1994), Chapter 6.

2. *The Prince of Tides* was released by Columbia Pictures in 1991. It was produced and directed by Barbra Streisand. The screenplay, by Pat Conroy and Becky Johnson, was based on the novel by Conroy. The video is available through Columbia Tristar Home Video, 1992. This film received seven nominations for Academy Awards in 1991.

3. Hans Conzelmann, *1 Corinthians: A Commentary on the First Epistle to the Corinthians*, trans. James W. Leitch; bibliography and references by James W. Dunkly; ed. George W. MacRae (Philadelphia: Fortress, 1974), 244.

4. F. F. Bruce, *1 and 2 Corinthians*, New Century Bible (London: Oliphants, 1971), 133; see also C. K. Barrett, *A Commentary on the First Epistle to the Corinthians*, Harpers New Testament Commentaries (New York: Harper & Row, 1968), 326.

5. See Krister Stendahl, "The Apostle Paul and the Introspective Conscience of the West," in *Paul Among Jews and Gentiles and Other Essays* (Philadelphia: Fortress, 1976), 78-96.

6. Rudolf Bultmann, *"aischynō,"* in *Theological Dictionary of the New Testament*, vol. 1, ed. Gerhard Kittel; trans. and ed. Geoffrey W. Bromiley (Grand Rapids: Eerdmans, 1964), 189.

7. Rudolf Bultmann, *"aidōs,"* in *Theological Dictionary of the New Testament,* vol. 1, 170.

8. Axel Horstmann, *"aischynomai,"* in *Exegetical Dictionary of the New Testament,* vol. 1, ed. Horst Balz and Gerhard Schneider (Grand Rapids: Eerdmans, 1990), 42.

9. Albrecht Oepke, *"kryptō,"* in *Theological Dictionary of the New Testament,* vol. 3, 957.

10. Georgia Brown writes in *Village Voice,* 24 December 1991, 72 that "The Wingos' main debility . . . is shame and fatal silence."

11. Jack Matthews, review of *The Prince of Tides, Newsday,* 24 December 1991, sec. 2, p. 47.

12. Bob Condor, "To Be Honest," *Chicago Tribune,* 22 April 1997, Tempo section, p. 1; see Brad Blanton, *Radical Honesty* (New York: Dell, 1997).

13. Condor, "To Be Honest," 7.

14. Barrett, *1 Corinthians,* 326: "something like the Bacchic frenzy of men believed to be overpowered and used by a supernatural force."

15. Karl Olav Sandnes, "Prophecy — A Sign for Believers (1 Cor 14,20-25)," *Biblica* 77 (1996): 15.

16. Joop F. M. Smit, "Tongues and Prophecy: Deciphering 1 Cor 14:22," *Biblica* 75 (1994): 184.

17. Carolyn Osiek, "Christian Prophecy: Once Upon a Time?" *Currents in Theology and Mission* 17 (1990): 293.

18. Walter Rebell, "Gemeinde als Missionsfaktor im Urchristentum: 1 Kor 14:24f als Schlüsselsituation," *Theologische Zeitschrift* 44 (1988): 124-32.

19. Rebell, "Gemeinde," 132.

20. This scene "struck a deep chord" in director Barbra Streisand, according to James Spada in *Streisand: Her Life* (New York: Ivy, 1992), 504: " 'That happened to me in therapy,' she recalled. 'My therapist touched my hand and I just broke down. I thought at the time, This must be what it feels like to be held by your mother.' "

21. See Gordon D. Fee, *The First Epistle to the Corinthians* (Grand Rapids: Eerdmans, 1987), 687; Graydon F. Snyder, *First Corinthians: A Faith Community Commentary* (Macon: Mercer, 1992), 285.

22. Archibald Robertson and Alfred Plummer, *A Critical and Exegetical Commentary on the First Epistle of St. Paul to the Corinthians* (Edinburgh: Clark, 1911), 318.

23. See also Fee, *1 Corinthians,* 686: "These two verbs [in 1 Cor 14:25] together imply the deep probing work of the Holy Spirit in people's lives, exposing their sins and thus calling them to account before the living God."

24. While Jami Bernard raises the question about what the psychiatric "ethics committee" might say about Lowenstein's "sleeping with her prized patient's twin" (review of *The Prince of Tides, New York Post,* 24 December 1991, 19), Janet Maslin is content to criticize the "gooey overtones" of this episode (" 'The Prince of Tides' Sidesteps Book's Pitfalls," *New York Times,* 25 December 1991, 13).

Notes to Chapter 3

1. *Babette's Feast* was directed by Gabriel Axel and produced by Just Betzer/Panorama Film International in cooperation with Nordisk Film A/S and the Danish Film Institute, 1987. The video is available through Orion Home Video, 1988. It received the Academy Award in 1987 for the Best Foreign Language Film, the first time a Danish film received this award.

2. See the recent study by Judith Crain, "The Communal Meal as Sacrament: 'Babette's Feast,' I Corinthians 11, and the Church Today" (M.T.S. Thesis, Garrett-Evangelical Theological Seminary, 1991).

3. Lynn Darling, review of *Babette's Feast, Newsday,* 1 October 1987, sec. 2, p. 7.

4. James M. Wall, "Seeking the Embodying of Our Hints of Truth," *The Christian Century* 105 (June 8-15, 1988): 563; cited by Crain, "Communal Meal," 19. See also Otis Carl Edwards, Jr., "Exempla V," *Anglican Theological Review* 72 (1990): 94: "The celebration of the founder's anniversary became a messianic banquet in which the peace of the endtime was experienced proleptically."

5. See Martin Hengel, *Crucifixion in the Ancient World and the Folly of the Message of the Cross* (Philadelphia: Fortress, 1977); Peter Stuhlmacher, "Eighteen Theses on Paul's Theology of the Cross," in *Reconciliation, Law, and Righteousness,* trans. E. R. Kalin (Philadelphia: Fortress, 1988), 155-68.

6. Raymond Pickett, *The Cross in Corinth: The Social Significance of the Death of Jesus,* Journal for the Study of the New Testament — Supplement Series 143 (Sheffield: Sheffield Academic Press, 1997), 123-24: "In remembering Jesus' death on a cross, the community is remembering one who is a victim of shame."

7. Francis J. Moloney comes close to this idea in the title of his article, "The Eucharist as Jesus' Presence to the Broken," *Pacifica* 2 (1989), but he does not articulate the dimension of shame in describing the tendency of the rich to humiliate the "have nots" (p. 168).

8. See Geoffrey M. Hill, *Illuminating Shadows: The Mythic Power of Film* (Boston: Shambhala, 1992), 148 and Clive Marsh, "Did You Say 'Grace'? Eating in Community in *Babette's Feast,*" *Explorations in Theology and Film: Movies and Meaning,* ed. C. Marsh and G. Ortiz (Oxford: Blackwell, 1997), 214.

9. Gerd Theissen, *The Social Setting of Pauline Christianity: Essays on Corinth,* ed. and trans. and with an introduction by John H. Schütz (Philadelphia: Fortress, 1982).

10. Peter Marshall, *Enmity in Corinth: Social Conventions in Paul's Relations with the Corinthians* (Tübingen: Mohr Siebeck, 1987), 283.

11. Pickett, *Cross in Corinth,* 42.

12. Pickett, *Cross in Corinth,* 120.

13. See Bradley B. Blue's discussion of "Commensality and Social Classes" in "The House Church in Corinth and the Lord's Supper: Famine, Food Supply, and the Present Distress," *Criswell Theological Review* 5 (1991): 221-39.

14. Isak Dinesen, *Babette's Feast and Other Anecdotes of Destiny* (New York: Vintage, 1988), 40-41.

15. Cited from the screenplay by Diane Tolomeo Edwards, "Babette's Feast, Sacramental Grace, and the Saga of Redemption," *Christianity and Literature* 42 (1993): 424.

16. Edwards, "Exempla V," 91.

17. Edwards, "Babette's Feast, Sacramental Grace, and the Saga of Redemption," 425.

18. Eva Kissin, review of *Babette's Feast, Films in Review,* 7 June 1988, 358.

19. Rob Baker, "Babette's Feast," *Parabola* 15 (1990): 89.

20. Edwards, "Exempla V," 93.

21. Dinesen, *Babette's Feast and Other Anecdotes of Destiny,* 27; cited by Baker, "Babette's Feast," 89.

22. Dinesen, *Babette's Feast and Other Anecdotes of Destiny,* 41-42.

23. David Denby, review of *Babette's Feast, New York Magazine,* 7 March 1988, 101.

24. Edwards, "Babette's Feast," 430.

25. Richard Schickel, review of *Babette's Feast, Time,* 7 March 1988, 72.

26. Cited by Rob Baker, "Babette's Feast," 88.

27. Peter Lampe, "The Corinthian Eucharistic Dinner Party: Exegesis of a Cultural Context," *Affirmation* 4 (1991): 2-3; Hans Josef Klauck, "Presence in the Lord's Supper: 1 Corinthians 11:23-26 in the Context of Hellenistic Religious History," in Ben F. Meyer, ed., *One Loaf, One Cup: Ecumenical Studies of 1 Cor 11 and Other Eucharistic Texts,* New Gospel Studies 6 (Macon, Ga.: Mercer, 1993), 64-66.

28. Although untouched by reflections on the dimensions of honor and shame, Klauck makes clear that the "principal mode" of Christ's presence in the Lord's Supper is "as head of the table and host who summons his own to the meal. . . . All without distinction were to receive gifts from his hand. That is, in essence, a dimension of the designation of the Lord's Supper as *kyriakon deipnon,* 'the Lordly (= belonging to the Lord) Supper' in 1 Cor 11:20" ("Presence in the Lord's Supper," 69-70).

Notes to Chapter 4

1. The rhetorical structure of this passage is adapted from Johannes Weiss, "Beiträge zur Paulinischen Rhetorik," in *Theologische Studien: Festschrift für Bernhard Weiss,* ed. C. R. Gregory et al. (Göttingen: Vandenhoeck & Ruprecht, 1897), 197-200.

2. *Forrest Gump* is a Paramount Pictures release of a Steve Tish/Wender Finerman production, 1994, directed by Robert Zemeckis. The screenplay was by Eric Roth, based on the novel by Winston Groom. The video was released by Paramount Pictures. *Forrest Gump* received six Academy Awards, including

Best Picture and Best Director. It had been nominated for six additional awards, making it the most celebrated film in 1994.

3. Gerald Forshey, "What Must I Do to Be Saved?" (paper presented at the seventeenth annual meeting of the Popular Culture Association, April 15, 1995), 5. See also Harry Pearson, Jr., *Films in Review*, 12 November 1994, 60: "It is, at heart, a fairy tale about American Innocence, i.e., our belief that an unspoiled child lives at the center of each of us."

4. Gordon D. Fee, *The First Epistle to the Corinthians* (Grand Rapids: Eerdmans, 1987), 626-28.

5. Margaret M. Mitchell, *Paul and the Rhetoric of Reconciliation: An Exegetical Investigation of the Language and Composition of 1 Corinthians* (Louisville: Westminster John Knox, 1993); see also Oda Wischmeyer, *Der höchste Weg: Das 13. Kapitel des 1. Korintherbriefes* (Gütersloh: Gerd Mohn, 1981).

6. On the text-critical question of why 1 Cor 13:3 should read "that I should boast," found in the earliest and most reliable manuscripts, rather than the option preferred in many modern translations, "that I should burn," see Fee, *Corinthians*, 633-34 and Bruce M. Metzger, *A Textual Commentary on the Greek New Testament* (London: United Bible Societies, 1971), 563-64.

7. See Fee's discussion of the verb *psōmisō*, "to feed by putting little bits into the mouth," in *Corinthians*, 633.

8. Fee, *Corinthians*, 634 cites Clement of Rome's letter to the church in Corinth (*1 Clement*) 55:2, "We know of many among us who have delivered themselves to bondage in order to ransom others; many have sold themselves into slavery and used the price paid for themselves to feed others," using the same verb for feeding morsels as used in 1 Cor 13:3.

9. In his great treatise on Christian love, *Agape and Eros*, trans. Philip S. Watson (Philadelphia: Westminster, 1953), Anders Nygren defines *agapē* as "a love described by God's love in Christ on the cross" (cited by Graydon F. Snyder, *First Corinthians: A Faith Community Commentary* [Macon, Ga.: Mercer University Press, 1992], 174).

10. Adolf von Harnack, "The Apostle Paul's Hymn of Love (1 Cor. XIII) and its Religious-Historical Significance," *The Expositor* 8, no. 3 (1912): 404.

11. Sidney E. Mead, *The Nation with the Soul of a Church* (New York: Harper & Row, 1975). See also Nathan O. Hatch and Mark A. Noll, eds., *The Bible in America: Essays in Cultural History* (New York: Oxford University Press, 1982); Gerald R. McDermott, *One Holy and Happy Society: The Public Theology of Jonathan Edwards* (University Park: Pennsylvania University Press, 1992).

12. See Josiah Royce, *The Basic Writings of Josiah Royce*, vol. 2, ed. John J. McDermott (Chicago: University of Chicago Press, 1969), 1149-63.

13. Jonathan Romney, review of *Forrest Gump*, *New Statesman and Society*, 14 October 1994, 41. Michael Medved offers a clearer vision of the moral dimension of love in his review of the film in the *New York Post*, 16 July 1994, 33.

14. Fee, *Corinthians*, 636.

15. Fee, *Corinthians*, 637.

16. Fee, *Corinthians*, 637; Hans Conzelmann, *1 Corinthians: A Commentary on the First Epistle to the Corinthians*, trans. James W. Leitch; bibliography and references by James W. Dunkly; ed. George W. MacRae (Philadelphia: Fortress, 1974), 224.

17. Archibald Robertson and Alfred Plummer, *A Critical and Exegetical Commentary on the First Epistle of St Paul to the Corinthians*, 2d ed. (Edinburgh: Clark, 1914), 295.

18. Jean Héring, *The First Epistle of Saint Paul to the Corinthians*, trans. A. W. Heathcote and P. J. Allcock (London: Epworth, 1962), 141; similarly Fee, *Corinthians*, 639, suggests the translation "in everything" or "always." It might be better to call this an "accusative of respect" or "of extent," using the categories of F. Blass, A. Debrunner, and Robert W. Funk, *A Greek Grammar of the New Testament and Other Early Christian Literature* (Chicago: University of Chicago Press, 1961), §§ 160-61, pp. 87-89.

19. Fee, *Corinthians*, 640.

20. I am therefore not convinced that Forrest Gump is simply "a kind of holy fool who succeeds brilliantly in life while nominally wiser folk get all bollixed up," to use Kenneth Turan's words in his review of the film in the *Los Angeles Times*, 6 July 1994, Calendar section, p. 1. See also the review by David Denby, *New York Magazine*, 50.

21. The most likely translation of the term *epiousios* in the Lord's Prayer is "tomorrow's" bread, referring to the banquet of the kingdom of God. See Joachim Jeremias, *New Testament Theology: The Proclamation of Jesus* (New York: Charles Scribner's Sons, 1971), 200; see also Robert Jewett, *Jesus Against the Rapture: Seven Unexpected Prophecies* (Philadelphia: Westminster, 1979), 122-38.

22. The idea of the reign of God as a banquet was developed in Isaiah's prophecy about the messianic age. In Isa 25:6-8 we have a picture of a future banquet that God will host to unite all the peoples on earth, overcoming the symbolic shroud that separates nation from nation, race from race, family from family.

> On this mountain the LORD of hosts will make for all peoples
> > a feast of rich food, a feast of well-aged wines,
> of rich food filled with marrow,
> > of well-aged wines strained clear.
> And he will destroy on this mountain
> > the shroud that is cast over all peoples,
> a sheet that is spread over all nations;
> > he will swallow up death forever.

23. Stephen Brown, "Optimism, Hope, and Feelgood Movies: The Capra Connection," in *Explorations in Theology and Film: Movies and Meaning*, ed. C. Marsh and G. Ortiz (Oxford: Blackwell, 1997), 231.

Notes to Chapter 5

1. *Mr. Holland's Opus*, from Hollywood Pictures, was produced by Patrick Sheane Duncan and William Teitler in 1995 and was directed by Stephen Herek. The screenplay was written by Patrick Sheane Duncan. The video was released in 1996 by Interscope Communications/PolyGram Filmed Entertainment, copyright by Beuna Vista Pictures Distribution, Inc.

2. In an interview published in *NEA Today* 15, no. 3 (November 1996): 42, Richard Dreyfuss attributed the success of the film in part to the fact that "all of us over a certain age have memories of powerful teachers who have shaped our lives, but whose impact has been obscured by the passage of time."

3. Dieter Georgi, *The Opponents of Paul in Second Corinthians* (Philadelphia: Fortress, 1986); Gail Paterson Corrington, *The "Divine Man": His Origin and Function in Hellenistic Popular Religion* (New York: Peter Lang, 1986); Jeffrey A. Crafton, *The Agency of the Apostle: A Dramatistic Analysis of Paul's Responses to Conflict in 2 Corinthians*, Journal for the Study of the New Testament — Supplement Series 51 (Sheffield: JSOT Press, 1991).

4. Georgi, *Opponents*, 229-314.

5. There is a debate over what such letters contained, since the evidence is entirely deductive. Dieter Georgi accepts the fact that philosophical instructions about such letters cautioned against self-display and arrogance, and he concludes that the letters were not about the superapostles themselves (*Opponents*, 243). But this is implausible, and the recent commentators on 2 Corinthians conclude otherwise, as do I. See Ralph P. Martin, *2 Corinthians* (Waco: Word, 1986), 51; see also Jerome Murphy-O'Connor, *The Theology of the Second Letter to the Corinthians* (Cambridge: Cambridge University Press, 1991), 32; and Francis M. Young and David F. Ford, *Meaning and Truth in 2 Corinthians* (Grand Rapids: Eerdmans, 1988), 49.

6. David E. Garland, "The Sufficiency of Paul, Minister of the New Covenant," *Criswell Theological Review* 4 (1989): 21.

7. Garland, "Sufficiency of Paul," 24.

8. There is a textual variant that attempts to smooth out this text, substituting "your hearts" for "our hearts," but it is weakly supported and as William Baird observes, the variant may be a "corruption . . . to harmonize the 'hearts' of vs. 2 with the hearts of vs. 3" (William R. Baird, Jr., "Letters of Recommendation: A Study of 2 Cor 3:1-3," *Journal of Biblical Literature* 80 [1961]: 167).

9. Janet Maslin, "A Teacher Who Once Had Dreams," review of *Mr. Holland's Opus*, New York Times, 19 January 1996, sec. C, p. 3.

10. Georgi, *Opponents*, 264.

11. Carol Kern Stockhausen, *Moses' Veil and the Glory of the New Covenant: The Exegetical Substructure of II Cor. 3,1–4,6* (Rome: Pontificio Istituto Biblico, 1989), 72-74.

12. Ralph P. Martin, *2 Corinthians* (Waco: Word, 1986), 81, referring to Johannes Behm, *"kardia,"* in *Theological Dictionary of the New Testament*, vol. 1,

ed. Gerhard Kittel; trans. and ed. Geoffrey W. Bromiley (Grand Rapids: Eerdmans, 1965), 609-16.

13. Alexander Sand, *"kardia,"* in *Exegetical Dictionary of the New Testament,* vol. 2, ed. Horst Balz and Gerhard Schneider (Grand Rapids: Eerdmans, 1981), 250.

14. Robert Jewett, *Paul's Anthropological Terms: A Study of Their Use in Conflict Settings* (Leiden: Brill, 1971), 448.

15. See M. Scott Peck, *People of the Lie: The Hope for Healing Human Evil* (New York: Simon & Schuster, 1983), 85-149. Peck has a more restricted notion that only certain people have this malady.

16. Baird shows in "Letters of Recommendation," 169-70 that the expression *diakonētheisa hyph' hēmōn* in 2 Cor 3:3 refers to a letter "delivered by us." "Since he views himself as the courier, Paul is not to be understood as either the writer or the ultimate recipient of the letter."

17. Crafton, *Agency of the Apostle,* 79-80.

18. James Wolcott refers to this scene as the climax of the "schmalz fest" that marks *Mr. Holland's Opus* ("The Love Bug," *New Yorker,* 9 January 1996, 93).

Notes to Chapter 6

1. *Groundhog Day* is a Trevor Albert production of a Harold Ramis film, a Columbia Pictures release in 1993, with Bill Murray as Phil Connors and Andie MacDowell as Rita Hanson. Harold Ramis directed the film, and the screenplay was by Danny Rubin and Harold Ramis, based on a story of Rubin. It is available as a Columbia Tristar Home Video, 1993.

2. David Denby, review of *Groundhog Day, New York Magazine,* 1 March 1993, 110.

3. See particularly John Marsh, *The Fulness of Time* (London: Nisbet, 1952); Thorleif Boman, *Hebrew Thought Compared with Greek,* trans. Jules L. Moreau (London: SCM Press, 1960), 123-54; James Muilenburg, "The Biblical View of Time," *Harvard Theological Review* 54 (1961): 225-71; A. L. Burns, "Two Words for 'Time' in the New Testament," *Australian Biblical Review* 3 (1953): 7-22; Oscar Cullmann, *Christ and Time: The Primitive Christian Conception of Time and History,* trans. Floyd V. Filson, rev. ed. (Philadelphia: Westminster, 1964).

4. See Gerhard Delling, *"chronos,"* in *Theological Dictionary of the New Testament,* vol. 9, ed. Gerhard Friedrich; trans. and ed. Geoffrey W. Bromiley (Grand Rapids: Eerdmans, 1974), 581-83; Hans Hübner, *"chronos,"* in *Exegetical Dictionary of the New Testament,* vol. 3, ed. Horst Balz and Gerhard Schneider (Grand Rapids: Eerdmans, 1993), 488.

5. Jonathan Romney, review of *Groundhog Day, New Statesman and Society,* 7 May 1993, 34.

6. See Gerhard Delling, *"kairos,"* in *Theological Dictionary of the New Testa-

ment, vol. 3, ed. Gerhard Kittel; trans. and ed. Geoffrey W. Bromiley (Grand Rapids: Eerdmans, 1965), 459-65.

7. Jörg Baumgarten, *"kairos,"* in *Exegetical Dictionary of the New Testament,* vol. 2, ed. Horst Balz and Gerhard Schneider (Grand Rapids: Eerdmans, 1991), 232.

8. Ernst Käsemann, *Commentary on Romans,* trans. and ed. Geoffrey W. Bromiley (Grand Rapids: Eerdmans, 1980), 346; cited by Baumgarten, *"kairos,"* 233.

9. Baumgarten, *"kairos,"* 233. He acknowledges that Paul's use of *kairos* has a fairly wide range of meaning and that it sometimes overlaps with *chronos.* This is quite different from the view expressed in Baumgarten's *Paulus und die Apokalyptik: Die Auslegung apokalyptischer Überlieferung in den echten Paulusbriefen,* Wissenschaftliche Monographien zum Alten und Neuen Testament 44 (Neukirchen-Vluyn: Neukirchener Verlag, 1975), 187. So he appears to have learned from James Barr, *Biblical Words for Time,* Studies in Biblical Theology 33 (Naperville, Ill.: Allenson, 1962), who rejected the simplistic semantics of the earlier biblical theology movement, which assumed that this theological connotation was inherent in the word *kairos* itself.

10. See the discussion of the antinomian tendency in the Galatian congregation in Robert Jewett, "The Agitators and the Galatian Congregation," *New Testament Studies* 17 (1970-71): 198-212; this view is accepted by Richard N. Longenecker, *Galatians,* Word Biblical Commentary 41 (Dallas: Word, 1990), xcix.

11. See Longenecker, *Galatians,* 281.

12. See David D. Gilmore, ed., *Honor and Shame and the Unity of the Mediterranean* (Washington, D.C.: American Anthropological Association, 1987); Bruce J. Malina, *The New Testament World: Insights from Cultural Anthropology* (Atlanta: John Knox, 1981), 25-50; idem, *Christian Origins and Cultural Anthropology: Practical Models for Biblical Interpretation* (Atlanta: John Knox, 1986); Jerome H. Neyrey, *Paul in Other Words: A Cultural Reading of His Letters* (Louisville: Westminster John Knox, 1990).

13. Matthew Giunti, "Bill Murray Grows Up?" *Christian Century* 110 (April 21, 1993): 430.

14. Richard Corliss, review of *Groundhog Day, Time,* 15 February 1993, 61; see also Giunti, "Bill Murray Grows Up?" 431.

15. Longenecker, *Galatians,* 281.

16. Hans Dieter Betz, *Galatians: A Commentary on Paul's Letter to the Churches in Galatia* (Philadelphia: Fortress, 1979), 309, citing Günter Harder, *"phtheirō,"* in *Theological Dictionary of the New Testament,* vol. 9, ed. Gerhard Friedrich; trans. and ed. Geoffrey W. Bromiley (Grand Rapids: Eerdmans, 1974), 309.

17. Ronald Y. K. Fung, *The Epistle to the Galatians,* The New International Commentary on the New Testament (Grand Rapids: Eerdmans, 1988), 295.

18. Jonathan Romney, review of *Groundhog Day, New Statesman and Society,* 7 May 1993, 34.

19. Stanley Kauffmann, "Fantasy and Fandom," review of *Groundhog Day*, *New Republic*, 15 March 1993, 24.

20. Audrey Farolino, review of *Groundhog Day*, *New York Post*, 12 February 1993, 31.

21. Ben Thompson, review of *Groundhog Day*, *Sight and Sound*, May 1993, 50.

22. Betz, *Galatians*, 281.

23. Longenecker, *Galatians*, 281.

24. Larry W. Hurtado, "The Jerusalem Collection and the Book of Galatians," *Journal for the Study of the New Testament* 5 (1979): 54-56, suggests in contrast that Paul may be referring here to the Jerusalem offering, but James D. G. Dunn, *The Epistle to the Galatians* (Peabody, Mass.: Hendrickson, 1993), 333, is correct in saying this is "hardly evident from the text."

25. See Robert Jewett, *Paul the Apostle to America: Cultural Trends and Pauline Scholarship* (Louisville: Westminster John Knox, 1994), 7-8, 73-86.

26. See Dunn, *Galatians*, 332.

27. Richard Corliss, review of *Groundhog Day*, *Time*, 533.

28. Jack Matthews, review of *Groundhog Day*, *Newsday*, 12 February 1993, 66.

29. Giunti, "Bill Murray Grows Up?" 432.

Notes to Chapter 7

1. Richard Brookhiser, "A Man on Horseback," *Atlantic Monthly*, January 1996, 50-64, reprinted in Brookhiser, *Founding Father: Rediscovering George Washington* (New York: Free Press, 1996), 127-36.

2. Brookhiser, "A Man on Horseback," 61.

3. Brookhiser, "A Man on Horseback," 62.

4. *Rules of Civility: The 110 Precepts that Guided Our First President in War and Peace*, edited and with commentary by Richard Brookhiser (New York: Free Press, 1997), 68.

5. Brookhiser, "Man on Horseback," 62.

6. Brookhiser, "Man on Horseback," 62.

7. *Babe* is a Universal Pictures presentation of a Kenneth Miller film released in 1995, with a screenplay by George Miller and Chris Noonan, with the latter serving as director. The story is based on a book by Dick King-Smith, 1995. Video by Universal City Studios, Inc., 1995. The film received the Academy Award for Best Visual Effects in 1995.

8. J. Budziszewski, "The Moral Case for Manners," *National Review* 47 (February 20, 1995): 62.

9. Nicolaus Mills, *The Triumph of Meanness: America's War against Its Better Self* (Boston: Houghton Mifflin, 1997), 165; see also Stephen L. Carter, *Civility: Manners, Morals, and the Etiquette of Democracy* (New York: Basic Books, 1998), 115-206.

10. Meg Greenfield, "It's Time for Some Civility," *Newsweek*, 5 June 1995, 78.

11. Judith Martin, *Miss Manners Rescues Civilization: From Sexual Harassment, Frivolous Lawsuits, Dissing and Other Lapses in Civility* (New York: Crown, 1996), 136-37; see also Letitia Baldrige, *Letitia Baldrige's Complete Guide to the New Manners for the '90s* (New York: Rawson Associates, 1990).

12. Martin, *Miss Manners*, 139.

13. Mills, *Triumph of Meanness*, 223.

14. Terrence Rafferty, review of *Babe*, *The New Yorker*, 4 September 1995, 100.

15. The tradition of dropping the definite article in modern translations and commentaries serves to generalize and decontextualize Paul's statement. Even the excellent study by Walter T. Wilson, *Love without Pretense: Romans 12.9-21 and Hellenistic-Jewish Wisdom Literature*, Wissenschaftliche Untersuchungen zum Neuen Testament 46 (Tübingen: Mohr Siebeck, 1991), 150, treats this statement as a generalizing maxim, translated without reference to the article.

16. James D. G. Dunn is the only commentator to mention the "love feast," in the context of "subsequent" usage in the early church (*Romans 9–16*, Word Biblical Commentary 38b [Dallas: Word, 1988], 739). The language of the "love feast," however, seems to have been used from the beginning of Christianity in Rome and elsewhere; see Bo Reicke, *Diakonie, Festfreude und Zelos in Verbindung mit der altchristlichen Agapenfeier* (Uppsala: Lundequistska Bokhandeln, 1951), 9-18.

17. Wilson, *Love without Pretense*, 154 refers to the "rational ability of . . . members to determine their ethical responsibilities and to discriminate between what is good and evil."

18. The word *apostygeō* ("abhor") occurs only here in the New Testament. In classical Greek, it means "hate violently, abhor."

19. This term is used otherwise by Paul only in the context of sexual intercourse (1 Cor 6:16-17); see Karl Ludwig Schmidt, *"kollaō,"* in *Theological Dictionary of the New Testament*, vol. 3, ed. Gerhard Kittel; trans. and ed. Geoffrey W. Bromiley (Grand Rapids: Eerdmans, 1965), 822.

20. Halvor Moxnes, "Honour and Righteousness in Romans," *Journal for the Study of the New Testament* 32 (1988): 74.

21. Hans Freiherr von Soden, *"adelphos,"* in *Theological Dictionary of the New Testament*, vol. 1, ed. Gerhard Kittel; trans. and ed. Geoffrey W. Bromiley (Grand Rapids: Eerdmans, 1964), 146.

22. See Ceslas Spicq, "PHILOSTORGOS (A Propos de Rom. 12:10)," *Revue Biblique* (1955): 497-510.

23. None of the prevailing translations has proven satisfactory. "Preferring" and "esteeming" one another lack lexicographic support. "Surpassing" and "outdoing" one another have been proposed by commentators on Romans, but these options lack firm lexicographic evidence and are grammatically difficult. The same grammatical difficulty weakens the translation "anticipat-

ing" one another. "Showing the way" to one another follows a version of this option. And "conducting others before you," yet another proposal, makes little sense.

24. See Walter Bauer, *A Greek-English Lexicon of the New Testament and Other Early Christian Literature,* ed. William F. Arndt and F. Wilbur Gingrich, 2d ed. (Chicago: University of Chicago Press, 1979), 712.

25. Johannes Schneider, *"timē,"* in *Theological Dictionary of the New Testament,* vol. 8, ed. Gerhard Friedrich; trans. and ed. Geoffrey W. Bromiley (Grand Rapids: Eerdmans, 1972), 169-80.

26. I am thinking particularly of Bruce J. Malina's analysis of the "dyadic personality" characteristic of the Mediterranean world, discussed in *The New Testament World: Insights from Cultural Anthropology* (Atlanta: John Knox, 1981), 25-50.

27. Otto Michel, *Der Brief an die Römer* (Göttingen: Vandenhoeck & Ruprecht, 1978), 384, mentions *m. Aboth* 4:15 and *b. Berakot* 6b in this context.

28. See Moxnes, "Honour and Righteousness in Romans," 74-75: "Paul here introduces an idea of equality with respect to honour which must have created tensions within the community. . . . In a challenging way Paul breaks with the competition inherent in an honor society. In a transformation of values, Paul claims that honour is now to be freely granted on the basis of love, regardless of status and merit."

29. Richard Schickel, "With an Oink, Oink Here," review of *Babe, Time,* 21 August 1995, 69.

30. Wilson, *Love without Pretense,* 179-80.

31. See H. Schlier, *Der Römerbrief Kommentar* (Freiburg: Herder, 1977), 380.

32. Frederic Louis Godet, *Commentary on Romans* (reprint, Grand Rapids: Kregel, 1977), 437. The literal sense of being directed "toward" others in the congregation must also be kept in view here. C. E. B. Cranfield tones down the distinctive use of *eis* ("toward") in order to coordinate this verse more closely with Pauline usage elsewhere and retain the relevance of the verse for those outside the church (*A Critical and Exegetical Commentary on the Epistle to the Romans,* 2 vols. [Edinburgh: Clark, 1975-79], 2:643). That it implies "outward conduct" is unfounded, and that Paul "has in mind specially the effect which their agreement (or disagreement) will have on those outside" misses the reciprocal connotation of "each other" (as noted by Bauer, *A Greek-English Lexicon,* 39). That "agreement among themselves is something which Christians owe to the world," as Cranfield states it, may in some sense be true, but it is not Paul's point here.

33. The close parallels in Rom 11:20 as well as in Phil 3:19 and Col 3:2 are directed against claims to possess superior mindedness. See my study, "Conflicting Movements in the Early Church as Reflected in Philippians," *Novum Testamentum* 12 (1970): 378-79 and Eduard Schweizer, *Der Brief an die Kolosser* (Zurich: Benziger, 1976), 133.

34. See the discussion of the Corinthian radicals' self-appellation "the

wise-minded ones" (1 Cor 4:10; 10:16; 2 Cor 11:19) in Walter Schmithals, *Gnosticism in Corinth: An Investigation of the Letters to the Corinthians*, trans. John E. Steely (Nashville: Abingdon, 1971), 182-83; C. K. Barrett, *The First Epistle to the Corinthians*, Harper's New Testament Commentaries (New York: Harper & Row, 1968), 231.

35. See Dunn, *Romans 9–16*, 747. Wilson contends in *Love without Pretense*, 183 that a connection with the "fear of God" motif in the Prov 3:7 citation was intended by Paul, as shown by the parallel citation in Rom 11:25. But the theme of fear is also deleted from that citation. I think it is more likely that Paul's redaction of Proverbs intentionally passed over the fear of God motif because there was now a new foundation for the ethic in Rom 12:1-2.

36. See Franz-Josef Ortkemper, *Leben aus dem Glauben: Christliche Grundhaltungen nach Römer 12–13* (Munster: Aschendorff, 1980), 105.

37. I follow Godet, *Romans*, 437; Cranfield, *Romans*, 2:644; M.-J. Lagrange, *Saint Paul: Epître aux Romains* (Paris: Gabalda, 1950), 306-7; and Ragnar Leivestad, *"TAPEINOS — TAPEINOPHRŌN," Novum Testamentum* 8 (1966): 46 in viewing *tois tapeinois* as a masculine plural ("the lowly people"). As Leivestad points out, the somewhat negative connotation of "common, poor people" is retained in this sentence, and it is inappropriate to transfer the more positive valence of Christian humility derived from Philippians 2 and elsewhere.

38. Halvor Moxnes, "The Quest for Honour and the Unity of the Community in Romans 12 and in the Orations of Dio Chrysostom," in Troels Engberg-Pedersen, ed., *Paul in His Hellenistic Context* (Minneapolis: Fortress, 1994), 227.

39. Wilson, *Love without Pretense*, 196.

40. See Otto Bauernfeind, *"nikaō,"* in *Theological Dictionary of the New Testament*, vol. 4, ed. Gerhard Kittel; trans. and ed. Geoffrey W. Bromiley (Grand Rapids: Eerdmans, 1967), 942-43; J. Rufus Fears, "The Theology of Victory at Rome: Approaches and Problems," in *Aufstieg und Niedergang der Römischen Welt*, II.17.2, ed. H. Temporini (Berlin: de Gruyter, 1981), 740-52, esp. 748-49: "Victoria in her various forms was an integral part of Roman cult, a supernatural power which had manifested itself to the Roman People and was capable of rendering benefits to the community of worshippers. . . . Victoria came to be the center of a rich and complex political mythology, the most critical element in an ideology to support the immense and fragile fabric of empire."

41. Fears, "Theology of Victory," 807; he refers also to the studies by S. Weinstock, "Pax and the Ara Pacis," *Journal of Roman Studies* 50 (1960): 44-58.

42. See William Klassen, *Love of Enemies: The Way to Peace* (Philadelphia: Fortress, 1984), 123: "In a society which boasted of the Pax Romana (the peace of Rome), which was maintained by force, Paul does not reject the military metaphor. He simply transforms it into the battle language of the Christian church." Klassen notes the contrast with the Roman use of the slogan, "If you want peace, prepare for war," described by Wolfgang Haase,

"'Si vis pacem, para bellum': Zur Beurteilung militärischer Stärke in der römischen Kaiserzeit," *Akten des XI. Internationalen Limeskongresses* (Budapest: Hungarian Academy of Sciences, 1977), 721-55.

43. See Wilson, *Love without Pretense*, 197.

44. Cited by Ortkemper, *Leben aus dem Glauben*, 124 from Heinrich Weinel, *Paulus: Der Mensch und sein Werk: Die Anfänge des Christentums, der Kirche und des Dogmas* (Tübingen: Mohr Siebeck, 1904), 253.

Notes to Chapter 8

1. *Edge of the City* was produced by David Susskind for presentation by Metro Golden Mayer in 1957. It was adapted from Robert Alan Aurthur's television production, *A Man Is Ten Feet Tall*, and directed by Martin Ritt. No video has ever been made available for this film, even though Leonard Maltin praises it as an outstanding, four-star movie in the *1998 Movie and Video Guide* (New York: Signet, 1997), 385.

2. See Carlton Jackson, *Picking up the Tab: The Life and Movies of Martin Ritt* (Bowling Green, Ohio: Bowling Green State University Popular Press, 1994), 41.

3. Arthur S. Barron, "Murder on the Waterfront," *New Republic* 136, 4 March 1957, 22.

4. See Robert Hatch, "Films," *The Nation* 184 (February 9, 1957): 125; Barron, "Murder on the Waterfront," 22: "Here, however, an entirely new pattern has been introduced. In this picture Negro and White appear as full equals, as close friends. . . . all without a shred of self-consciousness. The relationship is entirely spontaneous and open. For the first time, Hollywood has given the Negro the role of a warm, uncomplicated and natural human being." Bosley Crowther in *New York Times*, 30 January 1957, 33 agrees that this film comes "close to some sort of fair articulation of the complexities of racial brotherhood."

5. James D. G. Dunn, *Romans 1-8*, Word Biblical Commentary 38a (Dallas: Word, 1988), 254.

6. John C. O'Neill, *Paul's Letter to the Romans* (Harmondsworth: Penguin, 1975), 93.

7. See my study, "Ecumenical Theology for the Sake of Mission: Rom 1:1-17 + 15:14-16:24," in D. M. Hay and E. E. Johnson, eds., *Pauline Theology*, vol. 3 (Minneapolis: Augsburg Fortress, 1996), 93-97 and chapters 5-6 of my book *Paul the Apostle to America: Cultural Trends and Pauline Scholarship* (Louisville: Westminster John Knox, 1994).

8. Hatch, "Films," 125.

9. John Riches, *Jesus and the Transformation of Judaism* (New York: Seabury, 1982), 168.

10. See Marcus J. Borg, *Jesus A New Vision: Spirit, Culture, and the Life of Discipleship* (San Francisco: Harper & Row, 1987), 175-84; idem, *Jesus in Con-*

temporary Scholarship (Valley Forge: Trinity Press International, 1994), 112-16. For a discussion of the role of the cleansing of the temple in the sequence of events leading to Jesus' execution, see E. P. Sanders, *The Historical Figure of Jesus* (Allen Lane: Penguin, 1993), 254-62, 272-73.

11. Stanley E. Porter, *Katallassō in Ancient Greek Literature, with Reference to the Pauline Writings* (Cordoba: Ediciones el Almendro, 1994), 158; he cites Otto Michel, *Der Brief an die Römer,* 14th ed. (Göttingen: Vandenhoeck und Ruprecht, 1978), 136: "the enmity of men against God becomes an enmity of God against men. . . ."

12. The rejection of this evidence on the assumption of what the context requires is highly subjective, resting on an exegetical legacy that has always stressed the doctrinal objectivity of Romans and downplayed its situational orientation. In "The Argument of Romans 5: Can a Rhetorical Question Make a Difference?" *Journal of Biblical Literature* 110 (1991): 662-65, Stanley E. Porter has recently made a compelling case for accepting the more strongly supported subjunctive reading. Many commentators suggest that an early dictation error accounts for a substitution of the subjunctive for the indicative. However, this argument actually throws no light on which version was originally intended. While it is likely that the Greek *omega* and *omicron* were pronounced in virtually identical fashion by first-century speakers, the confusion could have gone either way. A computerized study of such confusion has found many instances where scribes intended to write *omega* and instead wrote *omicron* and vice versa. See Ian A. Moir, "Orthography and Theology: The Omicron-Omega Interchange in Romans 5:1 and Elsewhere," in Eldon Jay Epp and Gordon D. Fee, eds., *New Testament Textual Criticism: Its Significance for Exegesis* (Oxford: Clarendon, 1981), 179-83.

13. This is seen most clearly by Porter, *Katallassō,* 155: ". . . the parallelism of vv 1 and 10a with God as the common object illustrates that the securing of peace . . . is contextually synonymous with what is meant by reconciliation. . . ."

Notes to Chapter 9

1. For a discussion of the strophic pattern, see Gordon D. Fee, *The First Epistle to the Corinthians* (Grand Rapids: Eerdmans, 1987), 423.

2. *The Firm* is a Paramount Pictures release, 1993. It was directed by Sidney Pollack, with a screenplay by David Rabe, Robert Towne, and David Rayfiel, based on a John Grisham novel. The video is available through Paramount, 1993. *The Firm* was nominated for two Academy Awards in 1993.

3. See the classic study of patronage by Richard P. Saller, *Personal Patronage under the Early Empire* (Cambridge: University Press, 1982) and the recent analysis by John K. Chow, *Patronage and Power: A Study of Social Networks in Corinth,* Journal for the Study of the New Testament — Supplement Series 75 (Sheffield: Academic Press, 1992).

4. See Ronald F. Hock, *The Social Context of Paul's Ministry: Tentmaking and Apostleship* (Philadelphia: Fortress, 1980).

5. See the chapter on "Honor and Shame: Pivotal Values of the First-Century Mediterranean World" in Bruce J. Malina, *The New Testament World: Insights from Cultural Anthropology* (Atlanta: John Knox, 1981), 25-50.

6. Gerhard Dautzenberg offers a traditional, purely theological explanation of this passage, which fails to account for the rhetorical question and its social background, in "Der Verzicht auf das apostolische Unterhaltsrecht: Eine exegetische Untersuchung zu 1 Kor 9," *Biblica* 50 (1969): 212-32.

7. Ernst Käsemann, *Jesus Means Freedom*, trans. Frank Clarke (Philadelphia: Fortress, 1970).

8. For a significant but contrasting interpretation of the motifs of freedom and slavery in this passage, see Dale B. Martin, *Slavery as Salvation: The Metaphor of Slavery in Pauline Christianity* (New Haven: Yale University Press, 1990).

9. While overlooking the theological aspects of the film, Kenneth Turan comments that "The book's best-selling plot has been taken apart and put back together again in noticeably better shape. Subplots have been strengthened, characters switched around to make the jeopardy more emotionally involving, and increasing physical action has been added to the mix. . . ." (review of *The Firm* [Paramount movie], *Los Angeles Times*, 30 June 30 1993, Calendar section, p. 1). David Denby, in contrast, states: "*The Firm* was practically a movie between covers, so I don't know how the actual movie version could have been screwed up" (*New York Magazine*, 12 July 1993, 53). While also disapproving of the film version, Nick Adams provides the clearest grasp of the plot change in his review in *Sight and Sound*, October 1993, 44: "Prominent among many plot changes between novel and film is the way that the hero Mitch is allowed to come away from his ordeal almost unscathed. The novel is truer to the inflexible comeuppance of the Faustian pact: Mitch is allowed no way back into 'normal' society but has to become a permanent fugitive from the mob, cruising the obscure parts of the Caribbean on a never-ending limbo holiday."

10. This motif, not found in the novel, was explicitly affirmed by Robert Towne, one of the screenwriters for *The Firm*. He calls the law "the most sacred thing there is in a secular world," and he echoes Mitch's line in the film: "If you follow the law, it will be your salvation" (cited by Georgia Brown, *Village Voice*, 6 July 1993, 45).

11. The contrast between the film and the original novel is particularly striking at this point. The novel depicts Mitch as an unredeemed rip-off artist who loots millions from the firm and the mob, and escapes to a remote Caribbean island with his friends at the end of the story. This is a significant instance of "mythic alchemy," in which the film draws closer to a central religious archetype in the culture. See the discussion of parallel instances of this phenomenon in Robert Jewett, *Saint Paul at the Movies: The Apostle's Dialogue with American Culture* (Louisville: Westminster John Knox, 1993). But the

relation between film and novel creates confusion for some, as noted by Vincent Canby, "The Firm," *New York Times,* 30 June 1993, sec. C, p. 15.

12. See, for example, Stanley Kauffmann, "The Firm," *New Republic,* 2 August 1993, 32; Andy Pawelczak, *Films in Review,* October 1993, 336; David Denby, *New York Magazine,* 12 July 1993, 53; Michael Medved, *New York Post,* 30 June 1993, 23; Jack Matthews, *Newsday,* 30 June 1993, 49; Richard Schickel, *Time,* 5 July 1993, 58.

13. Barbara Hall, "All Things to All People: A Study of 1 Corinthians 9:19-23," in Robert T. Fortna & Beverly R. Gaventa, eds., *The Conversation Continues: Studies of Paul and John in Honor of J. Louis Martyn* (Nashville: Abingdon, 1990), 150.

14. David Sterritt, *Christian Science Monitor,* 6 July 1993, 12.

15. See Hall, "All Things," 138: "Paul's self-enslavement is his radical identification with all people."

16. Hall, "All Things," 142-43.

17. Hall, "All Things," 144.

18. *United Methodist Hymnal* (Nashville: United Methodist Publishing House, 1989), 421; the hymn was written in 1890.

Notes to Chapter 10

1. Robert Jewett and John Shelton Lawrence, *The American Monomyth,* foreword by Isaac Asimov (Garden City, N.Y.: Doubleday/Anchor, 1977; 2d ed. Lanham, Md.: University Press of America, 1988), xii.

2. *Unforgiven* is a Warner Brothers release in 1992, directed by Clint Eastwood, with a screenplay by David Webb Peoples. The video was released by Warner Home Video in 1996. It received four Academy Awards in 1992, including Best Picture and Best Director; it had been nominated for five additional Academy Awards.

3. See Richard Slotkin, *Regeneration through Violence: The Myth of the American Frontier, 1600-1860* (Middleton: Wesleyan University Press, 1973); idem, *Gunfighter Nation: The Myth of the Frontier in Twentieth-Century America* (New York: Atheneum; Maxwell Macmillan, 1992).

4. See especially the new sifting of the evidence by Martin Hengel, "Der vorchristliche Paulus," in Martin Hengel and Ulrich Heckel, eds., *Paulus und das antike Judentum: Tübingen-Durham-Symposium im Gedenken an den 50. Todestag Adolf Schlatters (19. Mai 1938)* (Tübingen: Mohr Siebeck, 1991), 177-294. See also Klaus Haacker, "Die Berufung des Verfolgers und die Rechtfertigung des Gottlosen: Erwägungen zum Zusammenhang zwischen Biographie und Theologie des Apostels Paulus," *Theologische Beiträge* 6 (1975): 1-19.

5. For the background of this violent zeal, see Torrey Seland, *Establishment Violence in Philo and Luke: A Study of Non-conformity to the Torah and Jewish Vigilante Reactions* (Leiden: Brill, 1995).

6. See Martin Hengel, *The Zealots: Investigations into the Jewish Freedom*

Movement in the Period from Herod I until 70 A.D., trans. David Smith (Edinburgh: Clark, 1989), xv, 146-212. For a balanced appraisal of the complex evidence concerning the impact of zealous ideology on the war, see David Rhoads, "Zealots," in *The Anchor Bible Dictionary*, vol. 6 (New York: Doubleday, 1992), 1045-52.

7. Hengel, *Zealots*, 183.

8. Hengel, *Zealots*, 224-28.

9. David M. Rhoads, *Israel in Revolution, 6-74 C.E.: A Political History Based on the Writings of Josephus* (Philadelphia: Fortress, 1976), 170.

10. In contrast to S. G. F. Brandon, *Jesus and the Zealots: A Study of the Political Factor in Primitive Christianity* (Manchester: Manchester University Press, 1967), my research in *The Captain America Complex: The Dilemma of Zealous Nationalism* (Philadelphia: Westminster, 1973; 2d ed. Sante Fe, New Mexico: Bear & Company, 1984) and *Jesus against the Rapture: Seven Unexpected Prophecies* (Philadelphia: Westminster, 1979) follows the mainstream of scholarship on this point, represented in recent studies by Richard Horsley, *Jesus and the Spiral of Violence: Popular Jewish Resistance in Roman Palestine* (San Francisco: Harper & Row, 1987); E. P. Sanders, *Jesus and Judaism* (Philadelphia: Fortress, 1985); and Marcus Borg, *Jesus, A New Vision: Spirit, Culture, and the Life of Discipleship* (San Francisco: Harper & Row, 1987).

11. Jewett, *Captain America Complex,* 15-47; *American Monomyth*, 169-97.

12. Harvey R. Greenberg, "Unforgiven," *Film Quarterly* 46.3 (Spring 1993): 52. See also Richard Schickel, *Clint Eastwood: A Biography* (New York: Knopf, 1996), 454-55.

13. In *Clint Eastwood*, 460 Richard Schickel reports that this ending replaces one that Eastwood had considered, "in which Delilah, the cut whore, and Will take up a life together." In making the superhero ride off alone into the mist, the film conforms to the American monomyth rather than to the classical monomyth, which would have featured marriage at the end.

14. John G. Cawelti, "What Rough Beast — New Westerns," *ANQ: A Quarterly Journal of Short Articles, Notes, and Reviews* 9, no. 3 (Summer 1996): 9.

15. See Greenberg, "Unforgiven," 52: Munny's "abasement is imbued with the quality of ritualized, Christ-like suffering seen in other Eastwood movies."

16. See Hans Hübner, "Gal 3.10 und die Herkunft des Paulus," *Kerygma und Dogma* 19 (1973): 215-31.

17. My first effort to explore this theme was published as "Zeal Without Understanding: Reflections on Rambo and Oliver North," *Christian Century* 104 (September 9-16, 1987): 753-56. This was followed by the essay written with John Shelton Lawrence, "Rambo and the Myth of Redemption," in Robert P. Metzger, ed., *Transforming Texts: Classical Images in New Contexts* (Lewisburg: Bucknell University Press, 1993), 63-83. There is also a chapter on this theme in my book *Paul the Apostle to America: Cultural Trends and Pauline Scholarship* (Louisville: Westminster John Knox, 1994).

18. An expression of national disquiet appeared in the *Omaha World-Her-*

ald in a lead editorial on June 5, 1997, "Too Little Known About McVeigh." "More needs to come out of the Timothy McVeigh trial than a guilty verdict. . . . We need to come away from the trial with the feeling that we understand enough about what happened that we can prevent future McVeighs from repeating this horror." The editorial reviews the background of the Branch Davidian episode and then poses the key question: "But how did McVeigh, a decorated war veteran, become a dangerously delusional anti-government terrorist? What motivated him and why?"

19. See the study by James William Gibson, *Warrior Dreams: Paramilitary Culture in Post-Vietnam America* (New York: Hill & Wang, 1994).

20. Cited by James C. Coates and Rogers Wortherington, "Far-Right Hates Government, Loves the Date April 19," *Chicago Tribune*, 23 April 1995, sec. 1, p. 17.

21. Andrew Macdonald, *The Turner Diaries: A Novel*, 2d ed., 6th printing (Hillsboro, W.Va.: National Vanguard Books, 1995; reprint, New York: Barricade Books, 1996). Pierce writes under the pseudonym Andrew Macdonald. The book was first published in 1978, and there are now more than 200,000 copies in print.

22. Coates and Wortherington, "Far-Right," 17.

23. Maurice Possley, "McVeigh's Unsettling Letter is Heard in Sister's Testimony," *Chicago Tribune*, 6 May 1997, sec. 1, p. 3.

24. "Unforgiven," *Magill's Survey of Cinema*, 15 June 1995, electronic publication with no page numbers.

25. Richard Grenier, "Clint Eastwood Goes P.C.," *Commentary* 97, no. 3 (March 1994): 51.

26. Christopher Frayling, "Unforgiven," *Sight and Sound*, October 1992, 58.

27. David Denby, "How the West Was Lost," *New York Magazine*, 24 August 1992, 119.

28. Greenberg, "Unforgiven," 52.

29. This critical category was developed in *The American Monomyth*, 49-51 and 311 as "a symbolic exhortation for members of an audience to conform their behavior to a mythical paradigm from popular culture."

30. Interview with Clint Eastwood on National Public Radio on 30 March 1993, hosted by Neal Conan, with reporter Ina Jaffe.

31. Grenier, "Clint Eastwood Goes P.C.," 51.

32. Harry Brod, "Unforgiven," *Tikhun* 8 (May-June 1993): 30. See, for example, Kenneth Turan, "Clint Is Back with a Vengeance" (review of *Unforgiven*), *Los Angeles Times*, 7 August 1992, Calendar section, F1, p. 12: "'Unforgiven' is also . . . a neat piece of revisionism, a violent film that is determined to demythologize killing."

33. Pat Dowell, "Film Reviews," *Cineaste* 19, no. 2-3 (December 1, 1992): 72.

34. Dowell, "Film Reviews," 72.

35. Judy Coode, "Unforgiven," *Sojourners* 21 (December 1992): 47.

Notes to Chapter 11

1. See Robert Jewett, *Paul the Apostle to America: Cultural Trends and Pauline Scholarship* (Louisville: Westminster John Knox, 1994).

2. See, for example, David Denby, *New York Magazine*, 26 September 1994, 94; Jack Matthews, *Newsday*, 23 September 1992, sec. 2, p. 82.

3. *The Shawshank Redemption* is a Columbia Pictures release of a Castle Rock Entertainment presentation in 1994, directed by Frank Darabont on his own screenplay based on Stephen King's novel, *Rita Hayworth and the Shawshank Redemption*. The video was released by Columbia Tristar Home Video. There were seven Academy Award nominations for this film.

4. Jennifer Rike, "Foundations of Hope," *Christian Century* (November 22-29, 1995): 1146.

5. Rudolf Bultmann, *"elpis,"* in *Theological Dictionary of the New Testament*, vol. 2, ed. Gerhard Kittel; trans. and ed. Geoffrey W. Bromiley (Grand Rapids: Eerdmans, 1964), 519-21.

6. For this reason I am not inclined to accept Andy Pawelczak's contention in *Films in Review*, 12 November 1994, 55 that "Andy is the film's representative of innocence traduced."

7. Rike, "Foundations of Hope," 1149.

8. Andy Pawelczak, *Films in Review*, 12 November 1994, 55 identifies "cleansing baptismal rain" as one of the "carefully orchestrated archetypal symbols developed by this film.

9. This may be one reason why reviewer Andy Pawelczak found that "the big, quasi-spiritual epiphany at the end left me unmoved and dissatisfied" (*Films in Review*, 55).

Notes to the Epilogue

1. See James D. G. Dunn, *Romans 9–16*, Word Biblical Commentary 38b (Waco: Word, 1988), 603 and M. Jack Suggs, "The Word Is Near You: Rom 10:6-10 within the Purpose of the Letter," in W. R. Farmer, C. F. D. Moule, and R. R. Niebuhr, eds., *Christian History and Interpretation: Studies Presented to John Knox* (Cambridge: Cambridge University Press, 1967), 289-312.

2. Michael Medved, review of *The Shawshank Redemption*, *New York Post*, 23 September 1994, 46.

3. Northrop Frye, *The Great Code: The Bible and Literature* (New York: Harcourt Brace Jovanovich, 1982). In "Northrop Frye on the Bible and Literature," *Christianity and Literature* 41, no. 3 (1992): 259, A. C. Hamilton shows that the "biblical heritage dominates" Western literature in Frye's view.

4. Frye, *Great Code*, 50.

5. Frye, *Great Code*, 171. He goes on to argue (p. 192) that the biblical narrative "becomes a series of ups and downs in which God's people peri-

odically fall into bondage and are then rescued by a leader, while the great heathen empires rise and fall in the opposite rhythm."

6. Randall Stewart, *American Literature and Christian Doctrine* (Baton Rouge: Louisiana State University Press, 1958), 3. For an account of the early formation of the United States as a "biblical nation," see Nathan O. Hatch and Mark A. Noll, eds., *The Bible in America: Essays in Cultural History* (New York/Oxford: Oxford University Press, 1982), 19-78.

7. Dunn, *Romans 9–16*, 607.

8. Otfried Hofius cites the close parallel to Pauline usage in the Roman political formula, "confess the emperor as lord" (*"homologeō,"* in *Exegetical Dictionary of the New Testament*, vol. 2, ed. Horst Balz and Gerhard Schneider [Grand Rapids: Eerdmans, 1991], 515).

9. Dunn, *Romans 9–16*, 608.

10. Dunn, *Romans 9–16*, 609.

11. Franz J. Leenhardt, *The Epistle to the Romans* (London: Lutterworth, 1961), 272.

Index of Ancient Texts

Index of Names and Subjects